Education, Work and Identity

Education, Work and Identity

Themes and Perspectives

MICHAEL TOMLINSON

B L O O M S B U R Y

LONDON · NEW DELHI · NEW YORK · SYDNEY

Bloomsbury Academic

An imprint of Bloomsbury Publishing Plc

50 Bedford Square	175 Fifth Avenue
London	New York
WC1B 3DP	NY 10010
UK	USA

www.bloomsbury.com

First published 2013

British Library Cataloguing-in-Publication Data
A catalogue record for this book is available from the British Library.

ISBN: HB: 978-1-4411-2192-9
PB: 978-1-4411-7411-6
PDF: 978-1-4411-4797-4
ePub: 978-1-4411-6142-0

Library of Congress Cataloging-in-Publication Data
A catalog record for this title is available from the Library of Congress.

Typeset by Deanta Global Publishing Services, Chennai, India
Printed and bound in Great Britain

CONTENTS

1 Introduction to key themes and perspectives 1

Education, work and identity: Introducing some
    key themes and concepts 3
Organization of the book 13

2 Social and economic transformations 17

From modern to late modern society 18
Individualization, reflexivity and the rise of identity politics 20
Globalization 27
Socio-economic change, education and the labour market 32
Chapter summary 35

3 The changing nature of work 37

From industrial to post-industrial economies 38
Work in post-industrial economies: Flexibility, skills and
    knowledge work 41
Post-industrialization and the feminization of work 43
Debating the impacts of work changes: Challenging the new
    post-industrial utopia 45
New capitalism, new challenges? Does work still
    shape identities? 48
From employment to 'employability' 53
Chapter summary 58

**4 Conceptualizing the relationships between
    education and work** 61

Historic linkages between education and work 62
Dominant theories on the relationship between
    education and work 64

Contested views on the role of education for economic
    development: Economic necessity or credential inflation? 68
Credentialism and positional conflict 72
Critical evaluation of these dominant theories 77
Chapter summary 82

5 Vocationalism, skills and employability 85

Education and employability 86
The skills agenda 90
Vocational education and training 96
Chapter summary 105

6 Lifelong learning, learner identities and
   work-related learning 107

Lifelong learning for a learning society 108
The social construction of learner identities 111
A closer look at the role of social class, gender and race 116
Work-related learning 123
Chapter summary 129

7 Managing transitions from education
   to work 131

Changing identities and the transition from education
    to the labour market 135
Education to work transitions in late modernity:
    Individualization, choice and mapping uncertain futures 141
Chapter summary 148

8 Transforming educational institutions for
   economic gain 151

Towards a new economization of education 152
Policy responses to economization 158
Economization and professional identities 164
Chapter summary 173

9 Higher education, social change and
    shifting identities 175

    The shift from elite to mass higher education 177
    Globalization, marketization and the new commoditization
        of universities 181
    Changing academic work and identities 184
    Students, graduates and the changing higher education
        experience 188
    Higher education and the changing graduate labour market 192
    Chapter summary 199

10 Conclusions 201

Bibliography 205
Index 227

CHAPTER ONE

Introduction to key themes and perspectives

Over the past half a century, significant changes have taken place in educational institutions and work organizations. This has resulted in disernable shifts in the dynamic interaction between education, the economy and the state. These have had far-reaching implications for people's relationship to, and experiences of, both education and work. Furthermore, changes in the wider economy and in work organizations have given rise to a number of contested views over the specific ways in which education regulates individuals' future economic outcomes.

These changes have, in turn, opened up some complex sets of issues about the purpose of education, or at least the ways in which educational institutions should best be organized. Over time, there has been a general convergence of the education – work relationship, which, in part, has been mediated by national governments' continued emphasis on education as both a source of national prosperity and a catalyst of social and economic opportunity. Changes in the political economy of nations have led to increasing concerns over the need for strong, fit-for-purpose and efficient forms of educational provision to meet the challenges of a globally competitive 'knowledge economy'.

Reworkings to the linkages between advanced systems of capitalist and educational processes, practices and structures – never straightforward at best – are now generating contested views about the type of learner that education needs to produce. Furthermore, the redrawing of the lines between education, credentials and occupational structures raises important questions about the forms of educationally related knowledge and skills that people require to progress within the labour market. Relatedly, issues have been raised over the ways in which educational institutions should be organized to meet these changing demands.

An increasing focus within the sociology of education and work has been on the ways in which these changes have been interpreted and managed by individuals as they seek to make sense of their wider economic futures. Broader structural and macro-level changes are likely to impact profoundly on individuals' lived experiences. A key goal of this book is, therefore, to examine and, where appropriate, problematize the different ways in which wider processes of social, economic and educational changes interact and coexist. The shifting interaction between social change, the labour market and educational change entails some significant reformations in the ways in which individuals orientate themselves to the social and economic world. This is likely to have a further significant impact on how individuals come to see the relationship between their educational experiences and future work-related activities and outcomes. But it also signifies some significant shifts in the role of education in regulating future work identities and positioning individuals in the social and economic world.

In addressing the issues outlined in this book, a broad range of disciplinary areas are drawn upon, including education, sociology, social policy, cultural studies and labour market studies. In attempting to unify these different disciplinary areas, this book is acknowledging the largely interlocking dynamics between wider social, economic and educational change: what occurs in the wider economic sphere inevitably shapes the fabric of educational institutions. It further impacts on the lived experiences of the key actors involved in education, namely, learners, teachers, managers and administrators.

In exploring the shifting dynamic between education and work institutions, key issues are raised about the role of education in both economic and social reproduction. In viewing educational institutions, and their related structures and practices, as being firmly wedded to economic and state-driven agendas, we are acknowledging the way in which educational institutions are positioned towards achieving economic, social and cultural goals. While, at one level, these goals may reflect increasing employer- and government-driven demands in the overall shaping of education, at another level they also map onto individuals' personal understandings of the link between education and future occupational reward.

As we will illustrate throughout the book, the changing economic context has altered somewhat the role of education in reproducing the types of employment-related outcomes and experiences that have been traditionally established. Ultimately, this is resulting in tensions around the role of education in structuring life chances and opportunities, and providing individuals with the necessary platform with which to negotiate their future place in the labour market.

Education, work and identity: Introducing some key themes and concepts

Education and social and economic change

The shifting dynamics in the interrelationship between education and work reflect broader social and economic transformations, all of which have a substantial bearing on individuals' formal (and informal) educational and labour market experiences. Changes in individuals' educational experiences have further taken place in the context of significant politico-economic pressure from governments around enhanced economic efficiency. As the economy has become more globally competitive and knowledge-intensive, nation states have looked to ensure that individuals and institutions are adequately equipped for less predictable and potentially more precarious futures. A range of policy responses have been developed with the aim of attuning educational institutions, and their practices, structures and governance, to the perceived needs and values of the modern economy. At the same time, the relationship between people's educational experiences and labour market outcomes has become more complex and open to a wider range of interpretations.

These developments have been reinforced by wider changes to the social and economic fabric. There continues to be much debate over the precise nature and extent of labour market change; indeed, many critically inclined commentators have taken some issue with utopian accounts of economic growth and opportunity (Bradley et al. 2000; Thompson 2004; Keep and Mayhew 2010). However, there is some significant consensus that occupational structures, forms of labour and the composition of the workforce have been reshaped over time. Changing labour market structures have altered the allocation of individuals to various positions in the workforce, as well as the types of skills and credentials they need to draw upon to attain and sustain employment.

Perhaps the most significant force underpinning socio-economic change is that of globalization, in its various economic, political and cultural forms. Globalization has not only altered the relationship between national states, markets and policy formations, but also human relationships and the way in which people live their lives. These developments resonate strongly with new conceptual movements within the social sciences that see social and economic life as becoming increasingly fragmented, complex and differentiated. At the same time, increasing responsibilities are placed on individuals to take charge of their lives. In short, people's social and economic experiences have become increasingly individualized (Beck 1992; Beck and Beck-Gernsheim 2002). Yet, somewhat paradoxically, as individuals' experiential frames of references have expanded through globalization, the individual self has become the main unit of resource and exchange within a socio-economic context that has generated greater possibilities and also greater uncertainties.

These wider changes have had a significant bearing on young people and adults in education and training, particularly in terms of their educational and labour market trajectories. They have also had a profound impact on the notion of youth, the transition to adulthood and the formation of adult identities. At one time, the majority of young people left school at 15, many with a fairly well-defined notion of what they wanted from the job market and what it would provide for them. This was set in the context of what was typically seen as stable and accommodating job market structures. For many young people, school was a rite of passage to particular jobs, most of which would be held for lengthy durations of their working lives. However, such certainties and expectations have been seriously upturned over the past three decades. Changing employer demands, the need for educational credentials, continued investment in further education and training, and expanded educational opportunities and pathways have all disrupted this once well-established transition. Many young people have now seen their period of youth extended and have had to align themselves with new labour market challenges. While all these changes are sometimes viewed as indicative of a new, positive relationship between education and the economy, they have also been seen to engender new risks and opportunity costs for those in formal education.

Identities: Linking structure and agency

The theme of identity is significant in the discussion of education and work as it relates significantly to individuals' interactions with, and relationships to, broader social structures and institutions, and how they make sense of the world. Individuals' experiences of education and their future work are dynamic and ongoing. Such experiences are likely to be derived from, while similarly feeding into, an individual's sense of self. Moreover, within educational contexts, people inhabit particular frames of reference that are likely to inform interpretations of their situations and, subsequently, their actual lived experiences and behaviours. Understanding what constitutes people's identities, however, is a challenging task, given the multiple ways in which this might potentially be approached and understood.

Such issues are further compounded by the often dualistic understandings of individuals' relationship to the wider social world. Is identity constituted by a core, kernel self that is stable, enduring and motors much of an individual's actions? Or is it socially situated, contingent and malleable? Are individuals capable of fashioning their identities through their own choosing, or are they more fundamentally constituted by the social arrangements through which they are developed? While there may not be agreement on the different ways in which people's identities are conceptualized, there is, nevertheless, some agreement that identities play a significant role in grounding people's social experiences and their relationships to the social and economic world.

A useful starting point might be Castells' (1997) definition of identity as: 'People's source of meaning and experience'. From such a definition, we might see identity as a fundamental resource from which individuals make sense of themselves and their place in the world. Individuals actively seek out meaning from their individual experience and find ways of connecting this to their wider existential quest for understanding their own being-in-the-world. The self-perceptions of people capture perhaps the wider ways in which people think about themselves and what type of a person they strive to become.

Nonetheless, individuals' self-perceptions and sense of self are often strongly informed by the perceptions of others. How individuals are perceived and related to by others can effectively frame people's wider sense of self and being-in-the-world. Goffman's (1959) classic work shows how identities are largely produced through the symbolically rich interactive spaces and specific social frames that people inhabit. In many ways, identities are produced through the 'categories' that we form about ourselves and others. The task of producing, projecting and maintaining a credible social identity is an important facet of our relationship to the social world. As such, we undertake significant 'identity work' in finding ways to achieve personal and social affirmation. Jenkins (1996) reminds us of the need to integrate the 'personal' dimensions of identity with the 'social' – that is, people's subjective experiences and sense of self are largely constituted by their wider social experiences. Identities are invariably contingent on the social and cultural contexts through which individuals' lived experiences are framed, and are seldom divorced from them.

A significant issue in individuals' relationships to educational and work-related activities is the extent to which identities influence action. As Fevre (2003) discusses, identities tend to transport deeply held values and ground people's understanding of their place in the world. It provides people with a framework of meaning, as well as action, and helps orient them to the social and economic world. Identities are, therefore, more than nebulous properties that passively resides in people's heads; instead, they serve to guide actions and subsequent social and economic experiences and outcomes. More significantly, identities constitute a significant part of people's embodied relationship with the social world; individuals are likely to play out their identities through the various behaviours they engage in and how they orientate to the social world.

Structuration approaches have been significant to the understanding of identities, particularly in terms of people's interaction with wider social institutions. The social theorists, Giddens (1984, 1991) and Bourdieu (1977), have been very influential in the advancement of this framework. These theorists have emphasized the significance of both agency and structure in the construction of identities. Agency refers to people's capacity and propensity for action and their scope for acting upon the world and producing outcomes, while structure refers to the wider social and institutional arrangements that bound individuals' actions. Yet, agency and structure are very much constitutive of each other and often represent two sides of the same coin. Archer (2007) discusses the potency of reflexivity, including people's 'inner dialogues' and conversations as a driver of action, influencing how people negotiate the social world. The reflexive self is an active, agency-seeking subject, who endeavours to establish some level of control over their place in the world.

Self-reflection and personal meanings are, nonetheless, derived from wider cultural and structural arrangements, including dominant cultural influences and frames of references. Bourdieu's theorizing, in particular his concept of habitus, very much highlights this dynamic. For Bourdieu, habitus refers to individuals' embodied dispositions, traits and ways of thinking and feeling. People's habitus very much shapes people's behaviours and choices and, at one level, are personal and idiosyncratic. However, Bourdieu also shows how an individual's habitus is largely constitutive of the wider cultural context of their life, not least their class and gender. In many ways, habitus is where the objective cultural and material forces meet the subjective properties of people's lived experience and reflections. Moreover, while people's actions may be shaped by their habitus, they may also be reflexive about their choice and actions, including an awareness of where they sit within wider social relations.

Education, opportunity and social reproduction

Any analysis of the inter-dynamic between education and work requires some degree of attention to education's role in regulating differential access and opportunities to different forms of paid employment. This is mainly because significant inequalities still exist within educational systems, reflected principally in marked differences in the nature and quality of people's educational experiences and outcomes. A core factor shaping these differences is socio-economic status, often more commonly referred to as social class. There are, of course, a range of other factors that shape educational and economic differences, not least gender and ethnicity, and these, in turn, often interact with social class. Exploring educational inequality is important as it allows us to further probe the various cultural dynamics that underpin individuals' and social groups' relationship to education, and the sets of values and identities that drive these dynamics. Moreover, it may help us better understand how class-based relationships to, and within, educational contexts shape and reinforce individuals' relative access to future economic opportunities. Peoples' relationship with the educational context, and their own learning experiences, do not take place in isolation. Instead, they tend to be inextricably related to wider social structures and experiences, of which their class is often salient. This, in turn, tends to inform individuals' understandings of their relationship to educational and economic life.

Sociological accounts of the relationship between learners' class background and their educational experiences and outcomes have drawn largely upon theories of social reproduction (Bernstein 1996; Bourdieu and Passerson 1976). In essence, social reproduction theory sees education as playing an active role in reproducing class structures and their links to future social and economic opportunities. It does this through actively affirming pre-existing class-based identities and values through its various practices, pedagogies and modes of curriculum. Furthermore, educational outcomes tend to determine labour market outcomes; the hierarchies and structural divisions that occur outside of formal education are reproduced through education, which, in turn, perpetuates inequalities in the labour market.

However, wider social and economic change has again complicated the link between education, class and social reproduction. The expansion of the middle classes, the erosion of traditional forms of class-associated consumption and lifestyles, and the blurring of traditional class-based labour divisions have disrupted time-honoured patterns of social reproduction. Occupational changes have altered the work experiences of all class groups, even though some individuals continue to undertake work similar to that of five decades ago. As Brown (2003) argues, there has been a gradual refocusing within the sociology of education from what have been seen as 'opportunity gaps' to what might now be viewed as 'opportunity traps'. As opportunities have expanded, the stakes have also risen for securing sought-after employment. More and more individuals are able to glimpse new economic opportunities, yet not all may get a chance to actually fulfil them. Patterns of social exclusion and closure still operate in many fields of education and in the wider labour market. Dominant social groups continue to deploy additional economic and cultural resources to achieve relative advantages. Significant here is the way in which these processes relate to, and are negotiated through, the identities that people carry, in terms of how they make sense of and approach the social and economic world more generally.

Traditional sociological analysis has tended to concentrate more on the experiences and attitudes of individuals from lower social class backgrounds, given that they are subject to greater inequalities and social exclusions. Perhaps sometimes missing in traditional sociological literature has been a more fine-tuned analysis of middle-class responses and behaviours to the changing educational and economic landscape (Ball 2003; Power et al. 2003). According to these authors, there have tended to be taken-for-granted assumptions that middle-class individuals will necessarily access the best social and economic opportunities on the back of smooth, positive and enabling relationships with the educational system. However, while this may be the case for many within the middle classes, this assumption tends to obscure the continued challenges experienced by middle-class individuals looking to use education as a route towards economic fulfilment. The expansion of the middle classes, new forms of labour market pressure and changing employer selection processes have all served to intensify the cultural tensions and struggles of those with traditional educational and cultural capital. In response to these pressures, the middle classes increasingly have to explore ways of expanding the scope of their opportunities. This often necessitates more flexible, strategic and competitive approaches to the educational and labour market fields.

Themes of class responses to education again map onto identity politics in terms of the ways in which individuals are 'positioned' and, to a large degree, position themselves in relation to social and economic life. The educational trajectories that individuals follow are still likely to be socially structured through, if not exclusively determined by, wider cultural experiences and identities. Individuals continue to make choices and decisions through the wider cultural reference points of their class, gender and ethnicity. This may be in terms of what particular further education course to choose, what university to study at or what type of career to pursue. In many ways, educational choices and pathways reflect the types of person that individuals want to become and how it fits in with their immediate and wider identity projects. Yet, continued debate abounds over the extent to which class and gender still work as major social forces in shaping individuals' experiences and subjectivities. While some continue to acknowledge its dominance in framing experiences and outcomes, others envisage greater fluidity in social relations and an overall dissolution of traditional class boundaries and categorizations.

Post-industrialism and the new economy: From employment to 'employability'

The changing labour market forms a significant contextual background in framing individuals' relationship with education, and their educational and future working life trajectories. It is, perhaps, the shifting nature of economic life that has most affected the inter-dynamic between people's educational and future labour market experiences. Traditional forms of work, work practice and work identities have been reshaped over time. So too have the types of work-related credentials, skills and knowledge that people draw upon in their work. One of the main manifestations of these changes has been the gradual movement from an industrial to a post-industrial and more flexible economy. This has seen an accordant decline in manufacturing jobs and other forms of work associated with the industrial past; and with this, various transformations to the types of work identity and identifications that people hold. The post-industrial economy purportedly signals some deep-seated changes in people's approaches to their work and careers. In this context, individuals are said to give more of themselves to their work and, in turn, can enjoy potentially more enriching working lives.

Another consensus is that the modern economy places increasing demands on individuals, in terms of how they approach their work and their wider career progression. The theme of flexibility has pervaded discussion on the nature of contemporary employment; flexibility in terms of the conditions in which individuals work; flexibility in the types of specialities they must draw upon; flexibility in the ways in which they plan and think about their careers; flexibility as a new condition of consciousness in thinking about one's overall labour market experience. This again has both positive and negative connotations. The more optimistic camp sees a fluid and enriching labour market that offers more scope for people to realize their potential, including social groups who have traditionally been held back. The increasing feminization of the workforce and the breakdown of rigid class-based labour divisions are evidence of the expanding possibilities that the new economy offers.

The reshaping of wider labour market relations has, nonetheless, been viewed with various levels of scepticism. New possibilities have given way to new risks and challenges. Not only are individuals experiencing more pressures and demands through the intensity of new capitalism, but they are also playing out more insecure and uncertain employment trajectories. These may be having significantly deleterious consequences for individuals' well-being and morale, as well as eroding the traditional types of work narratives and identities that guided people's experiences of paid employment.

The contestations over the current and future state of work and working life are clearly evident in discussions of a concept closely linked to post-industrialism – the so-called 'knowledge economy'. In many academic, government and corporate circles, the knowledge-based economy is the dominant motif of post-industrialism. This is predicated on the grounds that the economy has become increasingly driven by the knowledge, creativity and enterprise that individuals possess. It demands that employees do more with their heads than their hands; more brain work and less craft work. There has been a faith in what might be described as new 'knowledge work' and the growth in the amount of jobs requiring the higher-level skills and knowledge that were traditionally the preserve of the highly educated. Moreover, education and, in particular, further and higher forms of education, is seen to play a pivotal role in the production of knowledge workers.

However, the knowledge-based economy has been critically questioned. A degree of scepticism has been raised over its actual scale and prevalence, as well as the extent to which it represents a fundamental upgrading to many forms of work. Is its surrounding rhetoric matched by the realities of the contemporary labour market? Nevertheless, the idea knowledge-based economy has been potent in shaping the discussion of the future economy and the role of education in meeting its new challenges.

A further concept that has become closely linked to the discussion of the new economy is that of *employability*. The new challenges and demands brought about by post-industrialism have led to greater pressures on individual employees in securing and sustaining employment. The knowledge-based economy places new demands on individuals. They need to prove their worth. They need to adapt flexibly to new organizational expectations and pressures. They need continually to enhance their work-related knowledge and skills in order to stay fit in more volatile internal and external labour markets. Such demands have generally been seen to coincide with the erosion of the long-term, organizational- and job-specific career trajectory that individuals enjoyed in earlier periods of economic life.

The demise of the so-called 'job for life' has meant that an increasing onus has been placed on individuals to determine for themselves the various employment opportunities and outcomes. Moreover, this has become an ongoing, lifelong process and does not stop on leaving school and college. The concept of employability has been subject to various definitions and debate, some of which are ideologically driven. Policymakers have tended to view it as a measure of individuals' skills, competences and attributes, which can be matched up in a labour market requiring value-added skills. As such, questions have been raised over the extent to which educational institutions can, and should, enhance learners' future employability. However, more critical approaches have highlighted that individuals' employability is as much a function of the labour market and the scope of available employment as it is a measure of whatever skills they possess.

As with most debates on the future of work and individuals' place in it, there are important issues over the way in which individuals understand their working futures and adapt accordingly. This extends to their employability and the way they attempt to manage it. As a number of authors (Fevre 2003; Grey 1994; Sosteric 1996) have pointed out, work is not a purely technical matter that simply entails the deployment of technical skills and qualifications in exchange for pecuniary reward. It also equally entails highly subjective, affective and value-driven dimensions that compel individuals to behave in specific ways, including whether to undertake particular kinds of work.

Human capital and economization

Given the continued pressures from the labour market, some key issues have been raised over the ways in which educational institutions need to respond. Over time, there has been a strong ideological commitment to the role of education as a vehicle for future economic development. This has been evident in the sustained attempts on the part of national states to coordinate educational policies that are geared towards harnessing the activities of educational institutions towards perceived economic demands. Education is no longer just seen to be important in the economy, but is, instead, a key economic driver upon which national economic fortunes rest. As the economy becomes more knowledge-intensive and reliant on the skills that individuals bring forward, education plays a fundamental role in raising their so-called 'human capital'. The old tools of production based on machinery, manual labour and physical toil, or what can be termed physical capital, have gradually given way to more advanced, cognitively centred skills that now increasingly shape labour outputs. The more human capital that people can acquire, the more their productivity and value to the labour market will increase.

The increased emphasis on education's economic goal of optimizing human capital and workforce productivity has been strongly pursued by national governments globally. Education has been reconfigured as a commodity good that should be used towards the utilitarian ends of enhancing national competitiveness. It has become economized. Its increasing economization has a number of ideological and policy-driven underpinnings, both of which are largely conjoined. Ideologically, education has been increasingly dominated by instrumental values and goals, all of which are centred on future potential economic output and gain. Pervading this movement is the language of 'skills', 'employability', 'outputs', 'measurements' and 'competition', all within an overarching market framework. Moreover, this has tended to powerfully frame the overall purposes and values of education. It is now the ends rather than the means that count. Consequently, concerns have been raised that more traditional and 'softer' educational values relating to the growth of the individual and their potentially creative relationship with society may have become sidelined.

Economization as a new educational ideological creed has been actively propagated by national governments. This has been reflected in a range of state policies developed over the past three decades, which have tended to be based on the wider remit of economy, efficiency and effectiveness. Indeed, there have been sustained state-driven pressures to reshape education's practices and activities towards the goal of economic efficiency. This has been mirrored in most other public services, including health and social work, which have similarly been subject to state pressures to align their services with new market demands. The philosophy of 'New Public Management' (see Ferlie et al. 1996; Entwistle et al. 2007), with its strong agenda of target setting, performance measurement and stringent systems of audit and accountability, has penetrated well into the fabric of most public services. Moreover, governments have looked to impose a wide range of policy levers on educational institutions aimed at inducing responsiveness among educational professionals and managers and channelling practices towards advantageous economic ends. This has been further set in a much more market-orientated context where schools, colleges and universities have been encouraged to compete for funding and resources.

A problem with the predominately human capital and economistic approaches to education, as shall be illustrated throughout this book, is that they tend to be somewhat reductive and technicist in their understanding of the linkage between education and economy. Not only are national educational systems' relationship to the economy somewhat complex, but so are individuals'. The notion that education can generate economic prosperity places considerable pressures on it to deliver outputs whose impact may ultimately be contingent on the state of the labour market. In many ways, governments have tended to see education as both the source of and the solution to many economic problems; education is the panacea to meeting all economic challenges. Somewhat paradoxically, narrowly economistic approaches to education, as manifest in much state policy, may not actually have the intended effect of fulfilling economic goals. Short-term goals may lead to short-term practices, all of which may be inimical to the goals of sustaining economic development and reproducing a dynamic knowledge-intensive workforce.

The positioning of educational systems and processes towards economic competitiveness and growth has also generated a number of contested perspectives on the impacts of educational growth for individuals, social groups and society at large. These not only centre on the long-standing debate over utilitarian versus liberal academic goals and values, but also the extent to which education can genuinely facilitate access to economic goods. Human capital approaches tend to be located within a technocratic framework that sees educational expansion and growth as both economically necessary *and* socially just. The benefits of education are equally distributed to most individuals. The expansion of education and its associated policy theme of lifelong learning are seen to represent an inclusive model of social justice that engenders social mobility. Human capital empowers people and takes them to areas of economic life that they traditionally may have stood outside.

However, at a time when social mobility has halted and, in some cases, actually declined (Goldthorpe and Mills 2008), questions are likely to be asked about the extent to which educational growth can generate social growth. The expansion of the middle classes may be seen to reflect an expansion of opportunities through meritocracy and more inclusive educational practices. It could also be construed as engendering new forms of social contest and a struggle for sought-after and increasingly scarce social and economic goods. Some four decades ago, Fred Hirsch (1977) warned of the limits of social growth, questioning the economic capacity to absorb the increasing level of qualifications distributed by expanded educational institutions.

Over the past three decades, there has been an upsurge in the range of vocational pathways open to learners, both during and after leaving formal education. Vocationalism has been celebrated as fulfilling economic and democratic goals by expanding opportunities and meeting new labour market needs. It must also be seen in terms of its political and social function, and in terms of its regulation of occupational divisions and marshalling learners into particular segments of the workforce. There have been enduring tensions between academic and vocational pathways, particularly in economies such as the UK where these two routes map strongly onto the class structure. Learners' orientations to different educational routes are based on different types of learner profiles and orientations, as well as some deep-seated assumptions over the role of education and/or training in equipping people for future labour market roles.

Young people have been orientated towards vocational learning on the basis of its perceived labour market relevance and its compatibility to their learning orientations and identities. However, much of the success and efficacy of vocational education may rest on how well it is coordinated, valued and demand based. A continued concern among researchers about vocational education is that it has too often been ineffectively regulated to fulfil individual and economic needs; moreover, that it is likely to intensify inequalities between different learners and social groups if it serves to reinforce prevailing cultural–academic divisions.

We can see that there are a number of contested areas in understanding the links between education and work and their implications for individuals and social groups. These contestations invariably underscore much of the discussions in the various chapters in this book. While polarized debates on the nature and impacts of socio-economic changes are often a characteristic of social science research more generally, they often reflect some broader conceptual and philosophical perspectives on the nature of social and economic life. At their most dramatic, they offer utopian or dystopian versions of the nature of change and their impacts on the individual. In terms of individuals' relationships to education and work, tensions abound between consensus views of education for individual and socio-economic gain and those approaches that highlight deep-seated structural inequalities. While the aim of this book is not necessarily to juxtapose competing perspectives in order to highlight the relative strengths and weaknesses of each, it nevertheless attempts to illustrate the different ways in which themes and perspectives on education and work have been understood. These different perspectives ordinarily have a conceptual basis, which, in turn, have informed the types of research agendas and outcomes of academics working in this field.

Organization of the book

This book is organized around a number of key substantive themes, all of which relate to the interaction between education and work and people's relations to them. The first two chapters explore fairly broad, macro-level issues relating to social and economic change, and introduce themes and concepts relating to people's changing experiences of social and economic life. Chapter 2 explores some of the key areas in social and economic change over time, and considers their impacts upon identities and the way individuals live their lives. It examines, in particular, the dominant themes of reflexive modernization, globalization and individualization, and the reshaping of people's social experiences and relations. Chapter 3 looks at issues of the changing nature of work, exploring the themes of post-industrialism and the 'knowledge-based economy'. It considers how research has attempted to capture the effect of labour market change on individuals' lived experiences and identities and explores the extent to which work continues to shape people's identities. It explores the theme of 'employability' further by looking at the way this has been conceptualized and how it reflects aspects of people's changing relationship to employment.

Chapters 4 and 5 explore more closely the interaction between education and the economy and some of the dominant conceptual motifs and policy themes in this area. Chapter 4 examines the dominant conceptual approaches to the interrelationship between education and work. It examines how this relationship has been theorized and the competing perspectives within this area; in particular, the role of education for economic development and returns. The two dominant theoretical frameworks of 'human capital' theory and 'credentialism' are explored as both offer strong accounts of the evolution of educational systems and their role in regulating economic outcomes. They also relate to wider concepts of 'conflict' and 'consensus' that foreground debates about the role of education in economy and society more generally.

Chapter 5 explores some of the dominant policy themes in the education–work relationship, particularly the themes of 'employability', 'skills' and vocational education. This chapter shows how these themes are part of a policy orthodoxy that continues to place significant emphasis on the 'supply-side' of the labour market. The chapter also aims to critically engage with some of these themes and explore how they have been critically examined.

Chapter 6 looks more closely at individuals' experiences of education and their educationally related identities. It considers the wider notion of lifelong learning and explores how the notion of learner identities and careers fits into this model. This chapter highlights the social nature of formal learning and how it is closely linked to individuals' social and cultural contexts. It also explores the theme of work-related and workplace learning and draws upon some of the main conceptual and research themes in this area.

Chapter 7 explores the changing transitions from education to work and the nature of learners' transitions to the labour market and how this has both changed and been reconceptualized through broader social and economic changes. It also explores how the transition from education to work has been reshaped over time, particularly in the context of a changing youth labour market, and looks at some of the challenges this presents for young people making the transition from education into the world of work.

In Chapter 8, we consider the theme of 'economization' in education in terms of its main rationale, characteristics and manifestations, exploring how this movement has impacted on educational institutions and professionals. It explores some of the main features of economization and how this relates to the shifting ideological landscape of neo-liberalism. In so doing, it examines the manifestation of this movement in educational policy and some of the effects this has had on educational professionals' identities.

Chapter 9 explores the area of higher education, which has been subject to considerable changes over recent time, particularly in terms of its shifting relationship to the state and the economy. This chapter looks at changes in higher education over time and how they also affect the changing student and academic experiences of higher education. It also explores the changing links between higher education and the labour market and considers the impacts this has on graduates and their transition to work.

CHAPTER TWO

Social and economic transformations

This chapter examines the wider process of social and economic transformation that forms the backdrop to people's changing relationship to social and economic life. Social and economic shifts, in particular those relating to the move towards late modern and post-industrial society, have had a substantial bearing upon the ways in which individuals make sense of their place in the world. Furthermore, these changes have brought into greater focus the ways in which individuals respond to, and align themselves with, the new social and economic challenges that they face. The shift towards late modern society is seen to offer new risks and opportunities as people's life experiences and trajectories become less patterned around traditional forms of social exchange and practice. These processes further extend into individuals' experiences of education and working life; particularly in relation to the identities and subjective experiences they have within education and beyond in the labour market.

This chapter pays particular attention to some of the dominant forces of social and economic change, exploring the movement towards a more fluid late modern society and some of the consequences this entails for individuals. It draws upon two core themes that have dominated thinking and discussion of social change, namely, reflexive modernization and globalization. Both signal substantial changes to people's lived experiences and realities of social life, and the frames of reference through which they position themselves to the wider social world.

The process of reflexive modernization entails significant changes to individuals' subjective experiences, the formation of their identities and the rationalization of their life choices and trajectories. Similarly, globalization carries significant reformations to people's social experience and practices, as well as the wider external context through which individuals interact with the world. As a process, globalization has altered people's frames of reference, potentially lifting them out of very specific local contexts and exposing them to a wider network of images, ideas and modes of social exchange. Taken together, these processes have potentially altered the ways in which individuals make sense of and navigate the world around them.

The changing socio-economic context carries a number of consequences for individuals' experiences of education and learning. Educational systems, and the transitions that individuals make from education into the job market, have themselves been significantly ruptured through wider processes of social change (Willis 2003). Young people making the transition from education into employment are much less likely to anchor their goals and lived experiences around traditional economic structures and related opportunity structures from the past. Learners' and school-leavers' outlooks, expectations and self-images are discernibly different to what they were in the past. In addition, the relatively fixed identities around longer-term employment that young people may have held on leaving school have potentially given way to more fractured and pluralized identities. All roads do not necessarily lead to highly specified and predetermined forms of employment.

Economic and cultural globalization has also penetrated into the fabric of educational systems, and has also reshaped the wider process of national policy formation. The traditional insular operations of nation states and their educational and welfare systems have given rise to an increasingly globalized convergence and coordination of policy, provision and practice. Increasingly, national governments have looked to align their educational systems with fast-moving developments in a new, globally competitive, knowledge-driven economy (Rizvi and Lingard 2010). This new politico-economic settlement is itself characterized by fluid and cross-global flows in trade, innovation and investment, while also reflecting an increasing consensus between different national governments' policy strategies.

From modern to late modern society

One of the most marked shifts since the middle to the later part of the twentieth century has been the shift from a *traditional* society to what has often been termed a modern or *late modern* society. This has been described by a number of key sociologists, such as Giddens (1990, 1994) and Bauman (2000). Traditional societies are largely based on established and set social and economic boundaries, often fixed within fairly defined time and space dimensions and tightly regulated forms of social practice and consumption. Moreover, traditional societies tend to be predictable and routine. Customs dominate and past actions and practices are heavily drawn upon as a key reference point for understanding social life.

A combination of technological, economic and lifestyle changes since the early part of the twentieth century have gradually eroded the traditional underpinnings of society. The shift towards modernity, therefore, has seen widespread disruption to highly patterned and routine ways of life. For Giddens (1990), three core processes underpin modernity. These are *distanciation*, that is, the increasing separation between time and space; individuals' experiences are no longer strongly bound by fixed and immediate social exchanges and interactions. Consequently, people have become increasingly *disembedded* from very immediate, specific and localized social contexts. They have effectively become 'lifted out' of the confines of space and time and become subjected to a broader array of social experiences. Late modernity is also characterized by increasing *reflexivity*: individuals, and society at large, have become more prone to reflecting upon and evaluating social experiences, and ascribing meaning to them.

Much of these changes are a consequence of the move towards the information society, or what Castells (2001) refers to as the 'network society'. Clearly, advances in information technology have meant that human interactions are far less confined to the immediate, situated and physically constrained settings of the 'here and now'. The reordering of time and space through technology has considerably reduced physical and geographical constraints; social relationships have instead become stretched over longer distances. For Castells, this is an enabling process for individuals and social institutions as it allows us to become networked both in technological and social ways. New social ties are formed in ways that cut across traditional spatial and institutional boundaries. The communications revolution has potentially democratized societies – people are not just consumers of information but also producers as they are now exposed to greater levels of information and access greater knowledge of the world.

In many ways, late modern societies present greater opportunities to individuals, as well as greater risks and uncertainties. Giddens' (2002) notion of the *runaway world* very much captures the prevailing sense of uncertainty and dislocation in which people experience contemporary society. These uncertainties and risks are often of an abstract nature, given that they entail complexities that work beyond the immediacies of people's here-and-now realities. New forms of technological, economic and environmental risk are, at one level, external to individuals: both their source and momentum operate beyond the everyday experiences of human agents.

Giddens see a significant paradox at the heart of late modernity: while it has become knowledge-centred and fluid, it has also generated new uncertainties and instabilities. Advances in human knowledge have liberated people and expanded social experiences, yet they have not necessarily resulted in greater control over the course of future events. This has profound implications for people's immediate and future lives. It also means that individuals have to become more adept and reflexive around the management of risk.

Bauman (2000), through his metaphors of solidity and liquidity, has developed another way of conceptualizing the shift towards modern society. Early modern and traditional societies are characterized by what he terms *solid modernity*. Solid modernity is based on highly grounded sets of social protocols and practices that are very much underpinned by relatively rigid rules of social engagement. For instance, in the old industrial communities of the past, relationships were very much grounded by solid, or at least tangible, social relationships and modes of being. People's identities were not only set within the relatively fixed spatial and temporal contexts of work, home and community, but they were also shaped by clearly defined notions of what constitutes appropriate and meaningful behaviours. Values are based on the cherished ideals of the past.

Liquid modernity, on the other hand, is marked by far more open and contingent social and economic relationships. In essence, people's experiences have become more fluid as well as increasingly short term. The traditional points of reference and value frames that guided individuals' outlooks no longer have significant purchase. For Bauman, routinely changing location, jobs, relationships and pursuing multiple roles and activities has become an increasing part of the liquid landscape that individuals inhabit. This essentially means that individuals' personal narratives have become more fragmented and flexible. Increasingly central to this situation is the need for greater levels of life planning and adaptability in the face of continual and endemic change and uncertainty.

Individualization, reflexivity and the rise of identity politics

The concept of individualization has very much caught the sociological imagination over the past two decades, depicting a shift in people's relationship to wider social and economic life. Its central tenet is that the social bonds and relationships that have traditionally grounded individuals' place in the world and their relationship to others have weakened. Increasingly, it has become *the individual* who is become the principle resource in shaping social experiences and outcomes. The work of Beck et al. (1994) and Beck and Beck-Germsheim (2002) has been influential in advancing this theory, particularly in their account of the changing conditions through which individuals position themselves in wider social and public life.

According to the individualization thesis, the transition from industrial to post-industrial forms of labour and social organization has brought about significant changes to the formation of social identities. In traditional industrial societies, people tended to fix their identities around *collective* pursuits and endeavours, typically those of work colleagues, familial networks and other members of the community. The dominant point of reference is the collective *social other* in terms of shared commonalities in lifestyle, occupation and general biography. In industrial society, people's general social experiences and trajectories tend to be fairly uniform and follow fairly certain and predictable patterns.

In post-industrial contexts, however, these traditional frames of reference have significantly weakened; instead, individuals are confronted with a much broader array of possibilities around what they might become. It is now *the individual*, rather than the wider social arrangement of which they are a part, who shapes future outcomes. Individualization also means that people's life trajectories have become less stable and structured around established pathways. In many ways, the future has become less of a pre-given that people move towards with limited planning and deliberation; instead, it is increasingly riskier and uncertain, necessitating far more in the way of self-conscious and reflexive life planning. Moreover, individuals' outlooks and trajectories are made far less in relation to grand totalizing social structures, such as class, gender, workplace and community. Crucially, it is the individual, and their goals, aspirations and motivations that has become the primary frame of reference.

Writing on the changing youth labour market, Robert (1995) describes individualization as a measure of the decreasing likelihood of experiencing the same kinds of biographies and life trajectories as someone from a similar social background, cohort and age to oneself. In short, people's biographical experiences have become increasingly less patterned around shared experiences and similar points of reference. This has had a marked bearing on young people's transitions from education into the labour market, as they are confronted by a broader array of potential pathways and options. In the context of a more clearly defined youth employment market, such as that in the 1960s, transitions were more clearly structured. Young people were channelled into specific roles and socio-economic positions, based on clear expectations and frames of reference that firmly grounded their experiences. Moreover, they could effectively rely on traditional labour market structures and patterns of past participation to anchor their decisions and expectations for organizing their future aspirations.

According to Beck et al. (1994) and Beck and Beck-Germsheim (2002), the shift towards late modernity and post-industrialism has meant that individuals have become increasingly reflexive of their lives and their own future trajectories. The term they use to describe this process is *reflexive modernization*. The reflexive modernization thesis links closely to the concept of individualization in that it posits that individuals have become more self-consciously in tune with their own biographies and more prone to reflecting upon the shaping of their own life trajectories. As individuals become disembedded from the traditional structures and points of reference that may have once anchored their identities, they are then faced with the challenge of re-embedding themselves in new and multiple contexts.

The increasingly fluid and unpredictable conditions of the late modern age mean that individuals are continually trying to work out their place in the world, and the kinds of options open to them. This is likely to entail a range of existential deliberations around how to live one's life and how to negotiate the range of life options and challenges with which one is confronted. As people begin to follow less patterned and more individualized life trajectories, particularly in the job market, they must begin to forge their own destinations and secure their own fates. How do I live my life? What choices are open to me? How will my future be played out? These are the types of questions that reflexive modernization gives rise to, and must be negotiated by individuals trying to negotiate what the future holds.

As Bauman (2002) neatly describes it: 'individualisation consists in transforming human identity from a "given" into a "task" – and charging actors with the responsibility of performing that task and for the consequences (and side-effects) of their performance. . .' (Bauman 2002, p. xix). This clearly implies that individuals are no longer preconditioned towards following a very fixed and clearly defined social script, or one that forms a strong basis for their future actions. Instead, they have the active 'task' of working out what script(s) to follow and the means to realize the multiple goals they might pursue. Individualization therefore entails new existential confrontations: people face a continual struggle over working out how they are and how best to shape their current and future course of action. Their lives, and the identities they carry, need to be worked out, worked at and constantly negotiated.

Theorists of individualization acknowledge the paradoxical nature of individualization as both an experience and a process. They see the late modern, globalized and individualized human subject as both potentially empowered and ontologically disrupted. The process of being disembedded from traditional and fixed narratives produces new forms of potential insecurity and uncertainty that people have to negotiate carefully. The late modern age is characterized by continual change and a pervasive sense of risk and unpredictability. Yet, it is an age that can potentially open up individuals to new and exciting opportunities, particularly as they become less constrained by the dead weight of tradition and fixed expectation. The individualized individual has more flexibility to move around new and dynamic social spaces. This, however, inevitably carries risks and unknowns.

For individualization theorists such as Beck, processes of *institutionalized individualization* mean that individualizing processes are woven into the heart of most modern institutions, not least workplaces. The labour market, and the changing patterns of work and career that take place within it, is seen to mirror the flexible and fluid conditions of the late modern age. Beck and Beck-Germsheim refer to the labour market as the 'motor for individualization' given that it has become an institution that produces the same fractured narratives and individualized responses that are at the heart of the late modern age. This, in turn, places greater responsibilities on individuals to carve out favourable outcomes in the more precarious context of short-term capitalism where responsibility for work has gradually shifted away from the welfare state and employer organization and onto individual employees.

We can see how the concept has also become very much woven into contemporary discourses that emphasize individuals' propensities and responsibilities towards desired forms of action. It is now *the individual* who must take the lead in shaping their future outcomes. Moreover, the individual can no longer rely on social institutions, be they from the state or the labour market, to act as protective shelters in accommodating their immediate and longer-term employment fortunes and fates. In some ways, this has become reflected in policy discourses around the need for individuals to both invest in and actively manage their lifelong learning and future employability.

Rose (1996, 1999) has offered a critique of individualization when used as a political tool that places exclusive emphasis on individuals, including their deficiencies, instead of examining the wider conditions of the labour market. For Rose, the strong discursive framing of an active, striving and involved individual engaged in acts of self-responsibilization typically places almost singular emphasis on the individual and their motivational and ethical make-up. Consequently, people's relative success or failure within social and economic life can be explained by characteristics pertaining to *the individual*. This is invariably linked to their personal dispositions and capacity to act as responsive and proactive human subjects. For example, the unemployed person is recast no longer as a welfare dependent but as an *active* jobseeker, and therefore someone who must draw upon their personal resources and agency to elevate their fortunes.

Reflexive modernization and identity politics: From class to life politics

From the previous section, we can see how the individualization and reflexive modernization concepts present a challenge to the grander, more authoritative value and normative systems that may have traditionally formed the bedrock of people's identities and how they positioned themselves in work. Beck and Beck-Germsheim argue that forms of labour and social organization in the late modern age have rendered social structures, such as class and gender, as increasingly arbitrary influences in shaping people's identities, experiences and outcomes. Beck (2004) has gone as far as describing class as a 'zombie concept', almost akin to a ghost from a bygone industrial age, or an abstraction that has no immediate bearing on ongoing social relations and experiences.

A strong feature of early modern and industrial societies was the salience of social class, and indeed gender, in shaping individuals' identities. These were firmly embedded through individuals' experiences in the labour market, the immediate community and in their domestic lives. It largely fed through to how people conducted themselves and understood their place in the world. A highly class- and gender-based division of labour in industrial societies reflected and reinforced the salience of class as a mediating influence on people's identities and relationships. However, for theorist such as Beck and Bauman, the more fluid conditions of late modernity have eroded such normative frameworks, together with the tightly woven practices and ways of being which fashioned individuals' horizons and outlooks.

A major theme emerging from theories of late modernity is that of identity and identity politics, also referred to as life politics. Jenkins (1996) has discussed how identity politics has gradually replaced the influence of traditional class politics in organizing social relations. Class politics is based on ways of thinking and acting in accordance with the wider reference point of one's social class. Here, class can be seen as a totalizing influence that conditions people to act in habitual and non-reflexive ways. People's behaviours and outlooks are fashioned almost ostensibly by their class location and related social expectations. Identity politics, on the other hand, entails a greater range of possibilities to the types of identities that people seek and choose to play out. It encompasses a far wider range of existential and experiential concerns that relate to a potentially broader range of lifestyle and socio-economic possibilities. This has been reinforced by the shift towards a more consumer-driven society and the potential that people have to inhabit virtual space.

Giddens (1991) has made some strong connections between late modernity and identity, arguing that self-identities are reflexively organized and take the form of a broader *trajectory of the self*. Thus, identities are intimately linked to individuals' biographical narratives and the sequences of events that make up their own life trajectories. In keeping with the reflexive modernization themes, Giddens posits that identities are fluid and multiple and that individuals are prone to reflecting upon these and how they are developing. Moreover, identities are developed through the activities that individuals engage in and the life events they experience, particularly where these activities hold particular meaning and value. The construction of self-identities can be seen in terms of a wider biographical project, with key activities and events feeding strongly into one's sense of self.

As lived experiences based on individuals' biographical narratives, identities tend to centre on what Giddens has termed *life projects*. Life projects become the organizing practices through which individuals play out their identities and they help to establish a sense of self. These projects can be multiple and varied, or they may centre on very specific goals such as developing one's career pathway. Moreover, life projects are the kinds of endeavours that individuals invest in, in order to affirm a sense of self and a place in the world. Being a parent, a member of a club, a new employee or a traveller are all potential life projects that may all go towards making up a person's biographical narrative, informing how they may come to view themselves. Moreover, the shifting conditions of late modernity have facilitated the opening up of a range of life projects from which individuals can marshal their self-identities.

It is clear, therefore, that reflexive modernization theory places more attention on individuals, their changing relationships with contemporary social institutions and the increasing significance of identities in shaping their trajectories. However, it also points to a complex and potentially fragmented contemporary subject for whom stable and well-established pathways have given way to much more flexible conditions. Bauman (2000), in particular, has offered some cautionary warnings about the new individualized subject and their potential for substantial social dislocation. Furthermore, identity also runs the risk of saturation in terms of the way individuals in late modernity attempt to understand their place in the world. Identity, then, has the potential to be an exhaustive facet of personhood: individuals are faced with a bewildering array of notions around who, and what, they might be, or what Beck and Beck-Gernshiem (2002) refer to as the 'jungle of the self' (p. 33). At one level, people may actively seek out new forms of identity and self-expression in order to establish new ways of being. This might be liberating. However, the continual pursuit of identities may also produce a rudderless, destitute self that, far from developing a coherent and empowered personal narrative, engages instead in transitory forms of *identification*. Yet, identification, unlike identity, is merely a reference point, and is not necessarily embodied through individuals or integrated through to their wider sense of self.

But are we simply all just individuals now?

Reflexive modernization has, nonetheless, been critiqued in a number of quarters. One particular criticism has been towards its depiction of individuals as essentially free agents, who are both relatively unconstrained and uninfluenced by wider social structures. In the structure–agency interplay, agency tends to be the winner, not least because traditional social structures have weakened their grip in shaping people's outlooks and action frames. This tends to present individuals as highly voluntaristic and autonomous, as well as assuming that social structures have a minimal role in shaping people's experiences, outcome and identities. Is it really only the individual who shapes life outcomes, or are these still not significantly socially patterned? Is the representation of the free agent and individualized contemporary person at risk of underplaying significant social structures that may influence how people live and experience the world?

Significantly, the reflexive modernization thesis tends to rest uncomfortably with more traditional, class-based accounts of individuals' relationship to the social and economic world. Some critics have taken Beck's dismissal of class as a 'Zombie' concept as reflecting of a position that grossly underplays the significance of objective cultural and material conditions that shape social experiences (see Skeggs 2004). Moreover, the theory has been challenged for exaggerating the scale of social change and the nature of social relations within society and the economy. Social relations that were materially grounded and referenced against class have somehow dissolved into a landscape of free-standing individuals whose primary reference point is themselves. This, perhaps, somehow presupposes that the kinds of organizations and modes of experience within institutions such as the workplace have changed shape beyond recognition.

As discussed earlier, there is a danger that the individualization thesis falls into simplistic political caricatures. At one level, this tends to celebrate individuals as rugged, independent and fully responsible agents and citizens. At another level, it captures the popular notion of the 'classless' society, propagated by successive UK governments over the past four decades. Underpinning this is an ideological faith in the capacity of individuals to transcend social constraints and achieve the kinds of socio-economic outcomes they desire. In the 'classless' society, therefore, people negotiate their position in the world through their own design and choosing. Attributing socio-economic outcomes to predetermining social conditions like class is to negate the opportunities of most individuals.

The general consensus within sociological theory is that the nature of social class has become reshaped, if not dissolved fully as a social force (Devine 2005; Savage 2000). One of the key shifts has, perhaps, been a refocus away from the material and economic, to the more cultural and subjective ways in which social class is mediated and enacted. As Devine argues, class is as much a subjective condition that is embodied through cultural practices as it is a quantifiable measure of individuals' socio-economic and occupational standing. Yet, people acquire cultural resources, dispositions and ways of seeing, through formative class experiences, whether they are conscious or not. These frame, sometimes unconsciously, how individuals see the world and understand their place in it.

In a similar vein, Savage argues that the expansion of the middle class together with occupational changes at large have shifted class relations. The increased access to middle-class lifestyles and modes of consumption has expanded many people's frames of reference. For Savage, class itself has become increasingly individualized and the traditional formation of class identity weakened through modernity. However, class identities and their related cultural practice still have the capacity to reproduce themselves and in ways that serve to position individuals in the world. Significant here is the continued force that social class plays in regulating people's social experiences and outlooks, even though more individuals may see it as having less of a prevailing influence.

These types of issues also play out in relation to individuals' education and job-related experiences. A number of influential sociological works have pointed to continued patterns of social differentiation in educational and economic outcomes (Roberts 2001; Goldthorpe and Jackson 2008;

Goldthorpe 2003). This suggests that individuals are still located within a hierarchical social order, based on socio-economic origins and resources, which appears to pattern both opportunities and outcomes. As Goldthorpe argues (2003), for all the educational and economic changes that have occurred over the past four decades, there continues to be a normative link between people's social origins and their wider life chances and outcomes. This further implies that social class continues to be a pervasive force in shaping people's social experiences and outcomes, and that the scope of individual freedom as developed by reflexive modernists has been exaggerated.

Perhaps more than any other theorist, the work of French sociologist, Pierre Bourdieu, has demonstrated the essentially structured nature of identities and their embodiment through behaviours, outlooks and practices. His work (discussed further throughout this book) shows that not only is class embodied through practice, but it is also reproduced through the kind of material and intellectual resources of people. Not only does this provide them with the tools with which to negotiate the world, but it also frames their subjective experiences in influential ways. In Bourdieu's theorizing, individuals inhabit well-defined cultural spaces that are strongly linked to social origins. These ultimately determine people's educational and socio-economic experiences and the ways they orientate themselves in the world.

Globalization

The move towards a late modern society is closely linked to wider socio-economic developments in the transformations of nation states and their increasing interconnection and interdependence with other national economies. This is being driven by the process of globalization, a process that gained significant momentum during the latter stages of the past century. Yet, there is no shared or agreed understanding of the specific nature and impact of globalization. This, perhaps, owes to the fact that it takes a variety of forms, not least within the economic, political and cultural fields. As authors such as Held and McGrew (2007) and Green (1997) argue, it is perhaps helpful to see globalization as encompassing a range of objective, subjective and ideological dimensions as it involves structural shifts in social and economic relations, as well as changes to individuals' everyday lived experiences.

In ideological terms, globalization is closely associated with the neo-liberal political consensus that places a strong emphasis on the liberalization of free trade across national boundaries. This has tended to be strongly endorsed by national governments that have come to view it as imperative that national systems, including education, become responsive to the challenges of a globally agile economy (Olssen et al. 2005). While globalization is not necessarily an antecedent to post-industrial society, it is, nevertheless, likely to impact on its broader trajectory. Thus, the global competition has become an increasingly dominant feature of national economic policy.

Nevertheless, there are some common features to globalization (see Held and McGrew 2007). A relatively straightforward and commonly held understanding of globalization is that it involves a process of bringing countries and their citizens closer together. This has been brought about by the gradual dissolution of national boundaries and geospatial relations, caused by a combination of transnational economic trading and increasing cultural diffusion between nations. Globalization entails a greater interconnection and interdependence between people across the globe, and this has been accelerated by the advent of advanced technology and communication systems, not least the internet.

This increasing global interconnection between national cultures typically involves the gradual compression of social relations within time and space. Globalization has effectively made the world a 'smaller place' and the flow of knowledge, ideas and technological influences have generated stronger points of reference between people. Citizens from different countries and continents, who may have once felt culturally estranged, now share increasingly common experiences, interests and patterns of lifestyle and consumption. This has led to a growing convergence of life experiences and practices as reflected in the increasing orientation to, and consumption of, global services, products and brands. In short, globalization has made nations and their citizens more globally 'networked' and their experiences more wedded to contexts outside of their traditional cultural setting.

There are, of course, different forms of globalization that reflect its different levels of effect and influence, not least in the economic and cultural spheres. Economic globalization essentially relates to the extension of trade and commerce across national economies, and the freeing up of trading agreements between nations. This has been very much associated with the presence of transnational corporations that have emanated from traditional global super nations, traditionally the USA, and have monopoly stakes in the production and delivery of goods. Economic globalization is also linked to the increasing subcontracting of international labour from national to foreign locations as transnationals look to base themselves in other economies, often with cheaper labour costs and resources. International employment legislation has allowed greater capacity for international flexibility in labour mobility. This has permitted transnational companies to utilize international labour, and draw upon the physical and human resources within newly emerging economies. In previous decades, indigenous, national industries dominated the employment landscape in the national context and employees were offered greater protection and regulation.

Globalization is often intimately associated with the development towards what has been termed a 'post-industrial economy', the features and effects of which we will examine in more detail in the next chapter on the changing nature of work. Put simply, post-industrialism represents a movement away from a strongly nationalized, extractive and manufacturing economy to one based largely on service-sector jobs, communication-orientated work and the application of advanced information technology. The post-industrial economy has corresponded with the decline of core national industries that operated within the confines of so-called 'walled economies'.

Cultural globalization refers mainly to the sharing of cultural practices across nations. This relates largely to the growing convergence in lifestyle and consumption patterns and orientations, and shared exposure to 'global' icons, brands, film, music and products. Perhaps most significantly, cultural globalization has resulted in the increasing sharing of cultural experiences and outlooks, together with the movement away from more local and specific cultural understandings to globally universal ones. It has become something of a cliché to describe the world as becoming a 'smaller place', yet increasing cultural convergence means that we are now more likely to know about developments in remote parts of the world than ever before. Cultural globalization has, therefore, not only facilitated greater knowledge and understanding of other national cultures and contexts, but also the sharing of more universal global discourses and frames of reference.

Both forms of globalization have been strongly contested and critiqued. In keeping with the neo-liberal stance, supporters of economic globalization have tended to celebrate economic globalization for its capacity to bind nations through stronger trade links and a speedier flow of capital across national regions and boundaries (see Bhagwati 2007). Furthermore, the global regulation of markets has allowed national economies and their corporations to be more receptive to advancements in science and technology and other innovations in trade and commerce. Economic globalization also limits the capacity of nation states to intervene too strongly in the governance of corporate planning, and instead permits corporations to partake in new forms of competitive bidding and flexible labour organization. Supporters of economic globalization challenge state intervention and oversight for being a constraining and unsustainable influence that hampers the free market's responsive capacity.

However, critics continually point to what they see as the inherent inequality and instability of economic globalization (Griffin 2003). Indeed, one of the strongest criticisms of economic globalization is that it engenders marked inequalities within what is an uneven balance of economic power between national economies. This is reflected in an imbalance in the presence and influence of different national economies, some of which have much stronger economic infrastructures. It also maps onto a clear international division of labour and the relative ability for powerful national economic elites to capitalize on cheap labour and resources in poorer national locations. Furthermore, the notion that economic globalization entails a fair allocation of labour, or that it somehow allows economies to proliferate their productive capacity has been seen as something of a myth (Brown et al. 2011). If anything, economic globalization has intensified the global competition between national economies that continue to look to outsource production to low-cost regions.

Within the cultural sphere, there have been similar challenges to globalization's increasingly pervasive influence. While, in some quarters, globalization has been lauded for promoting greater overall cultural diversity and pluralism, as well as cultural openness and exchange, critics have interpreted this as representing a cultural homogenization and standardization (Klein 2000). Perhaps even more cynically, it is seen as a form of imperial 'Westernization' or 'Americanization' that has undermined the cultural forms, practices and identities of indigenous cultures. As with economic globalization, the influences and effects of cultural globalization are seen as uneven. The diffusion of global products, brands and ideas originate from dominant cultures and political economies, and so their influence could be construed as a form of cultural colonization. However, commentators such as Robertson (1995) point to a process of 'glocalization' – that is, the capacity for local national cultures to retain their indigenous cultural forms and practices, while also absorbing and appropriating the various influences and trends offered by globalization.

Globalization, personhood and identity

Sometimes missing from the discussion and debate on globalization are the impacts that it has on people's personal lives and identities. Thus, all too often, globalization is presented in abstract terms as encompassing wider politico-economic and geo-cultural shifts that operate above and beyond people's everyday lives and experiences. John Tomlinson described globalization as a process that 'alters the context of meaning construction . . . it affect people's sense of identity, the experience of place and of self in relation to space' (Tomlinson 1999). Significant to this definition is the potential reframing of individuals' personal narratives and relationship to the world. Viewed in this light, globalization is a social process that penetrates through to people's lived experiences; it affects not only our relationships with the world and others, but also how we act, how we choose to live our lives and the kinds of lifestyle we pursue.

Globalization, therefore, clearly has a strong subjective element in so far as it shapes people's conscious experiences of the world and their relationships with others. Giddens (2002) takes this theme further by arguing that globalization alters the fabric of everyday experience and people's ongoing relationship with the social world. Globalization is not an exclusively external construct that is related to complex structural rearrangements in the international flows of capital and technology. Instead, it should be seen as an 'in-here' phenomenon that is embodied through thoughts, actions and self-identities. Globalization influences people's intimate experiences and relationships, for example, in the sphere of family life and friendship, largely through reworking the rules of social engagement. Accordingly, we are not just passive recipients of globalization, but active agents and participants in the process, and this has penetrated through to people's lifestyles, choices and orientations. For instance, changes to the way that people conduct their intimate relationships and organize their domestic worlds are by-products of wider global changes and movements – including the global spread of women's rights.

Beck (1999) has similarly referred to 'globalisation of biography' in terms of the expansion of individuals' social horizons and points of reference. Globalization inevitably means that people become increasingly entangled in a wider web of relationships, often mediated through multiple contexts. In the traditional, pre-global society, individuals' conscious experiences are framed almost exclusively by the local context of their immediate social environments. The local is relatively spatially fixed and promotes practices and modes of being that tend to be very specific to their own particular contexts. However, globalization effectively lifts people out of the specific contexts that may have traditionally anchored their ways of acting and being. This has resulted in the potential broadening of individuals' experiences as well as the types of biographical narratives they play out. The fracturing of exclusively local identities, in turn, gives way to the formation of multiple and hybrid forms of identity that transcend narrower affiliations to traditional practices, customs and social mores.

Globalization clearly, then, facilitates new forms of social experience and engagement. Appadurai (2006) discusses the new 'social imaginations' that globalization produces; in effect, the old rigidities of time and space have disappeared as people become more attuned to a globally networked landscape. The advance of global technologies has enabled individuals to foster new virtual selves and identities and these are played out in more fluid social contexts such as the virtual world. The expanded communication nexus afforded by globalization is often played out in virtual arenas as in the case of the widespread participation in global social media forums such as Facebook, web chat rooms and internet dating. In these contexts, individuals are engaging in a form of connectivity with other virtual actors that is high speed, fluid and atemporal.

Additionally, individuals can exercise higher levels of control over their social experiences in ways that are difficult to accomplish in the non-virtual sphere. For instance, in instigating virtual modes of communication, individuals are opening up new and potentially creative areas of self-expression. As part of the remit of new social media, individuals are invited to project new types of personal identities that might have been unachievable in traditional temporally and spatially constrained settings. Thus, supporters of this new type of globalized, virtual interchange see it as generating new levels of enchantment and empowerment for individuals. Some critics, however, see this mode of social interaction as short-termist, superficial and representing the demise of more authentic and meaningful social exchange that takes place in real time and non-virtual communities (Sennett 2012).

Socio-economic change, education and the labour market

The conceptual themes on the more specific linkages between education and the economy will be outlined in later chapters. For the present purposes, we explore some of the challenges that these wider processes have on educational systems and the labour market.

Perhaps one of the most significant challenges facing national economies and their educational systems is how to respond to the opportunities, risks and potential new developments that the late modern, globalized and post-industrial society carries. A prevailing theme in the area of social and economic change is the potentially disruptive and destabilizing effects that these changes have on people's sense of social and economic location. Individuals have been lifted out of relatively certain and cosseted contexts from which they could base their identities and sense of being-in-the-world, or what Beck refers to as new global ontological insecurity. These clearly extend to people's experience of education and working life, as they attempt to align themselves with increasingly less predictable and certain futures. There are also significant issues about how national governments and states respond and look to meet the challenges, and opportunities, that globalization presents.

One of the more optimistic takes on the impact of economic change has been the *new growth theory*, which stipulates that the global spread of technology and labour will escalate the scope that people have to pursue rewarding, discretionary and high-paid work (Romer 2007). Advancements in technology and the post-industrial economy have effectively generated new demands for high-skill work that an increasingly educated core of prospective employees will embrace. Moreover, the global expansion of knowledge and technology correlates with the expansion of education, which itself feeds into the economy in productive and innovative ways. The advancement of educational systems, and the development of people's skills and aptitudes within them, contributes to an upwards spiral of opportunity. The demand for education and skills is therefore generative: economic globalization and the post-industrial economy warrants enhancement of individuals' skills and educative capacities, and this, in turn, stimulates growth, productivity and economic opportunity.

However, the view that globalization expands the scope of labour market opportunity has been brought into question. While largely celebrating the opportunities presented by economic globalization, Reich (1991, 2002) has, nevertheless, offered some cautious observations on the structural and occupational power imbalance that it also engenders. In particular, the growing division between a global super-elite and an increasingly disenfranchised and disempowered labour class, increasingly including traditional middle-class professionals. The economic nationalism that was based on relatively stable patterns of employment and growth has given way to the global liberalization of trade, and with it, changing patterns of work and occupational structures.

For scholars like Reich, forms of work that were traditionally wedded to national economies have fractured as large multinationals and their organizational elites seek to offshore production at cheaper costs. The effects of this are far from benign and confined to low-skilled workers in national labour markets. It also increasingly means that traditionally skilled and professional forms of work have become both contested and devalued through the emergence of corresponding forms of work in other countries. Furthermore, the global economy offers considerably more scope for some individuals over others. This is manifest in an increasingly divided opportunity structure that has emerged between a flexible and elite body of high-tech, high-powered, knowledge workers whose work has strong global purchase, and a core body whose skill sets and labour market potential is confined to domestic and inflexible forms of labour.

More recently, Brown et al. (2011) have further developed some of these themes in their work on transnational companies' approaches to human resource development and skill formation. Again, this work challenges the conventional orthodoxy of the new growth theory; in particular, the 'promise' propagated by national (mainly Western) governments that investment in education will necessarily stimulate new job opportunities and life chances. What Brown et al. (2011) illustrate is that transformations in the global composition of skills through the development of emerging economies' skills bases has effectively generated a new 'global auction'. In many ways, the first wave of economic globalization based on the offshoring of low-cost, low-quality production has been gradually superseded by a new drive among transglobal companies to integrate higher-skilled, higher-quality production to emerging economies. Ultimately, this means that the old divisions between the 'brain' work of the West and the 'brawn' work of developing economies has dissolved. Many emerging economies (e.g. China and India) are now executing high-level, high-skilled work at the higher end of the production value chain.

The rise in global competition and flexibility, and its attendant features of cross-national skills diffusion, labour auctioning and human resource bargaining, has invariably had a significant bearing on educational systems across countries. A major challenge facing national governments is how to adapt their systems in ways that are aligned with the changing demands that globalization brings, as well as ensuring that they fare successfully in an increasing global 'war for talent' in knowledge and ideas.

There has often been a prevailing view that economic globalization has weakened the role of the state as a regulatory force in matters of economic and educational policy. While this may be true in terms of the state's influence upon the trajectories of transnational companies and corporations' human resource policies, national governments have, nevertheless, been shown to be responsive to the wider challenges of globalization (Ozga and Lingard 2007). Thus, although economic globalization is seen to be synonymous with *laissez-faire* government involvement in economic matters, it has also somewhat paradoxically led to a resurgence in state intervention in much public policy. This has led to increasingly planned central coordination of educational policy so that it is attuned to anticipated challenges of global competition.

Scholars such as Marginson (1999) and Dale (2005) have argued that globalization has potentially placed more power in the hands of state actors and policymakers in playing a stronger role in regulating educational systems. Certainly, one of the most salient impacts of globalization has been a renewal of the state's role in steering systems of education. Most national states' responses have been a combination of top-down mechanisms designed to enhance the output and delivery of educational institutions, and a revived faith in education to fulfil the aims of social democracy. The types of measures and responses will be discussed further in Chapter 8.

However, as Kelly (2009) critically points out, this is not always to the advantage of educational institutions and the wider labour markets that they are meant to support. Such critical readings of the state's response to globalizing challenges sees government as pursuing policies that are based on reactive and short-term measures that often amount to a misreading of the nature and implication of globalization. The state's response to the pressures of globalization is perhaps most evident in policies that have tried to make educational institutions more responsive and in tune with the challenges of economic globalization. In many ways, national governments have looked to tighten their grip on educational institutions in the form of state policies that are geared towards enhancing their national economy's global economic standing.

At the same time, globalization has also resulted in new forms of convergence between national states in the formation of policy and national educational strategy. At one level, this is evident in the increased levels of 'policy borrowing' and modelling between national governments, including, for instance, the expansion of the post-compulsory sector and the increasing privatization and marketization of state education. At another level, it is also evident in the increased standardization of provision across national boundaries, for instance, in Europe with the Bolonge process in higher education. This has led to an increased calibration of educational qualifications, modes of study and quality assurance across the European higher education system. The aim behind this process is for greater national convergence of provision and also easier mobility and transferability of higher education qualifications across national boundaries. Similarly, educational provision and outcomes have become increasingly subject to global comparison and benchmarking, for instance, through the Programme of International Student Assessment (PISA), which allows comparison in maths, science and reading across the Organization for Economic

Cooperation and Development (OECD) members states. At the same time, competition between nation states has meant that education has, in many ways, become an increasingly global 'commodity'. Elite schools and universities have increasingly opened themselves up to the global educational market, resulting in increasing global bargaining for students and teachers.

Chapter summary

This chapter has examined how the changing socio-economic that frames people's lived experiences, focussing in particular on the shift towards a late modern and globalized society. Many of these changes have taken place over the past half a century and have entailed significant implications for people's lived experiences. The shift towards a late modern society in many ways represents significant ruptures to traditionally patterned modes of social engagement and the formation of social identities. Major advances in technology and the communication revolution have facilitated a more globally networked society that is more fluid and less spatially and physically bound than in previous generations. The concept of 'reflexive modernization', and its related concepts of individualization and reflexivity, offers some significant ideas about the changing nature of social relations and how individuals approach core social institutions, including education and the labour market. Yet, we have also seen how some sociologists have also been prone to question the extent to which traditional normative values and frameworks, not least those linked to social class, have fully dissolved.

Globalization, particularly in its economic and cultural forms, also carries significant implications for individuals, societies and governments. As a cultural process, we have seen how globalization has reshaped aspects of people's cultural frame of reference away from the highly specific (local) contexts in which they ordinarily inhabit. Moreover, the increasingly fluid global movement of labour across continents has corresponded with the global development of educational systems. This, in turn, presents significant challenges in meeting the increasing demands, imperatives and risks of economic globalization and in aligning educational systems with increasing levels of cross-national competition.

CHAPTER THREE

The changing nature of work

This chapter explores the theories and research on the changing nature of work in the context of wider economic transformations. It will highlight some of the main impacts of these changes on people's experiences of the job market, particularly through the transition from industrialism to post-industrialism. The chapter will examine a number of competing perspectives on the nature of employment change and and how these relate to wider understandings of the post-industrial and 'knowledge-driven' economy. The final part of the chapter will introduce the concept and theme of 'employability', and consider why this has become an increasingly prominent theme in debates on the changing nature of work.

Contemporary discussions on the future of work have tended towards either a utopian or a dystopian account of the nature and consequences of economic change. The former approach tends to portray a new work order that has heralded new opportunities and rewards. It sees wider labour market changes as engendering a progressive upgrading to the work-related skills and knowledge that employees draw upon. This is set within the context of more fluid, skills-rich and knowledge-intensive work settings that enable people to utilize their talent and draw upon their increasing levels of education. Moreover, this perspective sees work as becoming integral to people's lives and how they choose to express themselves.

By contrast, less optimistic interpretations of contemporary work tend to view the workings of modern-day capitalism as producing new forms of work intensification and insecurity that have potentially deleterious consequences for employees. This, in turn, is associated with an overall degradation of the forms of work that employees traditionally enjoyed, meaning that they can no longer organize their working lives from a coherent and stable platform. Therefore, the new work order carries significant uncertainties and pressures for individuals in the context of far more precarious labour market conditions.

Inevitably, there are limitations with both perspectives. As Grint (2005) has argued, accounts of the changing nature of work often tend to be coloured by an overarching view of the state of contemporary capitalism. This not only centres on how modern labour markets operate, but also their wider impacts on employees' work experiences and the types of skills they apply. The changes that researchers and commentators outline are sometimes presented as all-encompassing and their effects both widespread and uniform across the workforce. This, in turn, tends to overlook the breadth and diversity of people's experiences of work, both between and within particular job areas.

This chapter therefore seeks to map out different themes and perspectives on the changing nature of work. It first contextualizes this in relation to shifting patterns of capitalism and production and its wider implications for organizations, jobs and employees. It will also explore how these wider structural shifts have affected people's working lives and identities. Again, there is much debate here. While some commentators and researchers point to an overall fracturing of work narratives and identities in the new economy, others depict labour market change as entailing a broadening out of people's career scope and potential.

From industrial to post-industrial economies

One of the most significant economic shifts over the past half a century has perhaps been the overall transition from an industrialized economy to a post-industrial one. This transformation has been significant on a number of grounds. At one level, it captures a fundamental change in the nature and workings of capitalist organizations; in essence, the economy has transformed from one based predominately on the production and distribution of large-scale and standardized products, towards one based on service delivery and communication.

While the production of wholesale goods still occurs in post-industrial economies, there has been a substantial shift from mass-scale and homogenized products towards diverse, niche markets that meet a wider range of consumer demands. This shift is mainly characterized by the significant expansion of service-based labour together with a corresponding decline in the forms of industrial labour that were common in the early and middle part of the last century. This, in turn, is linked to the upsurge in communication-driven, customer-orientated and non-manual forms of work as found in many service-sector areas.

The way in which work is organized in the new post-industrial landscape is therefore seen to contrast significantly with forms of work in traditional industrial economic settings. The concept of industrialism is often associated with the concept of Fordism, a term that derives from the archetypal organizational structure of Henry Ford's manufacturing plant with its rigidly demarcated lines of production and highly specified units of work activity. Perhaps one of the most enduring features of work in traditional industrial and Fordist-based economies is the overall routinization and predictability of the work process. This is based on a high concentration of work activities that are geared towards producing very specific forms of outputs, mainly within confined and nationally protected markets.

Work in industrialized contexts is therefore based on visible divisions of labour within hierarchical working relationships, together with highly top-down bureaucratic control of labour processes and outputs. The guiding principle here is *scientific management*, a concept associated with the early twentieth-century management thinker Frederick W. Taylor (Taylor 1911). This concept is predicated on the premise that the best means of achieving organizational efficiency and output is through high levels of control and audit of the labour process. Workers are encouraged to operate according to the key principles of accuracy, efficiency, speed and measurable output. Furthermore, those working in production industries are effectively cogs in the labour process, exercising minimal autonomy and control over the conditions and practice of their work.

Indeed, classic research studies on Fordist work organizations by scholars such as Beynon (1972) and Burroway (1979) have highlighted the various feelings of alienation and disempowerment experienced by production workers, along with the high levels of control that managers exercised over employees' outputs. A large segment of the workforce undertook their work in a compliant and routine fashion, often with little intrinsic reward and very limited discretion. In many cases, their employment profiles were confined to very specific jobs that they performed for a large part of their working lives.

In contrast to the Fordist labour process, with its organizing principles of scientific management and top-down bureaucratic control, it has been claimed that work in post-industrial contexts has become much more flexible and multifaceted (Child and McGrath 2001; Handy 1995). In order to compete and survive in increasingly global and continually shifting markets, companies have looked to redesign organizational structures and practices in more flexible ways. The industrial mode of organizational efficiency and output has purportedly been superseded by one that encourages employees to apply a broader portfolio of skills and experiences. This is to the advantage of individual employees and workforces at large.

Piore and Sabel (1984) make a contrast between the functional rigidity of work in industrial contexts with the new *flexible specialization* of post-industrialism. In flexible and shifting markets, products and jobs necessarily change and so the types of work that people undertake necessarily becomes broader. As such, the workforce needs to be more multi-skilled, flexible and adaptable, as well as being exposed to a wider range of job tasks that demand a variety of skills. Similarly, employees are encouraged to exercise greater responsibility and discretion within organizational structures that are flatter, multilayered and more teamwork orientated.

The shift towards post-industrial labour inevitably raises significant issues over the way that work is organized and the types of skills that people draw upon. Work in post-industrial economies is said to be more varied and complex, so the work-related skills and knowledge that people draw upon is potentially much broader. Underpinning these transformations is the more widespread application of information technology and other modes of advanced communication. Consequently, the more information-rich and technology-driven nature of contemporary work is seen to require new skills sets and attributes on the part of employees.

An increasing emphasis has been placed on the significance of human relationships within organizations, and also the relationships between companies and stakeholders. The contemporary labour market is markedly more people centred and interactive, warranting new skills sets that employees need to draw upon. These have tended to have a more communication-orientated, behavioural and symbolic dimension to them, as much of the post-industrial work context is based on reading and manipulating abstract symbols and dealing with 'people'. Taken together, these changes have had some significant impacts on people's experiences of paid employment and the types of activities they undertake in their jobs. However, they also carry potentially significant educational and human resource development implications, particularly in terms of the promotion and diffusion of employees' work-related skills and aptitudes.

The scale of the transformation from industrialism to post-industrialism has inevitably been questioned by some scholars who have challenged the sometimes deterministic account of the labour market (see, e.g. Grint 2005 and Strangleman 2007). Thus, there is some degree of scepticism over the extent to which there has been a whole-scale paradigm shift from one form of capitalist organization to another. Related criticisms also point to the continued presence of manufacturing industries, as well as the prevalence of forms of work that conform to the classic industrialized model.

Furthermore, as Amin (1994) discusses, commentators have often discussed the whole-scale transition from one economic model to another without always detailing how these map onto the specific realities of working life and the variations within. He argues that there has perhaps been a tendency for commentators to depict industrialism and post-industrialism as representing somewhat homogeneous forms of capitalism, which have limited overlaps. Nonetheless, there has been a strong consensus that work has manifestly changed over the past four decades. While there is acceptance that service- and communication-based employment has not entirely supplanted manufacturing work, it is also seen as increasingly prevalent and a primary economic driver.

We now explore more fully some of the main features of the contemporary, post-industrial work landscape.

Work in post-industrial economies: Flexibility, skills and knowledge work

Perhaps one of the most prominent exponents of the post-industrialism thesis was the social theorist Daniel Bell (1973, 1999), who argued that advances in technology herald a new age of work. Several features of this new work order stand out. The first, as we have already seen, is the upsurge in service-based employment. For Bell, this is characterized by the rise of more technically demanding work which requires a broader level of skill and expertise. Post-industrial economies are increasingly dependent on a new cadre of technocratic, semi-skilled and professional workers who are able to meet the increasingly technological complexity in jobs.

According to Bell's thesis, post-industrialism has therefore generated the expansion of new occupational fields, as well as the technical upgrading of many existing jobs. At one level, this has served to blur the distinction between low-skilled, operative work and high-skilled, managerial labour: larger numbers of employees undertake the sorts of higher-skilled work activities that may have once been the preserve of a small body of employees. At another level, this places new challenges on employees who now have to draw upon a higher skills set and produce a higher level of output.

A further feature of the post-industrial settlement is the changing *character* of employment and the nature of human relationships in the work context. A prominent feature of the new post-industrial landscape is the rise in what might be termed 'human services', which are based on a new range of industries and associated products geared towards accommodating people's changing personal lifestyles. Increasingly central to this is *communication*. This has become the primary motor through which employees conduct their work and relate to other employees, as well as clients and stakeholders.

In the post-industrial work order, communication is more widespread and has become a significant resource for organizations' sustainability and success. If the traditional industrialized work order was based principally on people's manipulation of physical resources, then post-industrial work necessitates far more in the way of human interactions, communication and 'people'-based work. This has some significant implications for the ways in which work is conducted and the types of skills that employees draw upon. An increasingly significant component of employees' work activities is the harnessing of positive interpersonal relationships within organizations and with external stakeholders.

Another significant dimension of post-industrial work is the increasing significance of abstract knowledge, or what Bell terms *theoretical* knowledge. This is essentially knowledge that is advanced and conceptually rich, and requires a strong level of technical expertize and competence. In essence, the knowledge base that the contemporary workforce draws upon is much broader and complex and passes through a more variegated range of contexts and applications. Again, this is contrasted to the very specific, context-limited working knowledge that is applied in the industrial context.

This post-industrial concept has become closely associated with another prominent concept that has gained much currency over the past several decades: that of the 'knowledge-based economy' (KBE). The work of management theorist Peter Drucker (1993) has been influential to this concept. For Drucker, labour production has become more knowledge intensive: it is knowledge that drives production as well as consumption. In keeping with the post-industrial thesis, this conceives a shift from physically orientated labour (i.e. brawn-based work) to cognitively orientated labour (i.e. mind-based work). Ultimately, knowledge is a key resource to both workers and organizations and therefore needs to be effectively harnessed.

Within the KBE, therefore, it is seen as imperative that individuals acquire and apply their knowledge in labour market contexts that demand continual innovation, creative energy and intellectual brokerage. The acquisition, exploitation and diffusion of knowledge, argues Drucker, has become increasingly central to individuals' and organizations' success. Employees continually need to enhance and manipulate the knowledge they have at their disposal. Furthermore, they not only need to upgrade their skills through the course of their careers and through lifelong learning, but also learn proactively in the informal contexts of the workplace. Accordingly, 'knowledge workers' will be rewarded and empowered in the job market and will be able to access a wider range of job opportunities. But it is important that they adopt a flexible and proactive approach to the enrichment of their work-related knowledge and skills.

The idea of the knowledge economy has been strongly promoted by Charles Leadbetter (2000) in his related account of the 'weightless economy'. He argues that much of what is produced and consumed in the new economy is of limited physical or tangible value. Increasingly central to contemporary work is knowledge management through digital media, virtual communication and electronic data storage. Thus, the new knowledge-driven and 'weightless' economy marks a dramatic upsurge in a range of knowledge management services and operations that cut across real time and space, and are largely intangible. These include an ever-expanding range of knowledge management services, such as copywriting, research and development, advertising, digital media, financial and consulting services and other customer-focused activities. Moreover, these services all require the decoding and application of abstract knowledge and are driven by companies' and individuals' so-called intellectual assets.

The idea of the knowledge economy has gained substantial currency with national governments that, as Godin (2006) argues, have tended to portray it as an all-encompassing feature of modern economic life. Indeed, a dominant policy narrative over much of the past two decades has been the importance of meeting the needs of the knowledge economy through education and training (see World Bank 2003; OECD 2009). As Peters

(2001) discusses, by the late 1990s, the notion of the knowledge economy had become a central motif in policy discussions on national competitive strategy and was increasingly used as a key basis for policy formation. In many ways, the ideas of the knowledge economy had begun to underscore most policy texts on national competitive strategy. Its sustainability was seen to rest increasingly on the development of advanced systems of education and training for producing future 'knowledge workers'.

In its most optimistic form, the concepts of post-industrialism and the knowledge-driven economy view the changing nature of employment as highly positive for the majority of workers, not least because they bring potential new opportunities. They have replaced an industrialized and Fordist settlement that was based on low-trust employee relationships and employees' work outputs and profiles being significantly restricted. Instead, within the post-industrial economy, employees have become much more empowered and have much richer, more varied and creative employment experiences. Post-industrial accounts tend to depict a particular type of worker, as well as a particular type of citizen – one who is increasingly enterprising and autonomous. Moreover, within the new work order, employees need to continually update their work-related knowledge and stock of human capital in order to augment their economic positions.

Post-industrialization and the feminization of work

Perhaps one particularly notable feature of the new post-industrial economy has been the greater absorption of females into the labour market, often referred to as the 'feminization of work' (see Crompton 1999). The feminization of work not only signals the greater composition of females within the labour market, but an increased value to the kinds of skills and work that they undertake. Labour market feminization also signals greater levels of equality between male and female employees, not only in terms of pay and job opportunities, but also access to types of jobs that might have hitherto been the preserve of male employees. The shift towards post-industrialism is therefore seen as a significant factor in facilitating the greater absorption of females into the workforce. Compared to the essentially 'male-ist' working contexts of industrial economies, the post-industrial economy has seen the expansion of job areas and professional domains that have not only become more gender-neutral, but which also demand new sets of skills. Accordingly, females are seen to be highly adept at the types of 'soft' skills – communication-based, information and interpersonal skills – that the new economy requires.

There has also been evidence to suggest that females are finding it easier than in the past to attain management positions and break through to senior corporate levels (Alvesson 1998; Hakim 2000; Wajcman and Martin 2002). Proponents of the feminization concept tend to highlight the greater levels of scope and 'choice' that females have in more gender-neutral workplaces. This is particularly the case for more highly educated females, many of whom have equal, and sometimes better, qualifications than male counterparts. Hakim's (2000) influential 'preference' model posits the emergence of 'self-made' female workers – namely, career-driven females who have a full commitment to the labour market, seek full-time, high-paid and higher-status work and invest strongly in their human capital. This model also conceives of new 'adapting' females who are increasingly managing 'hybrid' roles and identities in both full-time employment and within the domestic sphere.

Wajcman and Martin's (2002) research on female managers illustrated how many felt unhindered in their career development and had adopted a dominant 'market narrative' about the role of work and career development in their lives. Yet, while a significant proportion of the female sample perceived the modern flexible work context as facilitating new career opportunities, some female managers still found a greater challenge between balancing careers and domestic challenges. Such challenges were far less pronounced for male managers who, while increasingly accepting changes to the meanings of marriage and fatherhood, still tended to invest their private identities more exclusively in work and career development.

While the shift towards post-industrialism is seen to entail many positive developments for females' experiences, opportunities and outcomes in the labour market, there has nevertheless been some degree of scepticism over the nature and scale of feminization. Bradley et al. (2000), for instance, argue that the increased proportion of female employees has often been misrepresented as the general substitution of male-orientated work with new forms of female-orientated work. What this representation tends to mask is the continued gendered division of work in terms of the relative presence of females and males in specific jobs and labour markets, as well as continued differences in skills and job performances between males and females. As such, the 'numerical feminization' of the workforce may also entail a large proportion of females in low-skilled, part-time, service-based organizations.

In a similar vein, Bolton and Muzio (2008) highlight the continued 'vertical stratification' and horizontal 'segmentations' that prevail in many professional organizations. The former indicates existing gender hierarchies in relation to professional positions, standing and pay, while the latter refers to the divided nature of job type, roles and tasks in these fields. These researchers demonstrated this through research among female professionals in a range of different occupations, including law and management. While these professions have seen a marked upsurge in females in these fields, they show that there are still marked divisions in the types of areas that females undertake, often leading to differences in pay, opportunity and career progression. This research also points to prevailing gendered codes and expectations around performance, behaviour and skills being embedded in the cultures of professional organizations. Indeed, there is continued evidence pointing to existing patterns of gendered pay differences, institutional discrimination and 'glass ceiling' challenges within the contemporary workforce (EHRC 2008).

So, while at one level the contemporary labour market has become more feminized in terms of accommodating more female employees and a greater absorption of their skills and human capital, there is still considerable debate over the prevalence, scale and nature of this shift. It would appear that while the changing nature and context of work has facilitated far more opportunities for females, continued gendered patterns of differentiated opportunity and outcomes still exist in various areas of the job market.

Debating the impacts of work changes: Challenging the new post-industrial utopia

For all the discourses on post-industrialism and the knowledge-driven economy, there has still been much critical scepticism over its prevalence and scale. Social scientists and labour market analysis over the past few decades have argued that the picture is somewhat more nuanced than many commentators and theorists had portrayed it to be, for good or bad (Bradely et al. 2000; Thompson 2004; Fevre 2007). While sceptics do not necessarily negate shifts in paid employment, or that the nature of work organizations and their practices have changed shape, they nevertheless question the overall scale of these shifts. Is, for instance, most of the workforce really now engaged in fulfilling and creative forms of knowledge work?

Underpinning these more sceptical approaches to employment change are concerns that the realities of paid employment, including people's experiences of the job market, are not quite in tune with the vision that is often presented. For such sceptics, accounts of change have either been exaggerated or presented in an overly normative fashion. Thus, there is a concern that an *agenda for change* has been conflated with an accurate description of change.

There are two particular currents of debate on the future of work agenda. The first relates to the nature of skills and its links to changing occupational performances and demands. As we have seen, utopian thinkers of the post-industrial economy have depicted greater opportunities for employees to apply their skills and knowledge and draw strongly upon their education and training. Increasingly, individuals are no longer constrained by rigid occupational structures as contemporary employment enables people to find genuine self-expression and draw upon a broader skills base. Yet, there have been various challenges to the premise that the so-called 'knowledge economy' has created more dynamic, fluid and skills-rich work contexts that provide abundant opportunities for people to apply, and cash-in on, their existing skills and talents. It also questions the optimistic win-win scenario that nearly all of the working population have the opportunity to undertake fulfilling knowledge work.

The second relates to the extent to which labour market changes have actually served to empower individual employees, or at least provide them with a platform from which to establish a coherent work narrative and identity. A body of theory and analysis has come to characterize the contemporary labour market context as representing a so-called *end of work* (Bauman 1998; Beck 2000; Sennett 1998, 2006). This postulates that the traditional work narratives that individuals hitherto enjoyed have given way to a much more precarious landscape of contingent and flexible employment, set against a background of discernible work insecurities and economic uncertainty.

This sceptical and more pessimistic view of labour market change first questions the general impacts of labour market change. Critically, it has challenged the idea that the general movement towards post-industrialism necessarily represents a fundamental sea change in employees' skills and experiences. In his critique of the new economy, Thompson (2004) questions the post-industrial thesis's depiction of wide-scale employment shifts and the ushering in of new forms of work flexibility and employee discretion. Moreover, he challenges the general depiction of service-based and so-called 'white-collar' work as being typically high skilled and discretionary; and conversely, the assumption that most industrial labour is characteristically low skilled and restrictive.

This author further argues that the new economy not only comprises a continued core body of employees occupying manual and low-skilled employment, but also a new layer of service-based employees undertaking relatively low-skilled, routine forms of employment within fairly inflexible work structures. The presence of more post-industrial forms of employment, therefore, does not necessarily collapse existing divisions of labour, including those within higher-paid and higher-skilled work. Furthermore, even within so-called 'knowledge-intensive' organizations, there are often a large body of low-skilled employees who have to perform menial tasks, for example, cleaners, receptionists and canteen staff.

In a similar vein, Brine (2006) argues that there has been a tendency for knowledge economy utopians to mistake information-driven and communications-based employment for high-skilled work. However, they might not necessarily represent two sides of the same coin, particularly as some employees are more involved in the operation and execution of this work than in its conception and planning. Just because a person may work in a knowledge-based industry does not necessarily mean that they undertake knowledge-intensive work, and there may also be significant variability between employees in terms of what they have to perform, even within a single company. A computer packager is likely to be undertaking considerably different work to the computer programmer down the corridor, who themselves will be performing using different levels of knowledge to the software designer upstairs.

Distinctions may therefore need to be drawn between work that is associated with knowledge industries and work that is genuinely knowledge-intensive. Indeed, some 'knowledge workers' may be routinely drawing upon fairly standard and fixed types of 'working knowledge', compared to others who may be more at the cutting-edge of innovation and new knowledge productions. Questions therefore remain over the presence and scale of the knowledge economy, including the extent to which it is equally distributed across areas of employment and, in many cases, geographical location.

Some researchers have gone as far as to suggest that, even within advanced and 'knowledge-intensive' organizations, the proliferation of technology has actually led to an overall deskilling and standardization of many technical, professional and managerial occupations (Brown et al. 2011). Braverman (1974) originally described the gradual dismantling of traditional craft-based and technical skills through the increasing automation and standardization of the production process. He conceptualized that, as a consequence of this, increasing numbers of workers become dispossessed of the traditional skills that allowed them to exercise high levels of discretion over their work. Braverman's 'deskilling' thesis was also highly critical of Tayloristic scientific management practices, which he saw as leading to new forms of worker alienation and disempowerment.

More recently, other 'deskilling' authors such as Rifkin (1996) have described the technological deskilling of many occupations, including those that have traditionally utilized higher-order cognitive skills. He argues that rather than technological advances 'trickling down' to all areas of employment and generating new skill demands, they have displaced an increasing body of skilled workers and led to a scaling back of many of their operations. For Rifkin, even management-level and professional workers have become part of an increasingly disenfranchised middle-class workforce. They have also witnessed their jobs becoming globally outsourced. Rifkin further argues that technological changes have generated a new division of labour between a mobile cadre of hi-tech 'winners' who are able to exploit their knowledge capital, and an increasingly disenfranchised traditional management class who are at the mercy of continued economic and technological change and uncertainty.

The research by Brown et al. (2011) was part of a wider study on the relationship between education, globalization and changing human resource strategies. Their research highlighted evidence of a growing standardization and routinization within many areas of employment, including supposedly knowledge-rich jobs. As these researchers starkly illustrate, there is growing evidence that old-style scientific management principles are being adapted to the new digital era in the form of 'digital Taylorism'. Increasingly, traditionally high-skilled work has become routinized and codified as companies view it as less costly to standardize work practices through digitalization. The digital Taylorism argument therefore challenges the knowledge economy utopia as a myth that is not matched by many companies' human resource management approaches.

This research also highlights an increasing division of labour between an elite minority of knowledge workers who are at the apex of advanced knowledge production, and a growing body of professionals who simply draw upon routine forms of working knowledge, or what they describe as 'grunt' work. This presents significant challenges for well-educated and skilled employers, many of whom may be significantly underutilizing their skills and credentials. This pattern is largely reinforced by the increasingly flexible and competitive nature of economic globalization. Not only have emerging economies increased their pool of skilled labour, but they have also tended to increasingly displace Western employees from much high-skilled labour. Multinational companies are increasingly compelled to relocate production to relatively low-cost regions, namely China and India, where high-skilled and high-quality work can be done at a fraction of the cost of developed economies.

New capitalism, new challenges? Does work still shape identities?

As we have discussed, there have been a range of competing interpretations of the changing nature of work in contemporary capitalism. Another significant issue in these debates is the extent to which wider labour market changes have affected people's relationships to their work. As illustrated earlier, labour market utopians portray new capitalism as engendering new opportunities that offer a platform for people to find genuine self-expression. On the other hand, the 'end of work' commentators see new capitalism as having potentially destabilizing effects on both individuals and the workforce as a whole. This, in turn, leads to a related set of issues around the significance that work has in people's lives and the extent to which individuals are still able to form strong and meaningful identities around their work.

Generally, there is an overall consensus that the sorts of work identities, or at least work identifications, that people developed in earlier periods of work have been reshaped – for better or worse. The 'end of work' theorists have tended to advance what Fevre (2007) has termed a 'nightmare scenario'. This forebodes that previously stable and coherent forms of employment have been superseded by a new landscape of contingent, short-term and non-standard work. This, in turn, has significantly disrupted people's work identities and the meanings they ascribe to their working lives. This 'nightmare scenario' therefore depicts contemporary employment as a fundamentally destabilizing and precarious force in people's lives to which they need to continually adapt. Nevertheless, Fevre questions the scale of this situation and points to macro-level evidence that shows continued patterns of relative employment stability across many job areas.

However, as Conley (2008) argues in a related commentary, the insecurity argument nevertheless points to some significant themes and resonates with genuine concerns among the workforce. In the more recent recessionary context, many employees are finding it increasingly difficult to control and predict their labour market destinies, even in job areas that have traditionally tended to be insulated from widespread instability – for instance, the public sector. While this may not be uniformly experienced by the whole workforce, periods of labour market contraction and cutbacks invariably produce greater risks and uncertainties for many employees.

In terms of the relationship between the changing job market context and people's work identities, several themes emerge. One of these was developed by Bauman (1998), who argues that work has lost its centrality as a focal point in people's lives. Drawing in part upon the theme of reflexive modernization, Bauman sees a splintering of people's identities into many different compartments. While work was traditionally a core compartment, it has now become only one facet in guiding individuals' sense of self. This has also coincided with the move towards the 'consumer society' and the extended opportunities to pursue goals and interests outside of paid employment.

According to Bauman's argument, individuals are more preoccupied with what they *consume* than what they *produce*, and the end goal of their labour is to enjoy relative affluence and material reward. Moreover, the decline in well-defined forms of industrial labour has seen further erosions both to individuals' work ethic and the meanings and values that individuals attach to their labour. This not only centres on the loss of autonomy and discretion experienced by workers, but also a decline in the relationships they form in what are seen as increasingly less stable and cohesive workplaces. Consequently, individuals are no longer able to forge strong and meaningful work identities and ethics.

The second main theme relates to the increasing fragmentation and instability in contemporary work and its individualizing effects. Beck (2000) has referred to this as the 'brave new world of work', and presents a vision of contemporary work as increasingly short term and fractured. He argues that the Western labour market is increasingly mirroring the more insecure labour markets of Central and South America. Employees are experiencing far more in the way of transitory, non-permanent and uncertain employment arrangements, as well as a significant breakdown of the traditional employment contract and career support structures. Like Bauman, he anticipates that changes in patterns of consumption, education and lifestyle have all heightened individuals' sense that they can no longer rely on permanent work patterns and structures to accommodate their wider life goals and aspirations.

The third theme relates to the impact that new capitalism has on personal well-being and relationships, associated with the work of Sennett (1998, 2006). This has pointed to the corrosive effects of modern working life on individuals, which adversely affects their morale and endeavours to find authentic experiences through their work. New capitalism has led to an intensification of work, placing significant demands on individuals. This further brings some potentially deleterious consequences both for people's lived experiences of working life and their lives outside it. Sennett argues that contemporary capitalism engenders a fundamental 'corrosion of character', preventing people from forming authentic relationships with themselves and others.

The corrosion of character, therefore, is seen to cut to the core of modern corporate life with its constant multiple demands for individuals to 'get ahead' and develop their career portfolios. This leads to a rudderless, powerless and exhausted contemporary worker who is continually on the move and unable to root themselves to a fixed or coherent employment setting. This is further likely to place a strain on individuals' personal relationships as well as their general health and well-being. Moreover, this condition may leave employees feeling somewhat dislocated and unable to establish a firm work identity from which they can build a meaningful career platform. For Sennett, the contemporary 'knowledge worker' is largely disempowered, forever at the perils of juggernaut capitalism, which he sees as having become increasingly short term and transactional.

These main perspectives have not gone without criticism. Aside from the aforementioned charge of exaggerating the extent of these changes and their impacts on individuals, they have also been criticized for taking a somewhat nostalgic view of previous forms of work (Strangleman 2007). Strangleman points out that the caricature of a fulfilled, work-centred and organizationally wedded industrial worker presents something of a 'golden age' image of traditional employment. Furthermore, this does not always capture the realities of traditional forms of labour, particularly for those workers involved in low-skilled, unrewarding and sometimes oppressive work. There is, perhaps, a danger of presenting industrial forms of work as supplying people with strong work identities while contemporary work does quite the opposite.

Research into employees' construction of work identities has shown that individuals are keen to establish meaningful identities and find value in their work. Furthermore, employees' work identities are often mediated by the specific organizational contexts within which they work. Strangleman's own research on railways workers in the 1990s (Strangleman 2004) resonates in part with some of the theorizing around the effects of work changes on identity. This research uncovered a growing sense of disidentification and disassociation from the specific work roles and activities these employees had traditionally enjoyed. Older workers, in particular, reflected on a loss of the work narrative they had previously enjoyed, particularly in the identities that had been forged through the specific tasks and duties undertaken, their sense of affiliation to their companies and the collective pursuits with other employees.

There appear to be some genuine impacts of organizational restructuring on people's work identities and narratives, in particular the move towards privatization, managerialism and performance-driven cultures. Many of the older workers in this study saw a decline in their autonomy and discretion, with most of their energies taken up by either fulfilling or resisting managerial dictates. These workers also acknowledged a new cynical instrumentality in their approach to work, namely, 'take the money and run'. However, younger workers who had been more acculturated in the values of managerialism were perhaps better able to seek out new opportunities and forge new identity positions.

Other research has also illustrated the significance of organizational cultures in shaping employees' self-perceptions of themselves within the work environment; in particular, their relations with others in the field, such as managers, colleagues and clients. Du Gay's research in the retail sector illustrated the ways in which performance-driven and customer-focused work regimes feed strongly into the way employees understand their role. It further illustrated how the dominant discursive framings around what constitutes an 'effective' employee, as propagated by company managers, very much influenced retail employees' self-images and sense of agency as workers. Instead of viewing themselves merely as cogs within a wider organization, the retail workers in this study were encouraged to view themselves as shape-shifting semi-entrepreneurs who, through proactivity and willing endeavour, could add substantial value to their firms. Du Gay illustrated that, through a combination of rewards, positive appraisal and active endorsement, these employees' sense of work identity was bound up in their 'excellent' performance in securing transactions and meeting specified company targets.

Similar evidence has been found in research on public service professionals, particularly among professionals making the transition to managerial roles (Halford and Exworthy 1999; Dent and Whitehead 2002; Newman and Nutley 2003). For many of these professionals, the transition from purely professional to managerial work invariably entails shifts in practice, as well as the pursuit of different organizational priorities. Through internalizing the values and principles of managerialism, these professionals were likely to experience marked transformations in their identities and the ways they experienced working life and practice. This was perhaps manifest in the shift from purely professionally orientated practices, based on professional knowledge and judgement, towards more managerial practices, based on strategy, direction setting and performance management.

Halford and Exworthy's research showed that, rather than resisting managerialism and its attendant pressures around accountability and compliance, these professionals instead tended to actively embrace these changes. Many saw it as important for their career progression and relished the image of being managers and leaders. It was perceived potentially to affirm aspects of their work identity and allow them to occupy new occupational spaces.

Recent research (Felstead et al. 2009a; Doherty 2009) also provides strong evidence that individuals are still actively able to construct identities through their work. Based on studies across a range of occupations, including IT specialists and personal trainers, Felstead et al. (2009) demonstrated the varying ways in which work informs both personal and collective identities. At one level, these are strongly influenced by the types of practices and activities that employees perform, which are very occupation- and organizational-specific.

Some employees in this study, most notably those in continual interaction with the public, experienced more of a conflict between their public and private identities. For instance, aerobics instructors engaged in continual interaction and 'front-stage' performance, tended to engage in highly collective and socially situated behaviours. However, other types of employees, such as software engineers, were able to achieve strong alignment between their personal goals and the specific demands of their jobs, leading to more authentic expressions of work as an extension of themselves and a manifestation of their personal identity. This research suggests that work still has the capacity to inform aspects of a person's self-perception and how they are perceived by others.

Studying a range of employees across different public and private sectors, Doherty (2009) showed the prevalence of values around autonomy, task execution and wider organizational participation among employees. While some employees in this study were able to forge more significant identities through the specific nature of their work tasks, others employees achieved identity affirmation from related activities, for instance, through participation in unions and other organizational networks. What this research illustrated is that work 'still matters' to a wide core of employees, both through the intrinsic nature of work practices and the activities they engage in around their work. It is clear from the interviews in these studies that many employees still see the potential for work to inform aspects of their identity and relationship with others. While this is clearly more integral for some, and far more tangential for others, working life is an area where people look to find meaning and project a sense of self.

Collinson's (2003) work with shop-floor workers vividly demonstrated the ways in which people perform identity work through their jobs, sometimes in ways that have little relation to the nature of the employment. So, while there is evidence to suggest a decline in work identity and associated levels of skills and discretion, this may not take place uniformly across the workforce.

Even where work has become more precarious, short term and uncertain job conditions, individuals may still seek some kind of identity platform to guide their actions within the work setting.

From employment to 'employability'

Perhaps a strong unifying theme in accounts of changes to working life is that there has become an increasing onus on individuals to more actively manage their careers and work profiles. A combination of organizational restructuring, continued economic uncertainty, increasing competition for desired forms of work, work intensification and ongoing corporate and government-driven pressures on employees, have transformed people's relationship to the job market. Furthermore, this has potentially reshaped expectations and attitudes towards what they might need to do to progress within it. Increasingly central to employees' relationship to the job market is the issue of *employability*. The notion of employability has become increasingly prominent in a range of popular, academic and policy-based discourses of contemporary work and people's shifting relationship with the job market.

Gazier (1999) illustrates that 'employability' was historically conceptualized in a fairly objective way, based on identifying specific labour market needs and attempting to raise productivity through the accurate and measurable utilization of manpower. In more recent times, however, it has come to be depicted as a new feature of individuals' relationship with the job market, both in terms of their expectations for meaningful and rewarding work and what they need to do to achieve this. Employability has increasingly come to capture people's changing understandings of their labour market futures and their trajectories when in working life.

At one level, the notion of employability relates quite closely to the wider restructuring of the labour market through post-industrialism, and the shifting dynamics of career mobility in this context. More specifically, the movement away from the organizationally managed career progression to individually managed ones. In more flexible organizations, career progression follows a less linear pattern in terms of a movement through clearly demarcated corporate hierarchies and technical specialisms. The traditional, organizationally managed career progression is perhaps epitomized by Whyte's *The Organisation Man* (Whyte 1956), based on an employee's long-term affiliation to one particular company and upon which their career profile and identity are anchored. Such an employee will have typically progressed through the corporate hierarchy, acquiring specific technical expertize along the way, and then been rewarded by promotion and higher status. Movement through corporate ranks therefore tends to be incremental, working through fairly demarcated occupational cycles and accumulating additional technical expertise.

However, this mode of career progression is far less evident in more flexible organizations, which are less likely to allocate employees solely on the basis of organizational experience, commitment and loyalty. As Adamson et al. (1998) discuss, contemporary organizations act far less as protective shelters for employees. In short, career progression has become altogether more contingent on employees' ability to add immediate value and manifest their assets to their organizations. Furthermore, aspiring managers and leaders have greater chances of being fast-tracked to senior corporate positions where high levels of responsibility fall on them. In a context where employees' career progressions have become less anchored around single organizations and jobs, so careers have increasingly become reconceptualized as fluid and variegated. Terms such as the 'portfolio', 'boundaryless' and 'protean' career have been used to describe the increasingly flexible ways in which people manage their working lives (Arthur and Rousseu 2001; Colin and Young 2000).

With the decline of the so-called 'job for life', it has become increasingly important for individuals to stay fit in both the internal labour market in which they have been trained, and also beyond in the external labour market. As such, individuals need to take responsibility for their employability. Watts (2006) highlights the significance of *career learning* not only for school-leavers and graduates, but also the professional making transitions through working life. This centres on a number of key dimensions, including employees' self-awareness (understanding of their skills, interests and potential aptitude), awareness of job opportunities (and how to negotiate them), decision-making skills and engaging in proactive transition learning (including negotiating access to jobs and adapting to challenges).

In researching portfolio workers, Fenwick (2003) depicts the contemporary career as a 'lifelong personal human resource project', based on the continual renewal of skills and work profiles in ever-changing job market contexts. In the context of a more contingent and fluid work context, it has become increasingly important for people to develop repositories of knowledge and work experience that they can trade-off at different stages of their working life. Reviewing the concept of employability, Clarke (2008) argues that the shift from organizationally managed to individually managed career development has placed an increasing onus on employees to invest more strongly in their personal career development. The more traditional psychological investments, or *psychological contracts*, that individuals made towards their organizations in terms of commitment and loyalty have turned more towards a psychological investment in one's own career development and marketability. Individuals are perhaps taking a more free-agent approach to their employability development, looking to trade-off a range of work-related skills and expertize in different phases of a much more fragmented career cycle.

In human resource development terms, much of the ongoing discussion has been around the development and application of appropriate job-related competences and skills required by employers. At one level, employability might therefore been seen as a measure of employees' capacity to acquire, develop and deploy the appropriate level of skills that are needed for specific jobs.

However, employability is a complex and much-contested notion, and there is much continuing debate about what it actually constitutes and how it can be developed. For instance, critics see it as simply an employer-centred concept: a corporate mantra that is built around placing ever-increasing demands on employees in the pursuit of greater output (Garavan 1999). Employability may therefore be little more than a way of making employees think that they have to do ever-more to meet employers' increasing demands and expectations. Once a concept such as employability has been established, and then gets embedded in various human resource and employment policy discourses, it has the potential to be taken as an all-encompassing facet of the employment experience. However, some have also argued that the employability notion is genuinely in tune with the new flexible work order, even facilitating employee empowerment by allowing them to take greater control over the direction of their working lives.

Dominant definitions have tended therefore to frame employability as being an individual problem that is largely determined by the work-related attributes and qualities they possess. This is clearly invoked in Hillage and Pollard's (1998) influential definition where they define: 'Employability is about having the capability to gain initial employment, maintain employment and obtain new employment if required' (1998, p. 1). For Hillage and Pollard, employability rests on factors relating to individuals' assets (including skills, knowledge and attitudes), the utilization and deployment of these in relevant job contexts and their presentation to (and endorsement by) employers. We might infer from this approach that employability is something that can, and needs to be, continually developed. Individuals need to ensure that they can take sought-after assets and competences to the job market and continually look to develop them during their careers. In that way, they will strengthen their chances of attaining the types of jobs they seek. Above all, individuals' employability can be further developed by acquiring the appropriate assets through various forms of education and training.

It would, therefore, appear to be the case that a key component of people's employability is around the types of assets and qualities they can bring to the jobs, as well as their ability to develop these during their working lives. Employees who can demonstrate that they have the appropriate attributes that are valued by employers are in a much better overall position to attain sought-after employment. It becomes imperative that job candidates match the required skills demands of target employers and then successfully demonstrate these skills within the actual work setting. At one level, this may be achieved through the possession and deployment of specific technical and occupationally related skills and knowledge that they may have acquired through their formal education and training, or through previous work experiences. At another level, it may also be achieved through meeting less tangible criteria such as fitting in with a specific organization's culture and ethos, and having personal and behavioural qualities that are deemed desirable for a specific job. This also extends to the types of attitudes they have towards jobs, including their resilience, ability to adapt to change and take initiative for their own work. All the above will no doubt strongly influence how employable one is, or at least is seen to be.

Perhaps one shortcoming with this approach to employability is that it focuses almost exclusively on individuals and what they can offer to the job market. Some have questioned whether employability can be captured simply by the matching-up of individuals to various job demands. For instance, McQuaid and Lyndsay (2005) have attempted to move the concept on beyond mere individual considerations, arguing that an individual's employability is more likely to entail an interaction between these and the features of the labour market they are working within. They argue that employability is likely to be a highly contingent problem that is not only influenced by the job-related assets and qualities people bring forward to jobs, but also features of the labour market. This may include the supply and availability of jobs in a specific field, the appropriateness of these jobs and the extent to which their requirements are commensurate with prospective employees' profiles. As we saw earlier, some of the analysis of the 'knowledge economy' has shown it to be geographically variable with certain types of 'knowledge work' concentrated in specific regions. This is likely to influence the opportunities open to individuals, some of whom may be more able to capitalize on the skills sets they possess. In short, employability may be as much driven by the demand and scope for particular types of employment as it is by the characteristics that individuals bring forward to the job market (Table 3.1).

Table 3.1 Dimensions of employability

Absolute	Relative	Subjective
Employability as:	Employability as:	Employability as:
• Individual assets • Key skills and competences • Job performance and technical capacity • Matching up of individuals to specific job	• Positional competition and positional advantage • Contingent on job market – supply and demand and availability of work • Appropriateness of work to individuals' profiles	• Work-related identities and dispositions • Attitudes and values • Subjective opportunities structures (including class, gender)

Also critiquing more popular individualistic discourses around employability, Brown et al. (2003) make a very useful distinction between the *absolute* and the *relative* dimension of employability. In the former case, employability is very much about matching up individuals to specific jobs. An applicant applying for a specialized and highly skilled job will only attain this if they have the requisite individual qualities needed for this job. Moreover, in the context of employment changes and other organizational restructurings, new performance pressures are placed on individuals and this inevitably means that people continually have to enhance their absolute levels of employability in order to negotiate these new demands. Viewed in this light, prospective employees are placed on a continuum that ranges from unemployable to highly employable. On this continuum, some individuals will inevitably be more employable than others and this will crucially determine their chances of attaining employment. It is imperative that the less employable look to develop their employability in order to increase their future prospects. Not doing so may result in them being unemployed or continually unemployable.

Yet, according to Brown et al., employability may also be seen as: 'The relative chances of finding and maintaining relative forms of employment' (Brown et al. 2003, p. 111). This again refocuses the issue more towards the labour market, including the laws of supply and demand for jobs. If more people apply for jobs than are actually available, then their success in attaining these may be determined as much by the nature of opportunity as it is by their absolute levels of employability. It may well be the case that a prospective employee can bring forward desired skills and attributes, but may actually not succeed in gaining employment if faced by competition from other candidates with similar profiles.

Seen in this light, employability is very much about the way in which individuals are positioned against each other in a competition for jobs, some of which may be attracting a surplus of interest. The higher the stakes are in this competition, the harder it becomes to simply trade-in one's skills and educational credentials for a sought-after job. Therefore, how employable an individual is, or is perceived to be, is largely referenced against the employability of others. Within a context of job shortages and with more intense competition for jobs, this issue becomes particularly salient. In many ways, the absolute and relative dimensions of employability are interrelated: there are increasing pressures for people to raise their absolute levels of employability in order to maintain a favourable relative position in the competition for jobs.

We can therefore see that employability is not a straightforward problem, although it has been somewhat easier for policymakers to frame the issue mainly as an individual problem. In adopting a somewhat broader and socially contextualized approach, then employability might be seen to involve a complex interaction between the individuals and the job market. At a basic level, this interaction entails the transfer of individuals' employment-related assets in return for desired jobs and other associated rewards. It is perhaps easier for individuals to control their own employability than it is to control, or even predict, conditions of the labour market, which may continually vary.

Furthermore, individuals' interaction with the job market is also likely to involve the way in which they make sense of the labour market and their place in it. If employability is about people's relationship to the job market, then this may also involve the meanings and values they ascribe to employment, including the extent to which they want to commit to finding particular employment. Employability may therefore have a strong subjective dimension, and this again relates back to people's self-identities and self-perceptions.

The subjective dimension of employability therefore relates to the complex and dynamic relationship that people have with the labour market, the wider attitudes, values and identities that this engenders, and the range of social influences that may shape these. We saw earlier how people's identities around work are likely to significantly shape the way in which they approach the job market, including the types of values that they form. This is also likely to be referenced against individuals' social class, gender and ethnic profiles, which might frame their perceptions of particular types of jobs and labour markets. This, in turn, may well shape how employable they perceive themselves to be for certain types of jobs. The extent to which individuals invest a strong sense of themselves in their work and careers is likely to have a bearing not only on the way they approach their career development, but also on their wider employment experiences and outcomes.

Chapter summary

This chapter has brought together quite a wide range of theory, debate and research on the changing shape of work, and the impact this has for individuals in the contemporary labour market. There has been some significant contestation over the scale and impact of labour market change. Overall, there is broad consensus that there has been movement towards a more flexible, knowledge-driven, post-industrial economy, driven by and reflected through changing modes of production and consumption. This, in turn, has some major permutations for the types of skills people draw upon, the structures of their working life and careers, and the way they make sense of their employment situations. However, the extent to which these and related changes have heralded a fundamental repatterning of working life and identities still remains open to debate. New skills demands and opportunities have clearly been generated in the labour market over time, although to what degree the post-industrial economy presents a new utopia of skills-rich, creative work, inhabited by a growing cadre of 'knowledge workers', is much debated. Similarly, while many work organizations have become reconfigured through more flexible practices, how much this has led to more flexible and fulfilling work has been critically questioned.

This chapter has also explored the relationship between individuals' identities and work. In some quarters, contemporary work represents a narrative of decline and a fracturing of people's working lives and identities. What is perhaps clear are the demands the contemporary labour market places on individuals to actively manage their careers, and take care of their personal employability. Having explored the wider context of work, we now turn our attention to the interaction between work and the educational system.

CHAPTER FOUR

Conceptualizing the relationships between education and work

This chapter examines the way in which the relationship between education and the economy has been conceptualized. This relationship has developed over time and has been largely shaped by the shifting economic context around which educational and work institutions operate. At one level, there has been a marked tightening of the relationship between education and the economy. This potentially signals a positive new dynamic between education and the economy, whereby educational systems feed into the economy in ways that promote economic development and well-being.

National governments have increasingly looked to harness this link, and to find closer alignment between the institutional arrangements of educational systems and the labour market. However, this generates associated pressures on educational institutions to meet various economic demands – education has been identified as *the key* institution for fulfilling changing economic demands. As such, efforts have been made to model its activities on the supposed practices and requirements of advanced capitalist economies.

At the same time, the interplay between educational systems and the wider economy has become somewhat blurred and increasingly complicated. There has been much contestation over the role of education in generating economic outcomes and returns, and the extent to which it should, and can, be more closely aligned to the economy. Related to this are debates over the extent to which education actually serves to regulate individuals' access to rewards in the labour market. The expansion of educational systems has coincided with shifts in the labour market, which are also associated with changes to occupational and class structures. This, in turn, has disrupted aspects of the relationship between individuals' formal educational experiences and outcomes and their future occupational positioning. This relationship was perhaps traditionally more clearly defined.

In this chapter, we examine the wider historical context of the interaction between education and work. We explore some of the broad conceptual terrain in this area; namely, the contrasting perspective of education as a social and economic good on the one hand, and education as a site of social conflict and inequality on the other. We then examine understandings of the relationship between the expansion of education and economic development, as developed by theories of human capital and credentialism. These two approaches have provided alternative ways of understanding the connection between education and future labour market rewards, mainly in terms of the ways in which education helps shape individuals' labour market outcomes. They further explain various dynamics between education and work in terms of the way in which both the structural and institutional arrangements between education and work interact. Educational systems clearly do not operate in isolation from the the wider demands of the labour market or from the various expectations of key social groups, including families, learners, policymakers and employers. These two approaches explain these interactions in very different ways, as well as the different socio-economic outcomes that participation in education is likely to engender.

Historic linkages between education and work

The relationship between education, economy and society has been subject to considerable change over time. At one level, these changes reflect a wider reframing of the role that education has in regulating wider national economic outcomes and individuals' returns and occupational location in the labour market. Socio-economic changes, not least those related to the advance of post-industrialism and economic globalization, have led to nation states repositioning education as a core public priority. For large parts of the twentieth century, the interplay between education and the economy had been built principally on the consensus that education played a strong role in maintaining economic stability and successfully allocating individuals into appropriate positions in the economy (Halsey et al. 1961). As Tomlinson (2005) argues, as part of the wider welfare settlement of the middle-part of the twentieth century, education was seen to have a key role in social-democratic development around the maintenance of a welfare state, social justice, stable employment growth and relative job security.

The expansion of education was seen to facilitate these developments as it provided individuals with broader opportunities to fulfil their economic potential and achieve social mobility. It was also linked to the increasing technical challenges of industrialism and the gradual expansion of professional- and management-level jobs. In many ways, the expansion of education, including higher education, was perceived by national governments as contributing to national economic prosperity and meeting increasing economic challenges. Yet, perhaps somewhat missing from the 'golden age' depiction of educational expansion and its positive linkages to economic growth and stability, are the realities of persistent inequalities within both education and the labour market.

Avis et al. (1996) have illustrated how the majority of individuals' educational routes, aspirations and outcomes were very limited during industrialism. This invariably shaped people's wider labour market trajectories, which, in many instances, were confined to low-skilled work. Relatedly, Finegold and Soskice (1988) have shown how educational systems during this period helped perpetuate a low-skill, low-wage economy. Education in industrial contexts was geared more towards channelling individuals to narrow segments of the workforce than on nurturing future human talent. This is reflected in a marked division of labour, characterized by a pronounced 'skills dis-equilibrium' within the labour market – that is, up to 80 per cent of the workforce undertaking low-skill, low-wage and low-opportunity work and a relatively small minority doing rewarding, well-paid work.

The coupling between education and the economy has been captured by Brown and Lauder (1992) in their conceptualization of educational 'waves' and how these have shifted over time. For much of the middle to latter part of the twentieth century, education came to be characterized by a 'second wave' that saw an increasing demand for skills and an overall raising of the human resource profiles of companies. Nevertheless, the industrialized infrastructure of the old Fordist work regimes still operated on a strongly demarcated division of labour. In turn, the majority of individuals' schooling was confined to the acquisition of limited qualifications and skills sets warranted by the relatively minimal skills these future workers would apply during their working lives.

In the Fordist context, therefore, wastage of talent through education was 'affordable' as the economic system still reflected marked occupational segmentation and differentials in opportunity. People's educational experiences helped lock them into relatively low-skilled, low-aspiration forms of labour. Furthermore, education is structured on the same 'bureaucratic' principles as workplaces; based on tight protocols and rules, and learners being groomed and socialized towards particular future work-related behaviours and expectations.

Critically, Brown and Lauder (1992) argue that economic transformations have rendered such an educational paradigm unsustainable; changing work regimes and the move towards more flexible and higher-skilled work mean that educational systems need more effectively to harness human talent. Their hypothetical 'third wave' paradigm is premised on a potentially new and economically productive settlement that benefits the economy as well as learners and future employees as a whole. Moreover, it means a fundamental reshaping of educational systems towards a 'high ability' system that is built around nurturing the 'wealth of talent'. Here, educational systems play a crucial role in helping more fairly and effectively to harness individuals' creative and natural skills and to equip learners for more positive engagement with continuous learning beyond education and into the labour market. This is ultimately a key to cultivating the 'collective intelligence' that nations need to draw upon in a globally developing economy and for ending a low-skill, low-aspiration society.

However, this ideal has been shown to be in tension with the realities of much educational provision and policy. Thus, Hickox and Moore (1992) argue that many UK policy responses have adversely disrupted what might be a more productive relationship between education and the labour market. Their criticism is centred on the way that government policies have tended to reinforce structural divisions in skills and opportunities in the economy. One element of the problem is in what they see as a competitive, market-based agenda that operates on a highly selective and segmented system of advantage that benefits a select few. Another is the inadequate coordination of vocational education, which has underserved both the economy and learners, and does not address longer-term economic goals. Both problems are underpinned by class inequalities and the continued divisions in access to modes of educational experience and outcomes that favour individuals in the wider economy.

Dominant theories on the relationship between education and work

In their outline of the different ways in which education and work relationships might be conceptualized, Maroy and Doray (2000) point to a number of different levels. At a broad macro-level, the relationship can be articulated as structural in terms of education helping to regulate both social and economic relations. This can operate in a reciprocal, two-way dynamic. At one level, educational activities can potentially feed into economic processes and outputs. In broad terms, education helps maintain productive activities within the economy and can be a direct cause of such activities. An example of this direct functional economic relationship might be training for specialized employment, needed by both employer and individual worker.

At the same time, economic changes themselves can significantly reshape the fabric of educational institutions. An example may be the direct reworking of an educational system to meet changing economic demands, such as the need for more highly skilled and knowledge-based workers. Innovations in training and vocational development may be one such area where education can impact on labour market outcomes, particularly if these are translated into productive labour market value. The inter-dynamic between education and the economy also has a strong discursive and symbolic framing, particularly in relation to the gradual reframing of educational goals and values. In market-driven economic systems, there is considerable emphasis on education being a productive resource and this has led to strong technicist framing of educational values and practices. This again is likely to feed into the agenda about how educational systems should be organized and whose interests they might serve.

In very broad terms, conceptualizations of the link between education and the economy have tended to be subsumed under either *consensus* or *conflict* approaches (see Lauder et al. 2006). These approaches present largely diametrically opposed views on this relationship, reflecting different philosophical and sociological traditions on social relations. Consensus approaches tend to conceive the relationship between education and the economy as socially productive and advantageous to individuals and social groups. Education leads to positive social and economic outcomes that help generate clear benefits to individuals and society at large. Conflict approaches, on the other hand, tend to characterize educational systems as reproducing structural inequalities based on individuals' differential cultural and economic resources. Accordingly, educational processes both reflect and actively perpetuate the inherent structural inequalities of a capitalist system that rewards some groups much more favourably than others.

For consensus theorists, education is seen to service the economy in a clear and equitable fashion, helping to promote social and economic cohesion. Moreover, it meets the needs of the economy by producing skills that are matched-up equitably in the labour market. The consensus approach typically belongs to the structural-functionalist school of thought that views education as having a productive social function in terms of its role in nurturing the productive capacity of individuals. It instils in individuals the appropriate attitudes and capabilities required for them to operate in advanced societies (Durkheim 1893; Davis and Moore 1945; Parsons 1959). The productive role of education is manifest in its potential power to shape both social and economic systems as functioning entities, enabling social actors to make meaningful societal contributions. In conceptualizing education as a powerful social good, the consensus approach also tends to view the benefits of education as more than simply economic development: they also extend to better social cohesion, stronger citizenship and more fluid forms of democracy.

Central here is the role of education in helping establish appropriate mechanisms of socialization, skills and selection. First, education helps develop the appropriate values and moral codes that allow individuals to integrate successfully into social and economic life. Individuals' formal and informal educational experiences provide them with the appropriate attitudes and behaviours that enable them to function successfully as citizens and workers. Secondly, education promotes necessary skills in order for individuals to make the appropriate technical contributions to the labour market. It helps structure and coordinate basic skills, specific job-related skills and a range of life skills, without which individuals' capacity to operate within the social and economic world would be limited. Thus, the skills that individuals acquire through education feed both directly and indirectly into the labour market and form the basis for their future economic capacity.

In terms of selection, education also has the function of sifting and sorting individuals into appropriate labour market categories and channelling them towards appropriate forms of work. It does this by allocating labour market placement on the basis of people's educational achievements and aptitudes. Individuals' differential positioning within the division of labour reflects their relative economic capacity as measured through their levels of educational achievement.

The conflict approach paints a markedly different picture of education's role in social and economic relations. Much of the earlier analysis of the education–work interaction was heavily informed by 'correspondence' theories associated with the work of Bowles and Gintis (1976), as well as the social reproduction theories of Bourdieu and Passerson (1976) and Bernstein (1996). Correspondence theories see the social relations in education as being closely matched to those within the economic system: educational processes and relations essentially mirror what takes place in the labour market. However, rather than forming a fair and harmonious alliance, these relations are characterized by deep-rooted patterns of structural inequality.

Bowles and Gintis (1976) illustrated the ways in which educational systems within capitalist economies continue to regulate young people's orientations to work, channelling them towards future work roles and functions. However, rather than this being based on the fair allocation of individuals to appropriate jobs, this process both reflects, and feeds into, fundamental inequalities at the heart of capitalist economies. Bowles and Gintis' correspondence theory is also a theory of *control*: the dominant capitalist class is able to exercise considerable control over the educational system and its workings. This crucially helps achieve the necessary levels of conformity and discipline among a future workforce that will ultimately contribute to capitalist operations. Bowles and Gintis point out that the correspondence between education and the economy is neither equitable nor economically productive, as people's relative location within the economy is not an accurate reflection of their potential economic utility.

These authors illustrate the role that schools play in establishing the similar types of reward mechanism that are applied in the labour market. The educational system is essentially organized in a way that distributes its rewards in an unequal way, assisting some young people towards better labour market outcomes far more than others. Some individuals are able to use the dominant reward structures of the educational system to advance their future position as occupants of more rewarding jobs. Yet, for others, the sense of alienation they experience through formal education depletes their educational aspirations and, consequently, their scope within the labour market. According to this approach, schooling significantly assists in the process of pre-work socialization: through formal education, young people learn their place within the economy. Less academically able or willing pupils are provided with the strong message that their destiny is for relatively lowly positions in the economy, and this is then confirmed by their low achievements and limited formal qualifications.

Conforming learners, or those who have the adequate educational and cultural resources to work the reward structures of formal education, learn to successfully align their goals and aspirations towards the potential rewards that schooling offers. Their achievement of these rewards sets them up favourably for their future work-related activities, which themselves are based on the same reward structures and requisite levels of compliance. The correspondence theory has been useful in helping to explain the perpetuation of structural inequality in paid employment resulting from the inherent inequalities that the educational system reproduces. It paints a picture of an educational system fundamentally divided on class lines, with such divisions directly feeding into the class divisions in the labour market.

In a similar vein, social reproduction theories have also exposed the linkages between education and socio-economic inequalities (Bourdieu and Passerson 1976). This theory again posits that structural inequalities operating outside of education are actively reinforced and reproduced within it. The class-cultural and social inequalities that underpin relations within the economy are reflected in the differential experiences and outcomes that pupils receive through their formal schooling. Bourdieu and Passerson's work has powerfully demonstrated the way in which educational systems serve the interests and practices of dominant social groups, namely, the occupational middle classes. It does this chiefly through the transmission and validation of middle-class cultural currencies, values and practices, or what they term *cultural capital*, that are transferred onto middle-class individuals informally outside of education. Significantly, it is precisely these currencies that underscore the dominant practices, contents and modes of transmission within formal education.

For Bourdieu and Passerson, therefore, the dominant cultural script is essentially a middle-class one: middle-class cognitive structures and cultural practices inform what goes on within educational settings. The curriculum and its modes of pedagogic transfer is a key area where this operates, given that it is based around the particular forms of cultural capital that some learners have more possession of through middle-class socialization. Consequently, formal education helps reproduce both middle-class practices and social advantages through establishing a more harmonious link between the cognitive and cultural practices of middle-class family life and the educational system.

A significant feature of the social reproduction theory is its exposure of the forms of inequality reproduced through formal education. It highlights the ways in which the cultural deficits of learners from lower social groups serve to crucially impede their educational and future economic fortunes. As a consequence of significantly lacking the cultural capital through which educational content and relations are mediated, learners from lower socio-economic backgrounds are placed at a significant disadvantage. This is reflected principally in their formal educational outcomes, which have historically always been far lower than those from higher socio-economic groups. But, it is also reflected in a general ambivalence towards formal education and a wider indifference to dominant educational values and practices.

Social reproduction theory, therefore, also helps to illustrate the regulation of people's attitudes and identities towards education and learning, and the way in which the educational system reproduces differential experiences and outcomes. As with Bowles and Gintis' correspondence theory, it exposes the conflict and inequalities that operate through education, sometimes latently, and the differential experiences and outcomes this produces.

Contested views on the role of education for economic development: Economic necessity or credential inflation?

Having opened up the broader conceptual terrain on education's role in regulating social and economic relations, we now explore how this has been applied to more specific conceptual understandings of the relationship between the expansion of the educational system and economic returns.

The two theories of *human capital* and *credentialism* are significant here and very much map onto the consensus and conflict approaches. They both advance distinctly different perspectives on both the causes and consequences of educational growth. Furthermore, both theories are related to a number of other conceptual notions, such as meritocracy, which themselves make some significant claims about the relationship between people's educational achievements and labour market outcomes. However, neither of these theories has been without criticism and both have been charged with exaggerating their claims (see Baker 2009). Table 4.1 presents an overview of some of the main arguments in each theory on both the rationale for educational expansion and the outcomes that follow from it.

Perhaps owing to its more economically based underpinnings, human capital theory (HCT) has come under much criticism from sociologists who have tended to question its overall explanatory value for understanding individuals' educational and labour market behaviours (see Granovetter 1985; Fevre 2003, Fevre et al. 1999; Schuller et al. 2000). Some of these criticisms are around the extent to which education genuinely facilitates economic demands, or indeed whether that should be its ultimate goal.

Table 4.1: Conceptual models on educational expansion and economic development

Conceptual position	Rationale for educational expansion	Outcome of educational expansion
Human capital	• Education as 'investment' • Enhancement of labour market skills • Increase 'marginal product' • Education for competiveness	• Better individual and societal returns • High-skilled workforce • Greater productive capacity • National competitive advantage
Positional conflict	• Expansion of middle classes → increased social demand for credentials • Pressures to invest and avoid opportunity costs • Employer strategy for 'screening' • Policy agenda for educational expansion	• Inter- and intra-class conflict → positional competition for jobs • Mismatches between level of education and labour market return • Extra pressures to demonstrate 'employability' • Over-education/ underemployment

Similarly, the more sociologically informed credentialist and social conflict approaches have been criticized for downplaying the scale of economic change, as well as the legitimacy and necessity of educational expansion and the changing nature of functional and cognitive skills in the labour market (Barone and Van de Werfhorst 2011). They have also been challenged for presenting a somewhat conspiratorial notion that education exclusively acts as a vehicle of social control and reproduction. This, critics argue, negates manifest changes that have occurred in the labour market over time.

The first dominant theory, human capital theory, tends to fall within the consensus school as it depicts a strong and positive interrelationship between education and social and economic development. The human capital approach, sometimes referred to as the technocratic approach, attributes much significance to the role of education in meeting economic imperatives. This theory has been champion by several prominent economists, including Thodore Schultz (1961) and Gary Becker (1976, 1993). It has exercised considerable influence over national governments' policy agenda towards aligning education to the continued challenges of the economy. The theory is built on a premise that education is a key driver of economic development, which feeds positively and directly into the labour market. It posits a direct and positive relationship between the expansion of education and future economic reward: education is seen as an 'investment' that will bring far-reaching benefits for the economy and the individuals participating in it.

Through expanding the supply of individuals with additional skills and knowledge through education, the overall productive capacity of the labour market is strengthened. Becker (1993) has referred to this as 'marginal product' – that is, the added value offered to the workplace in terms of better output and quality in products and services as a result of better-educated employees. The theory therefore ascribes considerable importance to the added skills and knowledge that people acquire through further education and training, seeing these as directly translating into greater job performance and economic returns. It is imperative, therefore, for individuals to 'invest' in their human capital, as they will be aptly rewarded in the labour market.

There is a strong *technocratic* basis to the human capital model as it places heavy emphasis on the enrichment of prospective employees' technical capabilities and potential skills utility. These can be converted into labour market productivity and ultimately help motor future economic development. The human capital model is largely predicated on the principles of economic necessity and perceived economic demand. The discourses of post-industrial, knowledge-intensive work tend to be strongly woven into human capital accounts of the role of education in meeting changing economic needs (Olssen and Peters 2005). There tends to be a cyclical logic to this technocratic thinking. Structural changes in the nature of advanced capitalism have altered the nature of employment and its associated demands on employees. Contemporary organizations, with their shifting organizational forms and changing job content, necessitate higher levels of education among workers. Governments must therefore respond by raising the human capital levels of their workforce, mainly through the expansion of education and training and encouraging higher levels of educational certification. As a consequence, the labour market will continue to expand as work organizations are more able to meet new economic challenges due to having a higher-skilled workforce who are able to both adapt to, and add value to, the labour process. A high-skilled society is likely to result, whose members are committed to continual education and lifelong learning.

The central tenets of the human capital model have tended to be actively embraced by national governments across the globe as part of an educational policy strategy to secure economic prosperity. The discourse has tended to remain similar over time: investment in human capital is fundamental in fulfilling the economic potential of advanced economies, and raising the profile of emerging ones (OECD 2003, 2009). Governments have tended to support their rationale through evidence of wealth and income differentials between educated and less-educated economies. Nations that more strongly invest in education and training will enjoy considerable trade-offs in the form of a more productive workforce who are also able to command higher wage returns.

A key policy response has therefore been to expand post-compulsory education and training with the aim of further enhancing the supply of skilled labour. In the past two decades alone, the number of individuals participating in some kind of post-compulsory education has doubled (OECD 2009). This has also taken place within emerging transition economies whose governments have also subscribed to the notion of education as a catalyst for economic growth.

A significant feature of the human capital model is its depiction of social systems and the way in which individuals operate within these. Consistent with the consensus approach, it conceives a relatively stable, direct and productive relationship between education and the economy. Any prevailing inequality within the labour market can be explained by individuals' differential levels of investment and/or achievement in education, which invariably shapes their overall economic success. Labour market opportunities are available to most individuals within an economic system that rewards the added-value knowledge and skills that they can bring forward. Structural inequalities in income and job opportunities can, in turn, be compensated by additional educational investment, as this will springboard people into more advantageous economic circumstances. Both governments and individuals have a responsibility to further invest in human capital: the continued supply of human capital will ultimately help generate its future demand.

HCT has developed a particular conceptualization of individuals' approaches to social and economic life. Like most concepts linked to the logical-positivist philosophical tradition, it assumes that individuals' behaviour can be explained logically and objectively and is conditioned on the basis of measurable laws and governing principles. This extends to their behaviour in relation to their participation in both education and the labour markets in terms of the goals they develop towards them. According to HCT, individuals make logical and rational decisions around their education based on an understanding of the rewards it will generate. Moreover, that people's motivations are strongly built on utilitarian principles, driven almost exclusively by a desire to maximize financial returns and to self-optimize their future labour market potential. Therefore, individuals' approaches to education are framed by a set of logical and instrumental outlooks that sees education as a means through which to generate future economic ends.

The human capital model is linked closely to a sister concept known as 'rational choice' (Abell 1991). Similar to the human capital account, this concept argues that individuals are rational, goal-directed and self-serving, and that their decision making is ultimately based on conscious deliberations and careful planning at an individual level. Rational choice theories posit that people's decisions are purely rational and derived from an elementary cost-benefit type of calculus that individuals either consciously or intuitively formulate. This largely takes the form of a deliberate, meditated process whereby individuals weigh the relative costs against the relative benefits of undertaking further forms of education and training. The costs might entail, for instance, delayed income, additional time and energy, as well as likely financial expenditure. The benefits are principally to be found in higher future earnings and much broader labour market opportunities. More likely, people's rational choice making is likely to be confined to a more intuitive, common sense understanding that they will benefit in the long run from further investment in education. People may assume, or indeed they may simply infer, that it is both logical and just that their achievements in education will equate to future economic gains.

A concept that relates to human capital, although from a somewhat different ideological family, is that of *meritocracy*. As an ideological creed, meritocracy strongly emphasizes the role of educational achievement in opening up life chances and enabling individuals to access the most desired social and economic rewards (see Swift and Marshall 1997; Goldthorpe 2003; Goldthorpe and Jackson 2008). It works from the basic premise that individuals' achievements in education are rewarded fairly in the form of better life chances: in effect, the relative merits of people's educational achievements facilitate greater access to social and economic opportunities. Traditionally, it has been common for governments to place considerable emphasis on education as a primary route towards securing the best jobs and associated life chances. The more a person achieves in education, the more scope they have for opening up job opportunities and their associated rewards of better pay, lifestyle and status.

Underpinning the meritocracy concept is the idea that if people work hard and achieve what they possibly can in an open educational context, they will be aptly rewarded in the economic system. Thus, hard work and application is ultimately a more determining factor in their success than the ascribed social characteristics they may possess. Successive governments across the globe have espoused the value of meritocracy as a positive model for organizing education on the basis that it represents the fairest means of distributing opportunities. The social-democratic governments of the middle part of the twentieth century saw individuals' educational achievements as a way of helping them access the types of social and economic goods that were the preserve of the privileged. The neo-liberal movement in the 1980s also very much saw meritocracy as the legitimate means for individuals to transcend social barriers in accessing future economic rewards. To this extent, it fitted with their representation of individuals as independent, resilient and socially adaptive. Above all, meritocracy places a strong emphasis on the role of individuals and their capacity to apply themselves in the educational system.

Credentialism and positional conflict

So far, we have outlined an approach to the relationship between education and labour market return that sees the interplay as essentially positive, transparent and economically productive. In contrast to the consensus approaches evident in human capital and meritocracy accounts, the theories of credentialism and positional conflict view education as a site for cultural struggle and power play. They also tend to challenge the orthodoxy that education necessarily results in improved social and economic outcomes, and that its practices cohere closely with the requirements and demands of society and economy. Like all conflict approaches, it instead highlights the role of education in reflecting and reproducing structural inequality and intensifying people's differential access to social and economic goods.

Credentialist theory views access to jobs and economic rewards as being shaped by individuals' possession of unequally valued social and educational goods, rather than on a transparent and fair transference of equally distributed educational achievements in the educational system. It conceptualizes a fundamental power play at work between groups and individuals in the pursuit of what is seen as relatively limited labour market resources and rewards. This approach challenges the idea of a fluid and open opportunity structure that rewards people's merit and human capital. Instead, it sees opportunities as being a limited preserve and accessible only to those who are able to forge an advantage within higher-stakes job markets.

Similar to theories of social reproduction outlined earlier, credentialism theory is concerned with the ways in which dominant social groups use the educational system to secure social and economic advantages. It looks to demonstrate how these inequalities are relayed into the wider economic sphere, helping to generate differential labour market outcomes and opportunity structures for individuals. The credentialist school is associated with theorists such as Randall Collins (1979), Fred Hirsch (1977) and Ivan Berg (1970).

All these theorists have, to some degree, been influenced more widely by Weber's (1948) theories of monopoly and control, which had much to say about the ways in which dominant social groups are able to monopolize access to economic resources. For Weber, class stronghold is achieved through means other than simply the possession of economic capital and the crude division of economic assets. While this no doubt plays a significant role in maintaining relative economic advantage, dominant social-class groups also achieve their stronghold over social and economic resources through the principles of *social closure* (Murphy 1988). This essentially involves the use of exclusionary strategies, mainly through the accumulation of social goods (credentials) that provide some individuals with the resources, status and power to secure social monopoly and control. This, in turn, helps legitimize their access to economic goods (jobs, occupational status and financial advantage).

The work of the social theorist Randall Collins (1979, 2000) has been particularly influential to the credentialist framework. Collins views educational credentials as resources that help people secure occupational rewards that are in relatively scarce supply. More specifically, they can be seen as positional goods that act chiefly as an exclusionary mechanism for certain groups and individuals to maintain a stronghold within the occupational structure. Credentials are, however, little more than 'signals' or 'markers' of an individual's educational and labour market potential: they signify an individual's achievements and distinctions that help legitimate access to specific jobs.

As markers of a person's future economic potential, credentials confer onto their holders a status badge that can be exchanged in a labour market that continues to place social value on educational achievements. The value of credentials is therefore derived more from their capacity to facilitate access to labour market rewards than from any intrinsic economic value. While in some cases, specific credentials may convey specialist knowledge required to undertake specific jobs, more often their significance lies in their symbolic value. On their own terms, credentials may add very little to individuals' productive capacity, but they nonetheless facilitate access to forms of employment that require 'suitably qualified' individuals to undertake purportedly specialist forms of employment.

For Collins, the expansion of post-compulsory and higher education cannot be taken to reflect a genuine economic demand for additional credentials arising from a need for increases in human capital. Instead, the expansion of post-compulsory education is associated with the large-scale proliferation of credentials, and this itself is linked to changes in both the class and occupational structures. Consequently, social demand for credentials has risen and this has exceeded their actual economic demand. This is perhaps reflected in the tendency for policymakers and other advocates of educational expansion to conflate the increase in educational credentials with actual economic demand for more qualified individuals. Collins refers to this as the 'myth of technocracy' in that there is limited evidence that the growth in educational credentials reflects a technical upgrading of the workforce.

The idea that the economy requires more qualified individuals might, at one level, be erroneous, but it has helped justify the expansion of post-compulsory education over time. However, the expansion of education, disproportionate to its actual economic demand, is likely to result in a mismatch between people's level of education and the content of their jobs. This is an example of what has been called 'credential inflation', or what Dore (1976) somewhat provocatively terms as 'diploma disease'. In short, too many individuals are acquiring educational credentials beyond what they need or can actually utilize in the labour market. At its most extreme, this may result in individuals being profoundly overqualified for the types of jobs they are undertaking, an example being a store operator with an MBA.

A further problematic consequence of credential inflation is the overall decline in the market value of credentials, particularly those that might have traditionally facilitated access to particular forms of employment. As more and more individuals attain higher-level credentials, they no longer convey the so-called 'badge of distinction' that they traditionally might have. Instead, they effectively lose their status value and, consequently, their effectiveness in shaping people's access to desired jobs. A paradox of this is that individuals are likely to feel increasingly compelled to accumulate additional credentials in order to enhance their chances of securing sought-after employment. This is regardless of whether it genuinely increases their efficiency or productivity. Further participation in education may become, to use the phrase developed by Thurow (1977) a 'defensive expenditure'. Accordingly, people's motivations for participating in education may not be so much based on maximizing their human capital, but an avoidance of anticipated opportunities costs in terms of potential foregone income and other related negative labour market outcomes. It is likely that individuals are conscious of the potential detrimental consequences associated with not participating further in education and training; increasingly, it may therefore become a default position if there are unavailable alternative job opportunities.

Both Berg (1971) and Hirsch (1977) have also discussed the social costs associated with large-scale educational escalation. Berg has framed the discussion around the growing sense of frustration experienced by an expanded and increasingly qualified middle class, which is likely to spill into wider social tensions and unrest. As more and more people are sold the meritocratic dream and continue to invest significant financial and personal resources to secure better job opportunities, increasing anger and disaffection may ensue if these aspirations become unfulfilled. Moreover, the unfulfilled, over-educated 'professional' is likely to project this anger onto those who have sold them this promise, not least government and employer organizations. For such authors, therefore, credentialism does not simply result in benign over-qualification, but also potentially strong levels of societal discontent and conflict. Such tensions are likely to cut to the core of increasing middle-class tension and angst over future access to the so-called 'good life' that they have come to expect and value.

At another level, the move towards credentialism is seen to place potentially greater power in the hands of employers rather than individual employees, given that employers have more opportunities to define the demands for credentials and the specific form that they take. In some cases, employers can demand more credentials from prospective employees and to be ever more discriminate regarding the types of credential portfolios they bring forward. This often takes the form of what has been described as 'screening' (see Bills 1988, 2003). In effect, employers are able to pick and choose prospective employees on the basis of their perceived credential value. In turn, they may reject those who, prior to credential inflation, may well have had sufficient skills to undertake their targeted employment. Employers may demand and expect more in the way of value-added credentials from employees in order to legitimize their hiring decisions when there is a large pool of job applicants. It allows them to demand that prospective employees bring forward more than is actually needed, enabling them to filter out those who do not fulfil increasingly stringent job specifications.

It is clear that the expansion of education, and accompanying credentials inflation, is leading to increasing concerns among individuals and social groups over how to position their educational experiences and outcomes towards future economic returns in the labour market. Drawing upon the similar neo-Weberian position as Collins et al., Brown (2000) has developed the concept of *positional competition* to explore the potential inter- and intra-class conflicts that may result from educational expansion. The positional competition approach sees access to desired economic goods as increasingly taking the form of a competition that has its own set of rules and protocols. The ultimate goal here is to achieve a positional advantage in a wider cultural struggle where the traditional 'rules of the game' in accruing future rewards have been redrawn.

As a result of witnessing a weakening of the links between educational achievement and occupational reward, the expanded and insecure middle classes have increasingly had to embark upon strategies that will enable them to gain a future positional advantage. This pressure is likely to be heightened during periods of financial uncertainty and labour market contraction. Part of this competition necessitates a stronger level of engagement with the educational and labour market in order to further accrue added-value credentials that may help give access to opportunities that are in scarcer supply. It has become increasingly imperative that the middle class understand and work 'the rules' of the market in order to achieve new transferable goods in a context where traditional educational assets have lost their strength.

The positional competition approach very much exposes the limitations of meritocracy, as it highlights how increasing numbers of well-qualified individuals from the middle classes are responding to a breakdown in the relationship between their achievements in education and its return in the labour market. This, in turn, demands a far more strategic approach to the educational system in order to find ways of gaining positional advantages in the competition for good jobs and financial returns. The middle classes have tended to be more adept at using the educational system to their advantage, capitalizing in particular on the emergence of educational market hierarchies. This is reflected in the typical caricature of the 'sharp-elbowed' middle classes who do all they can to secure the best possible educational advantages for their children, including the best schools, extra support and tuition, and participation in extra curriculum activities. They are all too aware that these provide crucial additional assets that may have future job market currency.

This approach has been particularly useful at highlighting the continued pressures around education and jobs, underpinned by constant concerns about ramping up levels of credentials and potential labour market assets.

It also highlights the relative positional advantage that some social groups have in both capitalizing on education and accumulating new layers of educational credentials. Research on parental engagement with the educational system and choice behaviour clearly illustrates the measures that middle-class parents will undertake in order to secure the 'best' educational advantages for their children (Gerwirtz et al. 1995). The Ball (2003) research has demonstrated some of the strategies employed by middle-class parents in securing access to desired schools that were positioned favourably within market hierarchies. These include the exploitation of existing class-based social networks for garnering information, pooling existing knowledge and resources for acceding certain educational institutions and trading-off professional achievements and influence to those who gatekeep access. In all cases, it entails an engagement with the rules and protocols of new competition within a more intense educational market.

Critical evaluation of these dominant theories

Does education always lead to better economic outcomes?

These two dominant, yet largely diametrically opposed, theoretical positions have offered important insights into the link between education and the economy; in particular, the shaping of people's potential labour market rewards. They have not, of course, been without criticisms. Critics have tended to highlight either the exaggerated nature of their propositions and the intellectual and ideological biases that frame some of their arguments. Moreover, there has been a tendency for a sharp conceptual distinction to be drawn between either 'education as necessity' or 'education as myth', with adherents of either position often framing their position through these lenses. Therefore, it has often been taken that education either inevitably leads to more favourable economic outcomes or that it provides increasingly valueless credentials that have limited genuine economic currency. Either way, this tends to overlook the sometimes complex variations in the education–economic link, which does not necessarily operate uniformly between different labour markets, as well as between individual nations (Lauder et al. 2008; Hansen 2011).

The human capital model, as already shown, has been influential in shaping the official policy framework on the role of education in the economy. However, critics have often challenged this theory for overstating the link between education and economic return, at both a collective and an individual level. Indeed, they challenge whether the expansion of education, and the purported increase in skills, has necessarily led to better overall economic outcomes (Wolf et al. 2006). They point out that countries with expanded post-compulsory education systems do not necessarily always have high-performing economies with strong economic output, and this has increasingly been the case in the USA. Conversely, other countries have performed well without, for example, mass higher education systems, and have been more able to marshal their output and growth around key indigenous industrial areas and more robust state-led economic planning (Ashton and Green 1996). This leads to the wider issue over the extent to which education alone is sufficient in shaping economic fortunes, as the more recent economic predicament demonstrates. Countries that have expanded educational systems have still experienced economic meltdown, irrespective of the levels of human capital that have fed into their economies.

Human capital theorizing has therefore been challenged for offering a somewhat simplistic input-output formula to education and economic outcome. As Lloyd and Payne (2003) argue, this approach does not particularly detail the ways in which specific forms of education may improve economic efficiency, or address the ways in which particular forms of educational content and provisions may facilitate this economic efficiency. The model therefore tends to work from a 'more equals better' rationale, concentrating more on economic outcomes than on the ways in which additional levels of education are translated into better labour market performance. Wolf et al. (2006) further highlight that different areas of the labour market typically necessitate different forms of educational provision and skills, owing mainly to the diverse range of skills utilized across different areas of the job market. Therefore, while specific forms of education and training may be important for certain job areas, these may not necessitate prolonged time and investment in lengthy periods of post-compulsory education.

These critiques relate to another critical concern around the education–economy link. This centres on the ways in which additional educational activities shape what individuals do in the labour market. If education generates additional skills and knowledge, then perhaps not quite enough is demonstrated in human capital approaches to explain why these enhance so-called marginal product. It is assumed that the knowledge acquired through education significantly bolsters the knowledge-based economy, yet the meaning of 'knowledge' in this context has tended to be under-explored. Young (2009) argues that there is a danger that 'knowledge' becomes a catch-all phrase whose utility is taken for granted. He points out that it is not always clear whether the more decontextualized and propositional knowledge that certain forms of educational provision (namely, higher education) transfer actually enhances individuals' capacity to undertake future knowledge-based work. Human capital approaches, therefore, place much faith in education as an economic good, but without necessarily examining how the knowledge acquired through it is applied and contextualized in the economy.

Sociologically inclined analysts have also been keen to show the ways in which the education–economy relationship is mediated through wider social contexts and relationships in ways that go much further than the notion of rational choice. They have further pointed out that people's relationship to education is much more socially contextualized and complex than HCT presents it to be (Fevre et al. 1999; Schuller et al. 2000). Moreover, individuals' educational experiences are framed within wider sets of social relationships, all of which are likely to exercise a profound bearing on how they understand their participation. So, even if some people might come to see themselves as rational actors whose approach to education is solely based on economic betterment, their decisions are nonetheless likely to be mediated by a range of factors, including their social background, gender, geographical location and the mode of educational provision to which they have been exposed. These are likely to frame decision making and participation as much as any deliberated cost-benefit calculations.

A key criticism of the human capital approach has therefore been its exaggeration of the link between education and economic outcomes, at both a broader economic and more specific individual level. Ultimately, the human capital, rational choice and meritocracy positions have been seen to adopt an overly utilitarian and individualistic approach in their account of people's relationship with the labour market. This also extends to the link between their participation and achievements in education and future labour market outcomes.

However, in placing a strong emphasis on the individual and their personal achievements and rationalities, it assumes that individuals' educational achievements are driven solely by *the individual* in terms of their motivation, hard work and effort. If individuals are dedicated enough and smart enough, then there is little to prevent them from achieving their goals. The only potential obstacle might be ability, but even with enough dedicated application this can be compensated for. This, in turn, tends to assume that people's relationship to education operates in something of a social vacuum. More significantly, it runs the risk of reducing complex and multidimensional notions, such as intelligence and motivation, to the level of personal traits and dispositions. These may be important components in shaping individuals' educational outcomes, but are nonetheless likely to be strongly influenced by their social and cultural milieu.

Goldthorpe and Jackson (2008) discuss how, as a concept, meritocracy has been shrouded in considerable myth, including the somewhat unparalleled faith in education to positively assist individuals' social mobility. They also argue that more populist discourses on meritocracy often grossly underplay the linkage between people's socio-economic origins and their wider labour market destinations. Moreover, they draw upon evidence to show that social class still has a significant role in people's educational achievements and continues to strongly mediate the origins–destinations relationship. Thus, individuals' achievements, motivation and attitudes within education are more likely by-products of prevailing social structures – and the differential levels of opportunity within these – than they are simply a rational response to anticipated future rewards.

Are people becoming too qualified?

In the same way that human capital approaches have been criticized for over-exaggerating the link between education and individual and collective economic returns, the credentialist perspective has also attracted criticisms for debunking this link. One particular criticism relates to credentialist theory's charge that economic and job-related changes are fallacious. Critics of credentialist theory such as Baker (2009) have pointed to the inherent problems with simply interpreting the growth of credentials as a way of conferring empty signifiers onto credential holders. This potentially risks divorcing credentials from the actual labour market context in which they are employed and validated, implying that they are devoid of any content, intrinsic worth or applied value. Similarly, it might be argued that any potential move towards credentialism is as much a consequence as an actual cause of expanded educational provision. Simply because increasing numbers of individuals possess educational credentials does not necessarily mean that they are of limited labour market utility and instead driven purely by a middle-class strategy to gain a stronghold in the labour market. A more optimistic interpretation of credential growth might even argue that the expansion of post-compulsory education has helped to democratize access to credentials that might have been hitherto confined to elite social groups (Brown D. 2001).

The link between credentials and labour market change is one particular area where credential theories have been challenged. The credentialists have been challenged for their assertion that the shift towards the so-called 'professional society' during the middle part of the twentieth century simply represents new forms of professional monopoly and control that gives increasing power to dominant social groups. This shift has also been interpreted more positively as a response to new forms of work and expertize that necessitate higher levels of technical knowledge and skill. These, in turn, have demanded new forms of specialized professional training (Evetts 2008; Eraut 1994). Furthermore, this has proliferated to wider areas of the labour market, including job areas that have traditionally operated from relatively low skills thresholds. Therefore, the increase in professional work, and associated technical upgrading of other areas of work, represents tangible changes that require additional forms of education, training and continued professional development.

Taking up the theme of professional growth in the modern labour market, Baker (2009) has offered a critique of credentialist theory, arguing that it pays scant attention to conditions of work in the modern professional labour market. He charges credentialism for negating some marked changes in the professional character and composition of contemporary workforces. Just as human capital theorist have tended to sidestep analysing educational processes, credentialist theory has also tended to downplay what goes on in formal education and how this might have genuine labour market and societal value.

In its most positive form, formal schooling may help nurture 'thinking and choosing actors', instilled with dispositions that help them make a meaningful contribution in their future work. In an optimistic interpretation of workforce change, Baker argues that the labour market has increasingly become dominated by a new kind of *personnel professionalism*, characterized mainly by an upsurge in jobs that require technical expertize, decision making and independent action. In short, the contemporary labour market bears little resemblance to how it looked in previous eras when large amounts of learners were schooled to limited levels. It now relies on new forms of academic capital that are embodied through the formal educational experience and credentials that prospective employees possess.

There is also a danger therefore of credentialist accounts painting a picture of credentials escalating out of control, consequently generating false demand. Yet, in many instances, demand for credentials is both real and, for many individuals, are still used to access desired economic ends. The problem, of course, is the specific matching of these credentials to the specific demands of jobs.

The major exponent of credentialist theory, Collins (2000), points out some important comparative trends in educational expansion, not least the global rise in post-compulsory education and training and the overall attempts by national states to coordinate this rise. However, some researchers have shown that there are still crucial differences in the ways that national economies regulate the supply and coordination of different qualifications and forms of educational provision. These tend to take different trajectories, and not all countries have facilitated the move towards credential oversupply or indeed an *academic drift*. Similarly, different countries' educational and training systems have followed different trajectories, reflecting different modes of provision in the field of vocational education. Comparing the German and US models of vocational education, Hansen (2011) argues that the German vocational system has adapted more favourably to changing economic demands, attuning itself more to the skills requirement of existing and emerging labour markets. This often translates into a better overall matching-up of the forms of education and linked credentials that vocational learners receive and their value and currency in the labour market. This compares to the more credentialist-orientated approaches adopted in the USA, and similarly in the UK.

Hall and Soskice's (2001) influential concept of *varieties of capitalism* might be used to explain this process, particularly in terms of the typology they developed to distinguish the ways in which different economies operate and coordinate their work activities and relations. They draw a key distinction between what are termed 'liberal' (sometimes referred to as flexible) market economies and 'coordinated' market economies. In the former, the linkages between educational systems and the labour market are open and flexible and not necessarily regulated on the basis of individuals' levels of educational experience and qualifications. The UK and the US labour markets are examples of this as both tend to be characterized by limited regulation, competition and relative lack of employment security. Coordinated labour markets, also referred to as 'occupational' markets, on the other hand, tend to have a closer relationship between education and the economy. In such markets, individuals more readily train towards a particular occupation; and, overall, there is a higher degree of matching-up of the individuals' educational profile to their future labour market position. This is sometimes referred to as *occupational specificity*. Thus, in coordinated or occupational markets, people's levels of qualification tend to be more commensurate with the specific requirements of jobs. In flexible market economies, however, there is less matching-up of educational training to jobs and therefore more potential for displacement, but at the same time greater flexibility.

Chapter summary

This chapter has considered the dominant ways in which the relationship between education and the labour market has been conceived. The interplay between the two core societal educational institutions of education and work is complex and far from straightforward. Over time, this relationship has evolved from a loosely coupled to a more tightly coupled relationship. This has at least been the aspiration of many policymakers keen to find stronger levels of concordance between these two institutions. But, it also signals wider historical shifts in the labour market, driven by technological and organizational changes, which further necessitate new forms of human capital, skill and personnel development.

More optimistically, the expansion of education and the recoupling between education and the economy is seen to reflect a positive need for skilled labour and an erosion of traditional labour divisions. Yet, as the education–economy relationship has tightened, greater attention has been given to the ways in which educational and economic systems might cohere, as well as how educational processes and outcomes translate into labour market ones. This has been widely contested.

We have seen how dominant approaches to understanding this link have fallen within different theoretical camps. These, in turn, represent contrasting views of wider social and economic relations and the role of education in regulating these relations. Both the human capital and credentialist perspectives offer powerful accounts of this relationship and the outcomes wider economic effects of educational expansion. Yet, the notions of education as 'investment', 'return' and catalyst for 'growth' do not rest comfortably with those of credential inflation, over-qualification and opportunity hoarding. Clearly, there is value to each of these conceptual approaches and, at some levels, they have helped to explain individuals' differential outcomes in the labour market. However, both have their limitations and are not always generalizable to all individuals, groups and particular national economic settings. There is clearly a demand for education and training and this still continues to shape people's access to particular work and how much scope is available to them. At the same time, whether it is human capital that solely shapes access and outcomes needs to be reexamined at a time when increasing amounts of people are accessing qualifications during periods of labour market change.

CHAPTER FIVE

Vocationalism, skills and employability

We continue the theme of the education and labour market interplay by exploring several of its dominant themes, namely, the increasing vocationalism of education, the drive towards improving school-leavers and graduates 'employability' and the skills agenda. Each of these themes interrelates and is part of a human capital-driven approach to attune educational systems more closely to the world of work. If individuals can raise their overall levels of employability, skills and vocational aptitude, then their labour market fortunes will be much healthier. It is therefore seen as important that these are enriched through their formal educational experiences, and that educational curricula are designed more favourably to equip individuals for the job market.

In this chapter, we will show that such an approach tends to be very *supply-side* dominated – that is, it focuses almost exclusively on the education side of the labour market more than the specific dynamics of the labour market and what people actually undertake when in it. It is also largely predicated on the notion that what is supplied by education to the labour market is relatively closely matched and harmonious. For instance, if educational institutions can equip individuals with the necessary skills sets, then these will be traded-off in the job market and translated into better overall individual and organizational performance.

However, the supply and demand relationship has proved to be somewhat more complex and unpredictable. The skills (and employability) that people acquire through their education and training are not necessarily transferred in direct and tangible ways. Nor are the ways in which employers actually organize and utilize them. Thus, while the skills, employability and vocationalism agenda is often presented as a panacea to fulfilling shifting labour market demands, some degree of criticality is required for assessing how this impacts both on prospective employees and work organizations. Moreover, concepts such as 'employability' and 'skill' are sometimes presented in a descriptive and under-contextualized way, even though they have contested and multiple meanings.

The chapter will also examine the rise of vocationalism and vocational education. While these are often two different things, they are linked to a similar overarching agenda: aligning learners' educational experience more closely to their working lives. The rise of vocationalism is linked to an overall agenda for transforming educational content and practice in ways that match the needs of individuals and wider society. However, vocational education relates to significant issues around social divisions of learning, equality of opportunity and the ways in which education produces and affirms labour market orientations and identities.

Education and employability

We reintroduce the notion of employability because it has come to dominate discussions on the role of education for much of the past two decades. As we have seen, employability is a concept that has been adopted from human resource literature, and is now a term that has increasingly become an organizing principle in the way in which people understand their relationship to the labour market. Yet, it is a concept that very much sits at the changing and complex interface between educational systems and the modern economy. This reflects the ever-changing demands and challenges placed on prospective employees, as well as the wider challenges for educational systems to enhance the labour capacity of future workers (Morley 2001; Lauder et al. 2006). The challenges facing advanced capitalism in the context of economic globalization, technological advancement and cross-national skills bargaining can only really be met if there is a state-led drive towards raising individuals' employability.

Returning to some of the earlier themes in this book, we've seen that dominant and somewhat popularized accounts of employability centre largely on people's work-related assets and capabilities. This is based on matters such as their competence and ability to perform particular tasks, the utilization of skills and knowledge and their willingness to develop these proactively within their respective employment. According to this popular account, individuals' employability can, and should, be enhanced through acquiring appropriate levels of education and training. This not only places a significant onus on individuals to develop their absolute levels of employability, but also for educational institutions to prepare them better for the challenges of a changing job market. As such, much stronger attention has been placed upon what educational institutions are doing to optimize people's employability.

At the start of the twenty-first century, strong calls were made in government for a renewal of educational systems so that they were more fully in tune with the demands of the economy. The efficiency and performance of the UK economy was seen as fundamentally shaped by the nature of the supply feeding into it from educational institutions. Thus, in the words of the Department for Education and Employment's 'Education into Employability Report' (2001):

> The DfEE's application of the Keynesian investment ethos to the supply side of our economy enhances productivity and economic performance. Incomes can therefore rise and demand will respond to the enhanced supply side of the economy. The economy will be able to cope with increased demand without boom and bust, thanks to the efficiency of the labour market (DFEE 2001)

This approach to employability also tends to focus exclusively on educational institutions as crucial supply-side components of the labour market. While it is ultimately individuals who need to take responsibility for enhancing their employability, it is also paramount that their educational experiences have placed them in a favourable position to do so. This is reflected in a drive to organize educational provisions and practices in ways that make them better equipped individuals when entering the job market. When employability is framed around the supply of adequately skilled and qualified school-leavers and graduates, there tends to be a more sustained focus on how this can be enhanced through the various forms of provision, curriculum and pedagogy contained within educational institutions.

This rationale is clearly underpinned by the human capital framework, as employability is often taken as a measure of individuals' extra investment in education and training. We have seen how human capital approaches tend to celebrate the expansion of educational provision and people's uptake of this: what people learn through education is of significant labour market value. Not only does learning equal earning, but it also transfers crucial value-added skills and knowledge that have direct as well as longer-term labour market impacts. Accordingly, the more individuals invest in their education and training, the more productive, effective and attractive they will be in the labour market. This, in turn, will make them more employable.

Human capital approaches therefore tend to place considerable faith in educational systems for enhancing the productive capacities of the future workforce. It is taken almost as axiomatic that whatever people acquire through education has significant intrinsic value that can be transformed into some future labour market value. Furthermore, individuals' lack of employability can be accounted for by their unwillingness or inability to invest in their human capital.

However, much of the supply-side framing of employability has often be cast within a critical appraisal of the role of education in meeting labour market challenges, as evinced in much policymaker and employer discourses. The Confederation of Business and Industry (CBI), for instance, has often been critical of the current UK educational system for failing to produce prospective employees who are equipped with functional skills, including appropriate levels of literacy, numeracy and decision making (CBI 2011). This has been extended to post-compulsory education, including higher education, which has also been charged with not doing enough to add value to graduates' employability. The underlying message is that educational institutions need to do more to prepare school-leavers and graduates for working life and to embed employability skills more firmly into the curriculum.

However, such approaches have, in turn, been challenged for adopting a narrow focus by reducing employability to the preparation and attainment of employment. The attainment of employment is, in itself, something of a general outcome. It doesn't necessarily tell us much about the actual nature of the individual's employment and how they engage with and develop within it. Nor does it capture the extent to which the employment that people attain is truly representative of their actual potential or indeed longer-term plans. Furthermore, it offers a somewhat simplistic framing of education's role in helping people attain employment, given that employability is also largely contingent on an individual's personal circumstances and those of the job market. Thus, Harvey (2003) argues:

> Employability is not just about getting a job. Conversely, just because a student is on a vocational course does not mean that somehow employability is automatic. Employability is more than about developing attributes, techniques or experience just to enable a student to get a job, or to progress within a current career. It is about learning and the emphasis is less on "employ" and more on "ability". In essence, the emphasis is on developing critical, reflective abilities, with a view to empowering and enhancing the learner (Harvey 2003)

The notions of *learning* and *development* are important here, and they might be taken to connote processes that transcend the more technicist and capability-based approaches to employability. The supply-side, human capital approach acknowledges these to be potentially significant, but only by default of people's investment in education. As educative processes that have wider impacts on a learner's personal and work-related development, they are not readily translated into harder labour market outcome measures – for example, earnings, speed of job entry and promotion prospects. However, if we take employability as something that is based on wider dispositions, for instance, critical abilities and social skills, then perhaps the educational processes that help facilitate learners' employability may not always be tangible or easy to measure.

There has often been an assumption that the value of vocational education lies in its transference of direct labour market skills, which are of immediate relevance and utility, to employers. The vocational learner has been appropriately 'trained' and is in possession of specific skills and credentials that are salient to his or her employment goals and potential employability. However, it may not necessarily be the case that these individuals slot easily into clearly predefined employment or even find work that actually utilizes this training.

One particular manifestation of predominantly supply-side approaches to employability is the preoccupation with performance indicators in higher education. In the current UK higher education market, it has become almost imperative that institutions collate and transmit market-based data to prospective students (Hemsley-Brown and Oplatka 2006). This has largely centred on an institution's teaching and research performance and, increasingly, the employment outcomes of their graduates. These data can be potentially used to inform a prospective student's perceptions of the likely quality and value of an institution. In terms of considering their future job prospects, they may well infer that if an institution's graduates fare well in getting employment, it is because this institution engages in practices that enrich their students' employability. This may be through more relevant courses, better resources, more helpful guidance and so on. As Maringe and Gibbs (2009) have shown, institutions are increasingly driven to capitalize on such indicators if they provide positive signals that give them a positional advantage in the higher education market. This is especially the case for institutions that are clustered within similar market segments and competing for similar profiles of student.

It may be easy to infer from such information that an institution has significantly facilitated a student's future employability through its various provisions and how well it has fulfilled key performance markers. A student's employability is closely correlated with their institution's performance outcomes, and may also be significantly shaped by them.

Harvey (2001) has highlighted the inherent limitations in this approach to employability, for again it tends to fall short in exploring individuals' wider employability-related experiences. A higher education programme may assist a graduate in finding a job by virtue of being employment orientated, relevant and skills focused. However, this doesn't explain how the graduate got this job, the nature of the job and their potential sustainability in that job.

The increasing emphasis on equating employability with institutional performance therefore tends to work from the premise that institutions can act as 'magic bullets' in triggering favourable future job market outcomes. It also places much faith in the role of market information, for example, graduates' employment outcome 6 months after graduating. This, of course, may be open to various interpretations. Indeed, such information may only provide a minor snapshot of the relationship between particular aspects of individuals' educational experiences and their job market outcomes.

Dominant understandings of employability therefore do not always strike a balance between the skills, competences and job-specific knowledge individuals bring forward from their education and training and the conditions of the labour market that may allow these to be fulfilled. The preoccupation with measuring employability and its various manifestations has often meant that less attention is given to the ways in which employability relates to processes and experiences that take place well beyond people's formal education. As Forrier and Sels (2003) discuss, employability is likely to be mediated by a wide range of both contextual and person-specific variables. These tend to involve processes that go beyond the simple supply and demand of individuals to the job market. They may, for instance, include training and professional development opportunities, the organizational mediation of learning opportunities, inter-professional relations and the nature and quality of management structures.

There are also likely to be a range of other personal factors that influence an individual's job market outcomes beyond their possession of employment-related skills and aptitudes. As we discussed in Chapter 3, employability often has a subjective dimension that is related to people's identities and how they see themselves in relation to the labour market. Researchers such as Fugate et al. (2004) and Yorke and Knight (2006) argue that personal factors such as self-efficacy, confidence, personal awareness, adaptability and risk taking, are all likely to play a significant part in shaping access to and outcomes in the job market. The way people think about themselves and plan in relation to future jobs is clearly mediated by individuals' wider educational experiences. For instance, students who have experienced more elite forms of education may be more compelled to orientate and seek-out employment that is perceived as best fitting their profile.

In essence, official policy orthodoxies on employability mainly presuppose that there is a clear responsibility both on individuals and educational institutions to strengthen employability, and to seek out and facilitate opportunities that will contribute towards this goal. Individuals need to do what they can to develop their capacity to find and maintain the employment they seek. There is also a strong performance-based agenda to employability here. People not only need to possess the requisite skills and attributes, but also make sure that these are applied to good effect for meeting new performance imperatives.

The skills agenda

Another major preoccupation among policymakers in relation to enhancing the supply-side of the labour market has been around skills and their continued enhancement. Policymakers have increasingly emphasized the centrality of skills for productivity and economic growth. Much of this is closely linked to concerns about the move towards a high-skills knowledge-based economy. As we have seen, the upskilling thesis posits that employees across nearly all employment spectrums have witnessed higher demands on their work through advancements in technologies and transformation in the way organizations operate.

In the context of more knowledge-intensive workplaces, work has become more complex and multifaceted. Consequently, the nature of employees' skills and expertize has been transformed. This necessitates that employees can draw upon a more extensive skills set which they need to update constantly. A consequence of upskilling is that professional and management-level workers, in particular, have witnessed a marked transformation in how they perform their work, with new demands on their work activities and practices. At the same time, those who work in traditionally semi-skilled employment have also had to adapt to new technological developments and changing work practices, including greater areas of specialism.

According to the dominant policy narrative on skills, the route towards a high-skills economy can therefore only be properly achieved through appropriate forms of education and training. As such, education is seen as the key means to achieving a high-skills and high-wage economy which, in turn, helps national economies maintain a global competitive advantage (see Brown et al. 2001; Keep 2009). One of the key roles of the educational system is to transfer the necessary skills that people increasingly need to draw upon in the labour market. The aspiration among governments is that these skills will become widely dispersed into the economy. It follows that if the workforce is in possession of higher-level skills, they will not only be able to compete effectively for wages, but also for good quality work.

The development and dispersion of higher skills is therefore seen to lead to the raising of the standard and quality of work, as well as to a greater capacity for employees to engage in innovation and more flexible ways of developing products. As Keep (2009) points out, the vision of the high-skills, high-wage economy is also premised on the widespread amelioration of significant skills divisions which have held back various segments of the workforce. Thus, as the overall skills base within the labour market expands, so the traditional divide between the 'skilled' and the 'unskilled' diminishes. The widespread and equalizing distribution of skills into the economy will effectively help generate the growth of new skills and areas of work.

The case has often been made for future employees' potential to be unlocked at relatively early stages of their educational lives. In order to establish a high-skills economy, it is seen by policymakers as imperative that young people are offered flexible, employment-driven and personalized provision to meet their potential. Meager and Hillage (2010) discuss how this has become an even more salient issue in light of continued recessionary pressures and the potential for increasing numbers of young people to be locked into cycles of unemployment. Providing better access to qualification-based provision and skills training will both help potentially disengaged learners such as those 'not in education or training' (NEETs), and also meet what they see as an increasing demand for skills within the service sector.

Measuring skills and the actual value and utility of skills within the labour market is not an easy task, given the multitude of potential skills that different employees draw upon (Gallie et al. 2004). There again tend to be contrasting sets of evidence, with some pointing to trends in upskilling and others to an increasing deskilling. The former also points to greater levels of worker autonomy and discretion over work outputs, as well as greater breadth and scope for skills utilization. The latter, as previously discussed, points to the growing standardization and routinization of much contemporary employment.

Large-scale reviews based on extensive survey analysis of workplace skills have generally shown a rise in jobs skills over time, although this is not necessarily uniform across the workforce (Felstead et al. 2007). This is reflected in the increased level of training and qualifications individuals perceive that they need to undertake specific types of work. Furthermore, continual skills development through the workplace has become a more prominent feature of people's work in light of increasing demands on employees' work outputs. This is reflected in extensions in the training period many employees are undertaking. In addition to this, technical job-specific skills are also being complemented with more generic skills, based largely on interpersonal or 'influence' dimensions, such as communication, negotiation and persuasion. The Felstead et al. review also highlighted gender differences in job skills, with more female employment-related skills being weighted towards generic skills and interpersonal skills and more male employees drawing upon skills based on technical 'know how'. At the same time, however, both genders equally utilize information literacy skills based on digitalized and online technology.

The skills agenda has been keenly embraced by policymakers who have propagated the importance of achieving and maintaining a highly skilled workforce. The Leitch review (2006) of skills outlined a comprehensive overview of the skills required in modern workplaces, and the specific areas where these need to be nurtured. The overall thrust of this review was on the linkages between skills and economic development, and the significance of skills to the formal and lifelong learning process. The review presented skills as not only integral to economic life, but crucial at all levels of production irrespective of the different forms that they take. Skills are defined principally as specialized qualities, but also more generically as:

> . . . capabilities and expertise in a particular occupation or activity. There are a large number of different types of skills and they can be split into a number of different categories. (Leitch Review, p. 6)

The familiar theme of economic efficiency being matched with social justice is also applied to the skills agenda in this report. Skills are the motors to economic productivity and their promotion through education and training helps to unlock many individuals' potential. They are economic and social goods whose impacts reach far and wide. Thus:

> In the 21st century, our natural resource is our people- and their potential is untapped and vast. Skills unlock. The prize for our economy is enormous – higher productivity, the creation of wealth and social justice. (Leitch Review, p. 1)

The report makes it clear that employers have properly identified the skills they demand, as well as the specific areas where they need to be developed. These are not only in the core basic skills of basic numeracy and literacy, but also more *generic* skills around communication, information literacy, personal adaptability, as well as job-specific skills used in particular jobs. Furthermore, the review calls for greater attention to the skills of all ages of the workforce, not simply school-leavers. It recommended that more is done to ensure that school and university leavers, as well as the majority of adults, are equipped with a broad and dynamic skills base that will raise their overall labour market productivity and effectiveness. It also called for much stronger levels of employer-led engagement and investment in qualifications and skills development for individuals entering the workforce, including the provision of skills-rich, demand-driven training.

A key recommendation of the Leitch review was to increase the number of young people accessing higher-level qualifications such as Level 3, as this will lead to more people attaining apprenticeships and A levels. It further highlighted the importance of access to higher education, which was presented as central to the formation of a high-skills economy; further recommending that increasing numbers of learners have access to degree-level qualifications. Indeed, the subsequent Labour government report, 'Higher Ambitions' (BIS 2009) outlined a rationale for ensuring that at least 70 per cent of individuals under 30 are engaged in degree-level qualifications and/or advanced diplomas.

> We will bring together employers, HEFCE and the UK Commission for Employers and Skills (UKCES) to identify and tackle specific areas where university supply is not meeting demand for key skills and will expect all universities to describe how they enhance students' employability. (Higher Ambitions 2009, p. 9)

Prior to the Leitch review, the influential Dearing report (1997) on higher education a decade earlier had brought the issue of employability-based skills to the fore in discussions of the wider role of higher education. The Dearing report made the strong case that one of the core purpose of higher education should explicitly be around the enhancement of graduates' employability and skills. This was linked to the related call for improved access and enhanced programme provision. This report argued that the traditional academic and disciplinary knowledge that graduates acquire through formal studies needed to be complemented with additional levels of added-value or 'key' skills.

'Employability skills' in the Dearing report are presented as being central to graduates' success and integration in a changing graduate labour market. Likewise, employability is strongly equated with the skills that graduates are in possession of, as well as their capacity to deploy these in employment settings. Higher education institutions that do too little to transfer key skills through their curricula are likely to undermine their graduates' chances in the labour market.

Like the Leitch review, the Dearing report was keen to outline the range of skills that needed to be nurtured, placing considerable emphasis on higher education institutions' role in incorporating them in curricula design and course programmes. Skills such as 'team-working', 'communication', 'self-management' and 'learning how to learn' were given particular weighting, as they were seen as skills that employers particularly valued. There were echoes in this report of earlier drives to make higher education programmes more vocationally relevant, particularly in terms of building up graduates' commercial awareness and enterprise skills (DES 1991).

The Dearing report highlighted the importance of skills-driven higher education learning in the context of mass higher education and the imminent financial contributions students would need to make to their studies. Acknowledging that mass higher education has witnessed a corresponding growth in vocationally orientated programmes, the report nonetheless called for a shift away from exclusively academic modes of learning and provision. It further urged employability skills to become embedded in course programmes so that learners are proficient in skills such as teamwork, presentations, collating information and independent research.

A central theme in the Dearing and Leitch reviews is the role of educational institutions, and in particular post-compulsory ones, to do more to enrich learners' skills and better prepare them for the workforce. Skills should be central chords in educational provision rather than token add-ons to existing practices. The core messages of these reports have been greeted with a mixture of support and criticism among academics. Supporters have endorsed the need for a renewed focus on what school-leavers and graduates can actually *do*, and how provision can be best organized to maximize their chances of meeting the changing demands of work. In a more fluid and increasingly turbulent economic climate, educators have a responsibility to assist learners in their quest to optimize their labour market fortunes. Moreover, in the context of economic uncertainty, school-leavers and graduates are likely to expect more in the way of applied and vocationally orientated learning that will aid their job market prospects.

On the other hand, there has been a degree of scepticism towards the skills agenda, in terms of not only what it represents educationally, but also regarding the way skills have been conceived. Keep and Mayhew (2010) make a forcible case that policymakers have often exaggerated the extent of skills deficits in the economy, instead presenting skills as a compensation for wider structural economic deficiencies. Related to this is the somewhat problematic relationship between skills and economic growth, a relationship that is often taken as casual and relatively straightforward. These authors point out that, while some skills may facilitate changing labour market demands, their whole-scale enhancement does not necessarily result in a fundamental upgrading in products and services.

A key issue raised by Keep and Mayhew is the tendency for policymakers to assume that once skills are fed into the job market, the demand-side of the labour market will take care of itself. However, skills utilization in the labour market and its potential for economic development often tend to be mediated by a wide range of corporate factors of which job design, organizational climate, governance and management structures and employee partnerships are often crucial. Thus, whatever skills people acquire through education are likely to be shaped by the labour market contexts they find themselves in. This is ultimately likely to facilitate their utility. At another level, as critics such as Hartley (2009) point out, there has been a tendency to conflate qualifications with skills, and much emphasis in the Leitch review was on providing access to higher levels of qualification.

Similar criticisms have been levelled at the wider policy narrative's tendency to under-explore the meanings of skills, how they are dispersed in the economy and how employers engage with them. Challenging the overtly supply-side focus to the skills agenda, Wolf (2007) questions whether policymakers have adequately engaged with what employers actually demand, or the degree to which employers are themselves proactive in promoting employees' skills throughout their working lives.

At one level, this raises concerns over the extent to which the skills that employers propagate are fully demand-led. Again, the prevailing concern is that employer strategies towards skills development have been mixed, if not fully negligible. Any genuine and long-term commitment to employees' skills requires a sustained targeting of resources that may be difficult in fragile labour markets where turnaround is fairly high. But, more importantly, Wolf argues that the supply-trigger approaches found in reviews like Leitch, significantly decontextualize skills as they largely fail to address adequately what skills actually constitute and how they are deployed in the economy.

Similar critical voices have been directed towards the post-Dearing skills-orientated approach to higher education. At one level, critics have challenged the onslaught of narrow employer-dominated competency approaches to university learning, which have devalued the role of traditional scholarship and academic values (Barnett 1994; Whitstone 1998; Hyland and Johnson 1998). Such critics have argued that 'employability' skills offer a narrow remit for university learning, which has traditionally been about higher levels of cognitive and intellectual development. These critics also argue that competency-based approaches have reduced the role of higher education to training, whereas it has traditionally been about enriching graduates wider dispositions and outlooks. The 'skills' agenda in higher education is therefore viewed to be narrowly focused and short termist. The 'list' approach to higher education skills is seen to be highly descriptive, tending to divorce skills acquisitions from their deployment in job settings. For instance, a learner's exposure to 'team-working' situations may make them better able to handle certain future work situations, but it doesn't necessarily capture how skilled they are in this area or how well they will fare longer-term in the job market.

The underlying premise in much of these critiques is that the *skills for employability* agenda represents a somewhat distorted notion of the role of education in promoting individuals' employability. As such, the relationship between the supply and demand of skills has often been simplified. Furthermore, education becomes reducible to training whereby its overriding goal is to fulfil vocational goals that have not been clearly defined. Skills are clearly as much driven by the job market context as they are by whatever educational practices are in place before individuals enter the labour market. In the context of educational policies designed to reinforce potential linkages between educational and work-based practices, the precise mechanisms through which skills translate to employee performance is not always well-defined.

Vocational education and training

A significant feature of educational policy over the past three decades has been the development of forms of vocational education and training (VET) and the related endeavour to align learners' experiences more fully to their future employment. This has been a response to shifting labour market conditions, in particular the shift away from more clearly defined forms of youth employment and job-related training. It also coincides with increasing numbers of young people participating in post-compulsory education. Consequently, the range and scope of vocational provision has expanded quite considerably in the period from the early 1980s. These changes have largely taken place against a backdrop of concerted calls from employers for more to be done to tailor young people's learning to their ever-changing needs.

Hodgson and Spours (2008) have discussed how vocational education connects to two salient policy agendas: skills in relation to economic performance and social inclusion. The official aspiration has been for vocational education to plug skills gaps and provide learners with transferable qualifications, while at the same time engaging more young people and giving them greater aspirations. Yet, the extent to which much vocational educational provision has addressed these issues has been much contested.

As these authors have pointed out, much vocational provision over the past three decades has been mixed and has sometimes exacerbated the differential educational experiences and outcomes between different types of learner.

The upsurge in vocational education is often seen as a policy response to changing labour markets and the changing needs of learners. As a mode of educational provision, VET has been promoted as a legitimate and potentially beneficial route, particularly among learners who like to know where their learning is likely to lead them and whose motivations are more strongly tied to paid employment. Winch (2002, 2009) argues that the process of being socialized in the ways of paid labour and acquiring future-orientated knowledge should not necessarily represent an anti-educational and overly instrumental approach to learning. If vocational learners' skills are properly harnessed and there is a strong degree of curricula balance that empowers learners, then vocational educational routes may be credible and worth pursuing. For many learners, finding greater interconnection between their immediate educational experiences and future employment activities is likely to provide them with strong levels of motivation.

Earlier research by Jamieson et al. (1988) and Spours and Young (1988) clearly demonstrated how schooling methods that help simulate actual workplace environments and practices enhance learners' motivations. Not only may these help provide genuine work-based insights which may be of benefit to learners, but they are also likely to be ascribed much value among learners who have not been particularly academically orientated. Thus, the moves towards vocationalism and more work-related provisions can, at one level, be seen as a legitimate way of engaging young people in the formal learning process. It is clear that a large core of learners continue to be demotivated by purely academic learning and instead want to 'see the point' of their formal education.

However, the structure of vocational education and the outcomes it generates has been held under considerable critical scrutiny. Concerns abound over whether vocational education is both fit-for-purpose and has genuine potential to address the deep-seated structural inequalities within educational systems. In some cases, it has been seen to reinforce inequalities. In the UK, for instance, there is quite a marked polarity between academic and vocational routes and this often reflects wider social class divisions and subsequent labour market outcomes between groups of learners (Ainley 1993; Raffe 2003). In many ways, these different routes are likely to determine access to different forms of employment as well as the formation of future employment outlooks.

Raffe (2003) has illustrated how vocational and academic provisions have come to represent distinct educational 'pathways' that have markedly different learning experiences and outcomes and fairly minimal overlap. As contrasting and divergent pathways, they invariably channel individuals towards particular future labour market options and outcomes; in the case of much vocational provisions, these tend to be quite specific and geared towards highly defined forms of future work. While 'academic' pathways are fairly generic and fluid, vocational ones can be highly specific. A consequence of polarized academic and vocational systems is that the different outcomes they generate tend to map onto social class inequalities. Thus, the acquisition of specific skills invariably equips learners for different segments of the labour market. Moreover, the lack of integration between pathways may often preclude learners from exposure to the varieties of skills and experiences needed for different jobs.

Young (1998, 2006) illustrates that there is a strong historical element to the vocational-academic division, which is rooted in the dominant modes of curricula provision within national contexts. Where academic modes of learning are given pre-eminence, clear hierarchies often emerge between academic and vocational provision. Here, the latter tends to be given less value and credence. This further reflects both the historical interlinkages between forms of educational qualification and paid labour, as well as the dominant educational philosophies within a national context. Young posits that the dominant and culturally valued modes of curricula in the UK are based almost exclusively on abstract and cumulative knowledge, geared towards instilling the learner with a core body of factual and theoretical knowledge. This has inevitably been more beneficial to certain learners than others. He also points out that the academic and vocational division is also strongly associated with occupational divisions and anticipated forms of work, and therefore tends to reinforce learners' differential labour market aspirations and opportunities.

The interaction between vocationalism and class clearly reflects learners' different orientations to various educational pathways (Bynner 1988; Fevre et al. 1999). Thus, perhaps a marked feature of working-class learners' educational identities has been the propensity to engage in forms of learning that have more immediate economic relevance, while discarding those that are likely to have minimal bearing on their anticipated working lives. By contrast, the routes to 'professional' employment are largely characterized by more abstract knowledge that is rich in symbolic meaning and strongly associated with traditional 'academic' curricula. Learners embarking on such routes, typically academically able, are aware that while not necessarily being 'trained', they are nonetheless being groomed for the types of skills and learning contexts that facilitate access to higher-level occupational pursuits.

However, such disparities are not so pronounced in other contexts where vocational provision is perhaps not only more coherent and better coordinated, but also more culturally and economically valued. The VET systems in countries such as Germany and Singapore, for example, have often been celebrated for providing rigorous modes of provision that favourably equip learners for the labour market (Green 2003; Winch and Clarke 2007). What tends to characterize these countries' VET systems is the relative esteem attached to them, their strong level of state coordination and their scope for integrating academic and vocational learning outcomes.

In the German dual system of vocational apprenticeship, there is more of a balance between applied, job-specific skills acquisition and the development of academic knowledge. In this system, vocational learners receive a broader and integrated mode of training and scholarship that helps them develop as learners while also facilitating their employment chances. Moreover, the system is given greater value, particularly among employers who have been shown positively to endorse much VET provision.

In the UK and the USA, vocational education has proved to be more problematic, partly owing to its lower cultural and economic status, as well as the ways in which it has been coordinated. The key challenge facing policymakers has been in constructing vocational provisions that are equitable and of genuine labour market value to learners. Thus, in countries where vocational education is weaker, the provisions have tended to function as a compensation for academic disillusionment. Unwin (2010) has argued that many of the VET policies over the last 30 years reflect a variation on a theme. Governments appear to have experienced consistent challenges in constructing a framework for vocational education that provides value to learners' longer-term labour market prospects and employability, and provides employers' with an adequate skills base. One of the central problems has perhaps been the sheer volume and range of available vocational qualifications, which has escalated since the period of the mid-1980s. While, in some cases, vocational provision has served some learners well, and provided them with a decent overall future platform, the picture has often been a mixed one.

The UK Conservative administration of the 1980s developed a whole range of vocational education streams, principally under the pretext of raising human capital in the workforce. Vocational education was promoted as being of wider economic value and helping fulfil changing economic demands. Various commentators, however, have interpreted the upsurge in vocational education at that time as a short-termist policy response in the face of increasing youth unemployment and the increasing reluctance among employers to offer job-related training (Ainley 1988; Roberts 1984). Nonetheless, the 1980s saw the emergence of a whole plethora of vocational programmes taken up largely by school-leavers who, hitherto, might have found employment fairly soon after leaving school. Out of the numerous vocational initiatives on offer, the National Vocational Qualifications (NVQ) and General National Vocational Qualifications (GNVQ) were perhaps the most prominent. The former was a competency-based qualification aimed at accrediting work skills, whereas the latter was mainly taught in educational institutions leading to a formal qualification.

However, there is some clear evidence that much vocational provision produced highly variable outcomes, in many cases being of minimal value to learners' future job prospects (McIntosh 2002). It also shows variability in the returns across different modes of provision. As McIntosh's research shows, where there is better overall compatibility between the mode of provision and employers' demands, positive outcomes are likely to occur. This has been the case for a number of advanced programmes such as Higher National Diplomas (HNDs). However, in numerous cases, vocational provision has often led to low-skilled, low-status employment, and has tended to be devalued by many employers. Again, once on such modes of provision, many learners may find it difficult to progress onto different pathways.

It would very much appear to be the case that many learners nonetheless continue to be drawn to vocational education, particularly when it is perceived as a viable route towards meaningful employment and helping them pursue the types of learning and skills that they value (Eccelston 2002; Hodgson and Spours 2008). At one level, this is partly a response to disenchantment with traditional modes of academic learning and its perceived lack of relevance to immediate employment goals. However, learners who are orientated towards vocational pathways also appear to be actively driven by a desire to acquire skills sets that will assist them in carving out an employment niche.

Research by Unwin and Wellington (2001) that explored young people's approaches to training, confirmed that many young people perceive vocational pathways as a potentially credible route towards achieving specific target employment. There appears to be a clear desire and commitment among young people to acquire useful and relevant skills and to find work that will give them a platform to operate in the jobs market. Furthermore, positive experiences of training often tend to affirm positive identities towards specific jobs and raise learners' overall work-related motivations. This, in turn, may be beneficial for employer organizations as the result of positive employee engagement, motivation and morale.

Perhaps out of the many vocational educational provisions to emerge over the past three decades in the UK, apprenticeships have proved to be the most beneficial and effective (Guile and Young 2001). One of the key strengths of the modern apprenticeship programmes is that they have been more specifically tailored towards employers' demands and have therefore been afforded higher employer value. Apprenticeships have many commonalities with the German dual system in that they are geared towards developing skills in particular employment areas, for instance, engineering or retail, while at the same time providing access to an NVQ Level 3 qualification. The duration of these programmes, their support by employers and their combining of work-related skills and educational qualifications have proved largely successful. As such, many apprentices have been able to use them as a positive vehicle in helping to secure positive employment. Steedman (2005) argues that apprenticeships lead to recognized skills that are nationally certified and provide many learners with relevant, flexible and adaptable modes of training that is more genuinely demand driven. They also have greater potential to meet employers' longer-term needs as well as providing learners with broader transferable skills.

Exploring the changing landscape of apprenticeships, Fuller and Unwin (2011) highlight the potential that apprenticeships have as a positive vehicle for vocational learning and development. They argue that part of the strength and robustness of the apprenticeship model lies in its universality across many employment domains and the fact that it is a recognized and valued mode of occupational formation. Most occupations, from relatively low skilled to elite 'knowledge work', draw upon the principles of apprenticeships for work-based training and skills formation. This is mainly based on the contextualized and transferable work-related knowledge and skills that genuinely aid employees' progression through their work. The success and potential sustainability of this model largely rests on its continued addressing of learners' educational and occupational needs, as well as the longer-term goals for employers' to plug skills gaps and generate better overall levels of cohesion within workplaces.

These researchers' earlier work (Fuller and Unwin 2004), however, points to both positive and less positive practices and outcomes associated with this model. Their research clearly shows that apprenticeships work most successfully when they allow learners to integrate fully into the work environment and practices, when they have better ownership over their own learning and are more constructively steered towards becoming rounded and competent employees. They also appear to work effectively when there are wider opportunities to learn outside the immediate work environment. This, however, is very often mediated by the specific characteristic and goals of an organization, some of which are more conducive to this kind of learning.

Reconfiguring the 14–19 landscape

The educational landscape has become increasingly complex over time. There appears to be an increasing demand for new and vocationally orientated modes of provision among young people. This is clearly a response to an anticipated need to acquire further qualifications and work-related skills. However, there are still concerns that much vocational provision reinforces the so-called academic and vocational 'divide', leading to discernibly different educational and employment outcomes. The difficulties of fusing these forms may be explained by the fact that once learners embark upon a particular pathway, they tend to stay on that pathway. Furthermore, individuals' orientation towards an academic or vocational route largely reflects more deeply formed learning dispositions, which, in turn, often have a class-cultural underpinning. This may also explain why learners who have chosen one particular route tend to experience difficulty in moving onto other routes.

Research by Hayward et al. (2008) found that students transiting to higher education from mainly vocational routes experienced challenges in adjusting to forms of learning, assessment and pedagogy that were largely dissimilar to what they had previously experienced. While the higher education institution under study stated an overt commitment to accommodating diverse learner profiles, the prevailing 'academic' climate presented challenges in adjusting to a significantly different mode of learning. This perhaps relates to a wider trend among VET students who largely tend to avoid what is seen as dominantly academic cultures of higher education. The process of 'academic drift' that many universities have undergone in the past several decades may well reinforce such challenges.

The variable outcomes from vocational educational provision have tended to frame concerns over their value among employers and other recruiting institutions such as universities. The prevailing lack of parity of esteem between vocational and academic provision in countries like the UK may invariably lead to certain academic institutions and employer organizations overlooking large amounts of vocational routes. As Pring et al. (2009) argue, most policy attempts at improving access to qualifications and subsequent job opportunities have only amounted to patchwork tinkering and not a genuine overhaul of qualification and curricula structures. They point out that continued educational and social divisions are likely to endure if two fundamentally different modes exist in parallel and are conferred significantly different status. Indeed, one of the key themes underpinning the Nuffield review of 14–19 year-old education in the UK was the need for a more coherent and unified system that meets the diverse range of learner and societal needs. The present system continues to operate within traditional boundaries, mainly reinforced by differential attainment on the General Certificate of Education and A-Levels. Alternative modes of provision and assessment have tended to be grossly marginalized.

One of the most significant attempts at restructuring the 14–19 curriculum in the UK came in the form of the government-commissioned review of the 14–19 curriculum (the Tomlinson review). This review called for the construction of a new overarching diploma framework for *all* 14–19 year-olds in order for academic and vocation pathways to converge. This new qualification framework was proposed in order to encourage greater integration between general academic skills and knowledge and vocational streams. This, in effect, would go some way to bridging what has been a traditionally divisive system where academic and vocational are largely mutually exclusive. The government's rejection of this core recommendation has been interpreted as representing a deep-seated reluctance to experiment with alternative provisions. This is particularly the case with new forms of provision that may disrupt the traditional and time-honoured routes to higher education and professional employment (Hodgson and Spours 2008). In response to this review, however, new 14–19 specialist diplomas were introduced from 2008. These include academic and vocational material covering each sector of the economy, and are led and designed by employers through the Sector Skills Council.

For all the developments in vocational provision over time, continued concern persists around the lack of efficacy and robustness of much provision. The Wolf review (2011), commissioned by the coalition government, raises a number of key criticisms of much existing vocational education provision. One of the main contentions outlined by this review was that vocational education in the UK continued to fall short of meeting the labour market needs of learners and employers. Too many vocational learners do not progress to higher education or to full-time or secure employment. One of the key recommendations of this review was for better provision of general educational skills, combined with better targeted forms of work experience and apprenticeships. The latter was identified as a key way forward and a way of simplifying and unifying a complex landscape of disparate and variable forms of provision; moving away from young people being steered towards irreversible pathways, particularly into low-skill, low-opportunity routes. The system is seen to require better coordination between educational institutions and employers in steering the direction of future vocational provision – in effect, a more *demand-driven* provision that is equitable and beneficial for both learner and employer.

It is clear that in countries such as the UK, vocational education has some way to go in order to reach its potential and meet the changing needs of learners and the economy. What should potentially be a robust and effective way of engaging learners and meeting both their needs and the needs of organizations has instead tended to be mired in loosely regulated and diffuse provision. The problem appears to stem from a fundamental lack of parity between vocational and academic routes and their perceived relative value. A number of commentators, such as Keep and Mayhew (2004), have highlighted the continued government propensity towards what might be seen as a 'higher' level skills strategy. Such a strategy invariably positions higher education as the key skills growth institution. The core rationale has therefore been to expand the numbers getting higher education qualifications on the premise that this is where economic demand lies. Aside from the issue of whether this may be beneficial for vast numbers of learners, it may be questionable whether this strategy meets genuine economic demands or fills existing skills gaps. Keep and Mayhew critically question the supposed linear relationship between higher education and expansion and the fulfilment of skills gaps and demands. Higher doesn't necessarily equate with better, particularly if higher qualified graduates eventually 'crowd out' less qualified school-leavers in jobs for which they are overqualified. There may also be consequences for skills diffusion in the labour market if intermediary-level skills get sidelined from educational policy.

These types of problems may well be exacerbated during times of recessionary strain. Young people, particularly those with relatively limited labour market experiences, continue to be one of the most vulnerable social groups during times of labour market contraction (Furlong and Cartmel 2007). One serious issue concerns school-leavers and graduates ability to break into jobs when employers decide to cut back on recruitment. Indeed, the evidence would suggest a cautionary conservatism on the part of employer organizations in their human resource strategies during recessionary and unstable market periods. Cost effectiveness appears to be the guiding principle in determining who, how and why they decide to recruit (Warhurst 2008). Employers may therefore be more inclined to retain older, more experienced employees who can offer immediate value and are cheaper in training terms, rather than recruit newly skilled, potentially flexible graduates who are likely to be more costly.

Research by Mason and Bishop (2010) has shown that the recession has caused many employers to lessen their commitment to offering work-related training. This, in turn, has implications for the hiring of newly qualified school-leavers and graduates who employers may perceive to be expensive to train. These researchers further criticize employers' approaches to vocational education for being too cost-driven rather than demand- and quality-driven. The well-publicized discontent expressed by employers over skills deficiencies among school-leavers is not necessarily matched by a sustained coordination of skills and training when many young people enter their workplaces. However, if there is inadequate on-the-job training within workplaces, it may be difficult for skills to be properly sustained over time given that this is the most significant context where they are utilized and evolved.

Vocational education has clearly evolved over the past three decades. But it still confronts major challenges around its supply and demand, coordination and planning. This also extends to its perceived parity and value. The integrated model found in European countries such as Germany is only partly rivalled in the UK. The way forward is clearly a fusion of generalist and academic skills with specialist skills training and development. This is likely to help socialize these learners more fully towards their desired target employment and provide them with more positive identities around learning and work. Moreover, it will make their routes more attractive to employers and give them a wider educational base from which to work. However, as Hodgson and Spours (2008) warn, if vocational education continues to be seen as the default route and compensation for lack of academic engagement, then perceptions around it will continue to be somewhat negative. Moreover, the hierarchy between academic and vocational pathways will persist, perpetuating unequal outcomes between pathways and some employers' continued reluctance to fully embrace vocational qualifications. In the UK, such perceptions have proven to be fairly deep-seated and relate closely to class-based perceptions of relative educational value. The middle classes in particular continue to value the traditional academic route towards attaining well-paid, desirable jobs.

Chapter summary

This chapter has explored and critically engaged with some of the key policy motifs in the education and work interrelationship. The role of education in improving people's employability has become a very salient policy theme and is set against the background of a shifting economy and new imperatives for upskilling, human capital development and meeting more acute international competition. Education clearly plays a fundamental role in raising school-leavers' and graduates' capacity to make meaningful and impactful contributions to the labour market. Additionally, it not only needs to provide them with extra skills but *the right* kinds of skills that have currency in the job market. These concerns are mainly underpinned by an aspirational vision among government that education can effectively generate a high-skills/high-wage economy and that the supply of skills will generate its own demand.

Wider policy goals have invariably raised expectations over the role of educational systems in enhancing people's employability and the skills they are able to transfer to the labour market. As such, much of the policy rationale of employability and skills has had a strong supply-side orientation – namely, that schools, colleges and universities have a fundamental role in raising the skills, and therefore the productive potential of the workforce. This is seen as a legitimate educational aim and one to which educational institutions have the capacity to respond. Yet, critical observations have pointed to the narrow framing of the skills revolution in terms of the supply-trigger effect that educational systems have for producing a future skilled workforce. This puts much responsibility on educational systems to raise the profile and supply of 'employable' and 'skilled' workers, while not always looking at the 'demand' side issue – for instance, the extent to which work organizations commit longer-term investments in workforce development. The vocational system has been presented as a key way of raising the labour market profile and aspirations of young people while meeting more specific economic needs. Clearly, vocational education has proven attractive, but its efficacy, economic value and parity with alternative educational routes, continues to be a cause of concern among educationalists.

CHAPTER SIX

Lifelong learning, learner identities and work-related learning

This chapter will examine the ways in which identities are produced within educational contexts, and how these identities predispose individuals towards particular forms of future participation in both education/training and the job market. The identities that individuals develop through their experiences of formal learning are likely to frame their future work-related orientations and outlooks. However, people's experiences of learning are ongoing and recursive and tend to form part of a trajectory through different phases and critical turning points in their lives. For some people, this may be fairly smooth, predictable and based on relatively stable and coherent learner identities. Such patterns may be further reinforced by dominant culturally derived sets of attitudes towards and expectations of the role that education has in an individual's life. Other individuals, however, may follow more fractured routes through formal learning whereby their progression is neither predictable nor clearly patterned.

The notion of learner identities and trajectories is important as it relates to individuals' specific frames of references, lived experiences and future orientations towards learning and work. Learner identities play a potentially potent role in framing the parameters within which people make choices and understand their wider position both within the educational system and beyond in the labour market. These identities often guide people's choices and their propensities towards various forms of future educational and work-related activity. However, people's learner identities are also socially and contextually mediated and not simply individually constructed. This works on a range of levels, from the broader socio-economic and policy context through which learner opportunities are structured, through to individuals' location within the social structure – in particular, their class position, gender and ethnicity.

The chapter seeks to further locate the analysis of learner identities in relation to wider sociological theories of learning, linking this to wider themes of the social and cultural mediation of the learning experience. This is linked to a discussion on the wider policy concept of *lifelong learning*, and how this has been conceptualized and applied in research with a range of different groups, not least those in post-compulsory and adult-based education. In particular, the way these are shaped by the wider social and educational contexts that frame their experiences. At the end of the chapter, we explore the issues of work-related learning and how this is mediated by the different contexts in which people work.

Lifelong learning for a learning society

The concept of lifelong learning gained increasing popularity in the 1990s, driven largely by the UK Labour government's attempt to create a so-called 'learning society'. The underlying rationale for lifelong learning is based on both economic and social justice imperatives. As the concept implies, lifelong learning refers to individuals' engagement in learning throughout their life course, moving beyond that which is confined to formal educational settings. Lifelong learning is presented as an economic necessity that helps meet the needs of a changing economy through the enhancement of individuals' skills. It also opens up opportunities to participate in learning among those social groups who have typically been excluded from formal learning opportunities (Coffield 2000). Clearly, governments have enunciated the significance of learning for both economic gains and as a mode of social inclusiveness. The DfEE (1998) report 'The Learning Age' thus expresses:

> Learning is essential to a strong economy and an inclusive society. In offering a way out of dependency and low expectation, it lies at the heart of the Government's welfare reform programme. We must bridge the "learning divide" – between those who have benefited from education and training and those who have not – which blights so many communities and widens income inequality. The results are seen in the second and third generation of the same family being unemployed, and in the potential talent of young people wasted in a vicious circle of under-achievement, self-deprecation, and petty crime. Learning can overcome this by building self-confidence and independence. (DfEE 1998, p. 14)

Governments have often presented lifelong learning as a social good that opens up social and economic opportunities to the learner. The goal therefore is to encourage more individuals to embark upon learning, and to provide greater opportunities for them to participate in learning continually throughout their lives. This represents something of a shift in the understanding of lifelong learning. The traditional view of lifelong learning centred predominately on learning for adult and mature students as a compensation for earlier educational underachievement. The contemporary approach instead tends to conceive lifelong learning as a condition that all individuals, across all social and professional spheres, must embrace.

The wider societal and individual benefits of lifelong learning are seen as abundant and far-reaching, potentially helping to build communities, promote civic participation and establish greater social cohesion (Schuller et al. 2004). In its broadest sense, therefore, lifelong learning refers to the multiplicity of contexts through which people engage in learning across different phases and stages of their lives. This is also likely to involve the increasing interplay between formal educational contexts and a range of other less formal social contexts through which individuals learn, including the workplace, community, the home and other personal domains.

In its more optimistic guise, the concept of lifelong learning indicates a more inclusive and egalitarian educational landscape. Indeed, the social justice dimension of lifelong learning has continually been emphasized by policymakers (Edwards and Nicoll 2001). The more opportunities that individuals have to pursue learning and gain access to relevant skills and credentials, the more empowered they will be. This is particularly the case for individuals who might have felt excluded or marginalized from formal learning opportunities, such as low educational achievers and those from lower socio-economic backgrounds. Thus, lifelong learning is potentially a key to expanding the 'pool of talent' from a wider demographic field and helping break down learning barriers that have often constrained some individuals' access to formal learning opportunities.

The concept of lifelong learning has, nonetheless, been held under much critical scrutiny. Field (2006) has challenged much of the normative and aspirational rhetoric that accompanies the concept, as manifest in various policy discourses. The normative element relates to the assumption that lifelong learning is both desirable and achievable for the majority of individuals. The opportunities for lifelong learning are extensive and so it is up to individuals to actively pursue them. But the concept is also highly aspirational as it tends to frame lifelong learning as an endeavour that generates unquestionable social and economic outcomes. Field (2006) also highlights the various tensions between policy goals and policy implementation, particularly as lifelong learning is not always easy to achieve both at the level of planning and individuals' resources. Instead, it has become the responsibility of individuals to seek out lifelong learning opportunities even when available provisions and access to learning opportunities are not always in place.

Grace (2009) has taken these criticisms further, arguing that much lifelong learning policy across most national contexts has a strongly instrumental and economistic undercurrent. He argues that much of the policy drive has been towards enhancing individuals' capacity for the challenges of global capitalism. However, an overly economistic agenda to lifelong learning, based on the drive towards upskilling and retraining, often means that other developmental and emancipatory features of lifelong learning become marginalized, not least it's potential for civic participation.

The economic imperative for lifelong learning resonates very strongly with the human capital approach that we explored earlier. Learning, in the form of continued education and training, provides a crucial resource that individuals can take forward to the labour market. Lifelong learning is central to a knowledge-based economy where skills are continually changing and upgraded, and where people need to learn how to learn (World Bank 2003). This again follows the circular technocratic argument of: globalized knowledge economy = educational expansion and lifelong learning = skills increase = fulfilment of changing economic demand and maintenance of a high-skills, knowledge economy. This, in turn, helps perpetuate a cycle of continued learning, as both society and individuals witness the benefits. It therefore becomes essential that individuals are provided with as many opportunities for both formal and informal learning throughout their lives, as this will be the key to unlocking their own economic potential.

However, the concept of lifelong learning remains somewhat ambiguous and diffuse. Not only does learning mean different things to different people, but it takes a variety of different forms and leads to a whole range of different outcomes. As Ingram et al. (2009) discuss, it is almost impossible to generalize from different experiences of lifelong learning given that they may take a variety of different forms. High-level training within a specialized professional domain clearly engenders different learning forms and outcomes from basic skills training for unemployed young people. They are also differentially provided for and take place in markedly differing learning contexts. Moreover, people's transitions to and from education also take a variety of forms and for some this may be more traditional and linear than others. Invariably, people's engagement with continued learning interacts with other facets of their lives and their wider biographies; therefore, there are likely to be different levels of constraint and facilitation to people's participation in different forms of learning.

Perhaps a strong criticism concerns the rather neutral and objective ways in which lifelong learning is presented. Jackson et al. (2011) critically point out that the concept of lifelong learning often depicts individuals as being equally resourced and possessing an equal understanding of various learning opportunities. This largely presupposes that all individuals have the means, resources and inclinations to engage in learning opportunities and to draw upon relatively high levels of personal agency towards this pursuit. Yet, as Jackson argues, learning opportunities continue to be patterned by class and gender, and these tend to shape the kinds of learning environments individuals orientate towards.

Such factors invariably determine the scope of individuals' engagement in different forms of learning and the opportunities available to them.

As earlier critics such as Riddell et al. (1997) and Rees and Gorard (2002) point out, popular discourses on lifelong learning tend to present learning opportunities as 'out there' and readily available. As such, it is largely seen as the responsibility of individuals to seek out and exploit these opportunities, often in order to compensate for deficits in skills, poor earlier attainment and low levels of employability. However, as these authors discuss, many individuals remain constrained from engaging in lifelong learning by a range of factors, including health, finances, familial constraints, learning difficulties and physical access, even if they have the inclination to do so in the first place.

There are also wider issues in relation to the outcomes that lifelong learning may potentially generate. When framed around the enrichment of human capital, lifelong learning is often equated with lifelong earnings.

Some critics have, therefore, discussed the problems around lifelong learning when it becomes a coercive, state-driven form of social engineering to compel individuals to undertake further education and training. If more individuals are obliged to invest in further education and training without perceiving or experiencing its benefits, then there is a danger that lifelong learning becomes part of a pattern of misplaced credential accumulation (Ainley 1999; Tight 1998; Wolf et al. 2006). Tight (1998), for instance, argues that the compulsion for individuals to embark upon lifelong learning may in fact lead to further disengagement with learning if it is actually at odds with what individuals wish to take from any additional education. Individuals' motivations are likely to centre on tangible personal benefits, intrinsic or economic, rather than being based on an obligation to simply participate per se.

Wolf et al. (2006) echo this view by challenging the generalized way in which lifelong learning has been presented in policy, often resting on the assumptions that it necessarily has direct and tangible societal and economic trade-offs. As such, the drive towards lifelong learning for its own sake may well undermine the true emancipatory value of learning and more specific ways in which it might contribute to wider personal well-being. In this sense, lifelong learning may become another shorthand for credentialism in the guise of raising opportunities and access to learning.

Lifelong learning and its related construction of a learning society is seen as a laudable policy goal based on a justifiable enough rationale that learning can empower and emancipate. Yet, educationalists have sought to critically engage with the concept and unpack the extent to which its ideals meet the realities that many potential lifelong learners experience.

The social construction of learner identities

Over time, there has been a greater exploration of people's educational biographies in terms of lived experiences of learning, transitions to and from education and engagement with future learning (Bloomer and Hodkinson

2000; Colley et al. 2003, Alheit 2005; Antikainen et al. 1996). The experiences people have of formal learning will invariably influence how they come to perceive themselves as learners and potential future workers. A learner's identity is very much at the heart of their wider educational biography. It is often what frames their lived experiences of education and their subsequent outcomes. However, in exploring learner identities, some consideration is needed of the factors that shape these identities and the different contexts through which this works. Individuals' educational biographies are very much the amalgamation of highly personal and subjective experiences that have been formed through formal and informal educational processes. At the same time, they are also inextricably bound by the educational, cultural and wider labour market milieus in individuals' lives, which frame their overall experiences.

There has been greater acknowledgement that educational biographies have become increasingly complex and fluid over time, no longer being forged from fairly fixed and stable experiences and built around clear linear movements from school, college (and potentially university) to work. In the context of more fluid labour markets, individuals may move between education and work fairly sporadically during their lives. Many may engage in new forms of formal learning at a significantly later period than their initial formal education at 16. Eccelstone et al. (2009) illustrate how identities are often central to individuals' construction of learning pathways and the ways in which they negotiate transitions within and beyond educational settings. Identities often form the fulcrum through which individuals make choices and understand and articulate their future possibilities.

The construction of identities in the contemporary context, however, is likely to be an ongoing process. Identities may shift depending on the changing contexts that individuals encounter; for example, people leaving a job to re-enter formal education during their middle years. Also significant are the ways in which individuals' learning experiences go towards shaping wider attitudes towards education, future participation in learning and their wider place in the labour market. Individuals' experiences of education are complex, highly contextualized and certainly not uniform between different types of learners.

The changing educational and labour market context is again very relevant in this area. Clearly, people's experiences of education are markedly different now to what they were in previous decades. Shifts in the formal organization of schooling, in modes of curriculum and types of qualification pathways open to learners will no doubt impact significantly on their experiences and outcomes (Pring et al. 2009). Hughes (2004) makes the case for a broader, more holistic understanding of people's learning experiences, which connects the micro context and private world of the learner to wider macro-level processes of socio-economic change. Thus, any sociological exploration of people's learning experiences needs to pay attention to the wider context in which learning takes place. Highly individualistic accounts of learning that simply see learning as the by-product of cognitive processes do not always capture the social dynamics that frame people's lived experiences of learning.

Hodkinson et al. (2008) also discuss the needs to break dualistic divisions in understanding the learning process, in particular the separation of individuals from the contexts that crucially define and shape their learning experiences. Learners' experiences are never divorced from context; instead, they are constituted by and referenced against them. A strong dimension of the learning process is the way in which individuals continually construct meaning and a sense of who they are and their place in the world. But this is highly situated and embodied through the action and dispositions of the learner, as well as through the interactive spaces within the learning context.

Indeed, constructivists have emphasized how learning is a highly personal process that draws strongly upon cognitive and affective processes as individuals strive towards meaning-making and developing a better understanding of their situation (Jarvis and Parker 2005). At the same time, they also show how learning seldom takes place in isolation and instead involves an individual's continued interaction with their immediate and wider social contexts. These provide the core medium through which meanings and learner identities are constructed. The social mediation of learning and people's learner identities, therefore, largely entails the interaction between individuals' agency and wider social structure. Individuals clearly draw upon degrees of personal agency in their learning, encompassing actions, goals and rationalities. At the same time, this is bounded by overarching structural arrangements through which their lived experiences of learning are formed. These not only relate to the various cultural and material resources they have through their class and gender, but also the institutional context in which their learning takes place, including the interaction between the learner and teacher, and between learners.

There has perhaps been a tendency for economically based approaches to learning to place heavy emphasis on individuals' agency towards their learning. For instance, the human capital approach is highly individualistic and presupposes high levels of conscious rationality and volition on the part of learners. Moreover, by subsuming individuals' goals under the framework of economic rationality, important and subtle biographical elements that shape attitudes and outlooks are often overlooked. As Fevre et al. (1999) highlight, the goal of economic return may constitute only one element in shaping people's learning behaviours, including decisions to participate in future learning. While this is clearly a strong rationale for some individuals' learning, others may choose to learn for a variety of reasons. This, for instance, may incorporate other values such as self-improvement and becoming a more rounded citizen. Therefore, the overemphasis that rational choice approaches place on people's agency and rationality often overlooks the broad range of possible variables that ground people's decisions to participate in learning.

Learner identities and learning careers

Early work on learner identity explored the way in which identities were mediated through the pedagogic relationship between learners and teachers, and also between learners (Weil 1986). It placed strong emphasis on the experiential dimension of learning and its influences on people's self-perceptions in the learning process. In many ways, people's experiences of formal learning shape the way they perceive themselves as learners and the way they interpret the immediate and wider learning context. Weil's (1986) work highlighted the affective dimensions of learning, and how it potentially informs individuals' sense of self. Engagement with learning is a dynamic and recursive process, involving some degree of continuity between previous and current experiences. She discusses learner identities in terms of:

> Learner identity suggests the emergence or affirmation of values and beliefs about "learning", "schooling" and "knowledge". The construct incorporates personal, social, sociological, experiential and intellectual dimension of learning, as integrated over time, (Weil 1986, p. 223)

This approach very much posits that individuals develop highly personal responses to learning and the way they perceive themselves as learners. For some learners, their experience can affirm a positive perception of their role and potential as learners. For others, their experience may be less positive and cause indifference, and sometimes resistance, towards the learning process. Thus, learning experiences might serve to disaffirm or affirm identities around learning and towards education more generally. In a context such as adult education, learners face the challenging task of establishing a coherent and meaningful learner identity in the face of ongoing life circumstances and challenges. They may also need to compensate for fractured learner identities based on unsuccessful early experiences of education.

Some adult learners' ongoing experiences may serve to affirm or disaffirm their perception of how well they have progressed into new learning contexts, as well as the extent to which they have been able to transcend their previous educational experiences. Zukas and Malcolm (2007) highlight that, in many cases, significant transitional hurdles need to be crossed in order for some learners to feel motivated, engaged and valued within their setting. Learners who are able to establish positive and coherent learner identities may develop a sense of personal emancipation that may propel them towards future learning. Moreover, such learners are more likely to engage in continuous learning throughout their life – formally, informally and professionally.

The concept of learner identity has been developed further by Rees et al. (1997), who were keen to highlight its sociological dimensions. They argue that learner identities 'encapsulate how individuals come to understand themselves as learners and, thus, their relationships to learning opportunities' (Rees et al. p. 932). Like Weil, they highlight the affective and subjective dimension to learner identities and how it encapsulates deeply formed values and attitudes towards the learning process. At the same time, they also emphasize the ways in which these are also socially structured and patterned. To this extent, learner identities may also be the by-product of wider cultural and structural patterns that operate outside and beyond learners' immediate educational experiences. This is likely to be partly shaped by individuals' class-cultural make-up and wider sets of cultural expectations towards the learning process.

In a similar vein, Bloomer and Hodkinson (2000) develop the concept of *learning careers* in terms of the continuities and changes that many learners experience over the course of their educational lives. This concept pays similar attention to the way in which students' approaches towards learning develop across the different phases of their educational experiences. These authors highlight that the role of identity and personal agency is significant to people's learning careers, but that these are ultimately shaped by the material and cultural context of the individuals' lives. They show that many young people's approaches and attitudes to learning develop through significant episodes and 'turning points' both within a formal educational setting and outside in their wider social and cultural domains. Crucially, these experiences go towards forming significant *learning dispositions* that guide choices and decisions both around future learning and possible career pathways.

Learner identities and dispositions are therefore very much linked to the wider social milieu, including the availability and opportunities to engage in learning. People's learning also occurs beyond formal education and is also played out informally through their social engagements and interests and, significantly, in the workplace. All these varied social experiences will go some way towards shaping learner identities. Rees et al. further argue that any participation in learning forms part of a trajectory that significantly influences the way learners navigate their way through formal learning opportunities. The kinds of learner identities that individuals form are therefore likely to have some bearing on their learning trajectories, particularly their orientations towards different forms of learning and their decisions to further participate in post-compulsory education and training.

Learner identities will shape, for instance, a person's decision to participate in higher education or their decision to leave formal education at the earliest opportunity. For some individuals, there may be a strong level of continuity between different stages of their learning. Others may have formed negative learner identities through indifferent formal educational experiences. As such, they may develop a 'functional avoidance' of formal learning, perceiving learning as both a waste of time and a threat to other aspects of their identity (Fevre et al. 1999). At its most extreme, this may generalize to other areas of a person's life, including an avoidance of formal learning at work.

However, while there is some degree of patterning to individuals' learning trajectories, they do not necessarily follow stable and predictable patterns. Increasingly, individuals may develop fractured learning trajectories, including periods away from formal study and returning at much later stages. This may itself lead to challenges in the formation of their learner identities, and the ways these are played out in formal educational settings. This has been illustrated in a range of research on adults making transitions to higher education (Crossan et al. 2003; Gallacher et al. 2002; Warmington 2003). As these researchers have found, even when learners undertake further learning, this does not necessarily lead to the construction of positive and affirmative learner identities. This may clearly be the case for mature students who have struggled to make transitions from previous learning to their current learner contexts. Some of these learners may still harbour hidden injuries through negative past experiences, which are not always resolved by participation in post-compulsory education. As this research suggests, the wider educational and cultural baggage that individuals bring to the learning context is likely to mediate their lived experiences and how well they make transitions into new learning settings.

We can see from this work that, at one level, learner identities are highly subjective and embody strong affective and attitudinal dimensions through which individuals make sense of themselves as learners. At the same time, they connect to wider aspects of people's lives and the social contexts through which they move. Crucially, these identities influence individuals' orientations towards learning, as well as to future participation. For some people, this may involve a clear avoidance of learning altogether as it may be perceived to play little part in their immediate and future lives. For others, learning is strongly related to immediate and future goals, for instance, the progression to further and higher education. Yet, even when individuals share similar learning trajectories, their values and rationalities may differ significantly. Some individuals may engage in learning due to an intrinsic interest in learning 'for its own sake', whereby learning is seen as a form of self-development. In other instances, individuals may participate in learning more passively as it is seen as a 'means to an end' to achieving a desirable qualification that may assist their job prospects. In all cases, learners' approaches are likely to be guided by a sense of what role learning plays in their lives as a whole.

A closer look at the role of social class, gender and race

It is clear from academic research and discussion on learner identities that there are some significant structural factors shaping them, in particular those relating to individuals' social location in terms of their class position, gender and ethnicity. These structural dimensions are likely to form a significant prism through which learners construct a sense of themselves within the wider educational landscape. Wider social dimensions are therefore crucial in mediating the ways in which individuals understand themselves in educational contexts. In many ways, learner identities interact quite strongly with wider cultural identities, rather than in isolation.

Much of this is likely to be informally channelled through discursively mediated interactions between learners and significant others within the educational context. In some ways, these interactions may bring about conformity to cultural stereotypes and expectations, as in the case of working-class students playing out dominant images of antipathy and resistance to formal schooling (Willis 1976, 2003; Mac and Ghail 1994). In other cases, they may result in active attempts to subvert dominant expectations and establish new forms of identity that may provide them with new sources of meaning and empowerment.

Social class has remained one of the most salient social variables in mediating people's relationship to the educational world, and has been a long-standing focus of the sociology of education (Gewirtz and Cribb 2009). Sociologists of education have been keen to highlight its continued significance in shaping educational relationships, processes and outcomes. The continued prevalence of social class as a key educational variable very much challenges the more recent policy slogans of the classless society. Instead, the link between social origins and destination outlined in much historical research (Halsey et al. 1980) continues to be mediated through people's educational experiences.

However, this has taken place against not only a changing class structure, including the expansion of the middle classes, but also transformations in the way in which class is conceptualized more broadly and understood in terms of social relations. Savage (2003) discusses the 'changing paradigm' of class, mainly through its reconceptualization from a purely economic and material condition measurable by individuals' location within clear occupational divisions, and towards a more nuanced cultural understanding of how people engage with the sociocultural world. This extends to their behaviour and actions, including the way they negotiate more challenging and competitive socio-economic environments.

This change in emphasis is also reflected in shifts in the sociology of education. Gerwirtz and Cribb (2009) have viewed these shifts in terms of a general move away from grander and normative understandings of social reproduction, towards a more nuanced account of people's lived experiences. This contemporary approach also pays closer attention to the ways in which learners are positioned in class terms through language, discourse and symbolically rich interaction. It also focuses more strongly on how class is linked to individuals' own sense of agency and the way they make sense of their place within the wider educational and cultural spheres. As such, greater attention is given to the nuances in individuals' different social experiences and the fact that the late modern environment has facilitated new and multiple modes of expression and identity. Thus, while the grander social reproduction approaches associated with the work of Willis (1977) portrayed fairly homogeneous cultural identities and practices, contemporary approaches tend to emphasize the richness and diversity of individuals' experiences.

However, this shifting perspective does not downplay the significance of class as a continued potent social force in shaping people's outlooks and lived experiences. As Reay (2001, 2006) discusses, class remains a core dimension in learners' identities. She argues that, far from social relations within education now entailing a dissolution of systemic class-cultural inequalities, social class remains embedded in educational processes. This is further mirrored in the pedagogic relationship between teachers and learners, as well as the interactions between learners. Working-class learner identities have tended to be characterized by fracture, ambivalence and a large degree of cultural disconnect between familial and educational contexts. This is likely quite profoundly to penetrate learners' attitudes, engagement and levels of educational confidence. In many ways, the fractured nature of many working-class students' learner identities may reflect the marked tensions between learners' root identities and the cultural contexts of formal education. This, in turn, may result in feelings of alienation, disaffection and educational resistance, as well as significant underachievement.

The ambivalent nature of working-class learning identities has been illustrated in studies exploring learners' engagement with the changing educational landscape of choice and extended provision. Archer and Yamashito (2003) have also explored some of these issues through research on post-school choices. A clear theme in this research is the fractured learner identities carried by working class and ethnic minority pupils in inner-city state school settings in the UK. It is clear that the micro contexts of educational institutions are important for mediating individuals' perceptions of themselves as learners. These settings facilitate forms of relationships and interactions that produce and reinforce messages to the learner about their place in both formal education as well as the wider social and economic system. Here, students are fed ideas about their potential, educational worth and likely future educational and employment 'success'. These may ultimately delimit certain learners' horizons, providing them with an overriding sense that various future educational routes are outside their grasp and capability.

As Archer and Yamashito's research exposes, educational policies that are geared towards instrumental goals around maximizing pupil school 'performance' are likely to reinforce pre-existing feelings of indifference to formal learning and guidance. The attendant pressures of 'high achievement', 'competition' and 'performance outcomes' may be at profound odds with the existing values that certain groups of working-class pupils hold, even where some of these students have genuine motivations to succeed.

Other research has shown how these processes can extend to other areas of education, particularly among mature students in higher education (Crozier et al. 2008; Jackson and Jamieson 2009). Located within the highly class-differentiated landscape of contemporary UK higher education, Crozier et al. (2008) showed how the class background of mature students significantly influences the way in which they locate themselves within both the academic and cultural environs of the university. In some cases, there are manifest tensions between the identities these students carry outside their formal study, sometimes as parents, part-time workers and members of working-class communities, and the ones they seek to develop within the predominately middle context of the university.

Crozier et al.'s study shows that these tensions are likely to be most marked for mature students in traditional and elite universities, particularly when there are less shared points of class reference. However, this research also shows that not all working-class students share similar identity challenges and hurdles, as some students make the transition (and transformation) to the new cultural context more smoothly than others. Again, the institutional context and its class composition are likely to mediate this process given the relative levels of congruence between students' class profile and the institutional context. Some students may therefore be more adept at negotiating new class positions and working with the dominant cultural codes and discourses of their new environments. In many cases, there are challenges for students in taking on hybrid identities and facing the inevitable 'cultural struggles' between their home lives and formal study.

Research has also shown the construction of learner identities among middle-class pupils, while again emphasizing the variation and richness of middle-class experiences (Power et al. 2003). Overall, middle-class learners have tended to develop learner identities that are more positively aligned to the cognitive and cultural structures of the educational system. As Ball (Ball et al. 2001; Ball 2003) and Reay (2008) illustrate, middle-class learners have largely been primed for the notion that educational success leads to the 'good life' of social and economic rewards and status. These learners and their families are therefore more prone to making higher levels of emotional and personal investment in education as it is seen as the key vehicle to future economic success. This is likely to be actively affirmed by significant others and the reward structures within formal education, not least exam performance.

Both Skeggs (2004) and Reay (2008) have discussed the pervading *culture of entitlement* that underpins many middle-class families' approaches to the educational system. This is largely predicated on the view that participation in further and higher levels of education is the natural and inevitable course, while also based on an active attempt to avoid the fates of working-class *others*. These sets of attitudes invariably entail the deployment of strong levels of emotional, social and cultural capital in order to open up access to future reward and opportunity structures within the educational field. The relatively high levels of emotional labour and identity work that middle-class individuals make towards formal education further helps militate against the increasing risks and uncertainties in both the educational and labour market spheres.

Compared to the more fractured and ambivalent learner identities developed by working-class pupils, it is more common for middle-class learners to have developed more positive and engaged learner identities. This may be largely based on an almost semi-conscious sense that they will move towards post-compulsory education and that continued learning will be a salient feature of their future lives, within and outside formal contexts. This notion is also likely to be actively reinforced by parents, teachers, peers and career advisors. As with working-class learners, however, there are likely to be variations in the form this takes, reflecting in part the expanded and differentiated middle classes. Moreover, the identities that middle-class learners inhabit may also be mediated by a range of lifestyles, familial and value orientations within these groups (Power et al. 2003). As Power et al. argue, it is problematic to treat the 'middle classes' as an homogeneous category given the breadth of middle-class occupations and cultural profiles. For instance, middle-class parents who have been educated privately and work in the private sector may approach the educational system in different ways to traditional middle-class state professionals. They also point to the continued problems experienced by some middle-class learners, including truanting, discipline and low educational motivation.

The gender dimension of learner identity has also been reported in research over time. A dominant theme in the analysis of gender experiences and outcomes in education has been the gradual reshaping of female and male learners' educational expectations and outcomes. It has been widely reported that the traditional patterns of gendered socialization and identity formation within formal education generations have been transformed, allowing for new forms of engagement with formal learning (Sharpe 1994). Indeed, Sharpe's earlier work (1976), along with other prominent feminist scholars (Spender 1982) offered an account of formal education as serving to reproduce substantial gendered inequalities. These inequalities were channelled through the valorization of male-dominated and orientated educational practices and the overall subjugation of female learners. Such processes were seen inevitably to affect females' educational experiences, as well their future labour market prospects, as they were socialized to think of themselves as economically subordinate. This was reinforced by a male-dominated curriculum and forms of pedagogy and symbolic interaction that alienated the majority of female learners.

However, the picture has changed quite significantly over time as reflected in higher levels of female educational attainment and participation, as well as the transformation and modernization of the curriculum (Arnot 2002). Indeed, official and popular representations of gender and schooling have tended to highlight the relative underperformance on the part of male learners (Arnot and Miles 2005; Gorard et al. 2001). However, as Gorard et al. show, there has been a tendency for policymakers both to exaggerate and distort the nature of this issue by focusing on extreme ends of the achieving spectrum.

Nonetheless, the relative achievement between genders has led to increased interest in the contemporary experiences of disengagement among male learners in conjunction with wider changes to the structures of schooling and beyond in the labour market. Arnot and Mac An Ghail (2006) have discussed how the apparent *crisis of masculinity* among certain groups of males can be partly read as a wider identity crisis brought about by the decline in traditional male forms of employment and other traditional modes of self-expression. At the same time, there has been an increasing celebration and utilization of female-orientated dispositions and skills in the labour market.

Other scholars such as Arnot (2002) have also interpreted the reshaping of gender relations in formal education as reflecting a myriad of societal, educational and labour market changes. These have ultimately altered the ways that male and female learners come to define themselves and understand the nature of their participation in education. The increasing feminization of the labour force and the opening up of economic opportunity structures has potentially resulted in more female learners viewing education as a productive means of fulfilling their future economic potential. This is mainly reflected in the continued high levels of females participating in post-compulsory and higher education.

While the experiences of female learners have undoubtedly changed and improved over the past three decades, continued attention is given to the ways in which patterns of gendered socialization and reproduction take place. This points to the fact that much of what take place in education, training and in wider social relations is seldom gender neutral. This further relates to the ways in which education continues to channel male and female learners' orientations and outlooks around particular choices. One salient issue here is subject choice (Whitehead 1996; Francis 2000; Mendick et al. 2008). This research shows that there are still marked differences in the types of subjects that males and females orientate towards across all levels of the educational spectrum. Much of this is to do with deeply formed attitudes and perceptions around the appropriateness of studying particular subjects – for instance, females undertaking science, mathematics and engineering. For female learners, such subjects may still be considered as essentially 'male' and at odds with their existing identities, outlooks and earlier patterns of socialization. This also reflects the wider occupational goals that different learners harbour, which tend to link to different subject disciplines.

Such patterns have also been found in the area of vocational training (Beck et al. 2006; Colley et al. 2003). Exploring subject orientation around apprenticeships, Beck et al. found that many female learners were often highly reluctant to cross the 'gender line' by choosing male-orientated options. Even though many of the female students in their study perceived greater opportunity and flexibility in the scope of potential options and future pathways, many still orientated to gender-specific forms of provision. While female students may have expressed greater levels of confidence towards potentially undertaking most subjects, this is not necessarily reflected in the choices these young people make. Their research revealed prevailing perceptions among females of being more suited to particular female-dominated courses, and that they would fare more favourably and 'fit in' more with the learning cultures associated with different provisions. This was also perceived as a way of militating against the various risks associated with participating in post-compulsory learning.

Colley et al.'s (2003) research also revealed the ways in which different forms of vocational provision serve to affirm various gendered images, ideals and discourses. Subject disciplines, and the dominant 'learning cultures' through which they operated, were found to strongly inform the emerging dispositions and 'vocational habitus' that learners were developing. This very much interacted with the wider cultural dispositions of the learners, not least class and gender. There was found to be marked differences in the emerging vocational identities between females in health and social care and males on engineering and construction courses, both of whom had pre-existing gendered dispositions reinforced through their training cultures. It is clear that early formative processes of socialization within formal educational settings can play a substantial role in engraining male and female learners with dominant discursive ideas about what constitutes appropriate gender behaviour. This, in turn, is likely to have a strong bearing on their learning choices and orientations (Renold 2005).

A range of ethnographic research has also shown how wider cultural dimensions linked to ethnicity can significantly shape learners' identities. Classic literature on the relationship between ethnicity and inequality has illustrated some ethnic minority learners' sense of marginalization within formal educational settings (Gillborn 1990). This research has shown that this is mediated largely through learning contexts that often implicitly, and sometimes overtly, devalue and subjugate the experience and profiles of some ethnic pupils. This again is channelled through the symbolically charged interaction between teacher and learners and between learners from different ethnic backgrounds. Gillborn shows how many ethnic minority learners' experiences of alienation have resulted from their inability to conform to the image and expectation of the 'ideal client' who could demonstrate the 'appropriate pupil behaviour'. As such, many were cast as the 'deviant other' who were seen as unable or unwilling to conform to the dominant cultural script of the school environment.

More recently, ethnographic research by Youdell (2003) and Shain (2003) has drawn upon more critical discourse approaches to illustrate how the pre-existing cultural identities of ethnic minority learners are sometimes in significant tension with the identities that they are expected to perform. This research has drawn upon the concept of *hegemonic discourse* in terms of the dominant ideas and beliefs that are imposed by dominant (non-ethnic) cultures. Youdell's research showed how some black Caribbean pupils are represented and positioned as problematic others and 'undesirable' and 'intolerable' learners. As such they are perceived by teachers and other learners as inhabiting subcultural identities that are fundamentally at odds with the goals and expectations for conformist and cooperative learning. Moreover, the identities associated with some ethnic minority learners' subcultures were seen as fundamentally incompatible with the goals of successful and compliant learning. Thus, the model of the pro-school and integrated learner appeared to be at odds with subcultures that expressed identities and attitudes that were mainly removed from these ideals.

Shain's (2003) research exploring Asian girls' educational experiences in the UK showed how many of these students actively sought to challenge the dominant representations and stereotypes with which they were associated. Instead of accepting the dominant expectation of themselves as passive, subordinate learners, they instead made active attempts to assert their identities and challenge the expectations of teacher and peers. This often entailed active attempts to assert their agency and construct alternative learner identities that subverted the wider cultural expectations of their educational attitude and performance.

Work-related learning

Learning in formal educational settings, particularly that which occurs before individuals enter the labour market, is a significant component of an individual's learning biography. But it is only one component, and context, of their wider learning experiences. Formal educational experiences clearly have a bearing on people's future working life, not only in terms of transferring skills and knowledge but also preparation for specific forms of work. Furthermore, learner identities developed in formal education are likely to impact significantly on career orientations and identities, which explains why the formation of certain learner identities orientates and equips learners for particular work – for instance, traditional university students for professional employment. However, also important is the learning that takes place in the context of people's working lives and within their workplace. This will influence how individuals come to understand themselves as employees and their overall location within the workplace.

There has been an increasing interest in people's experiences and patterns of learning during their working lives. The workplace is seen as a significant context through which people learn, not only in relation to the skills and knowledge they need to utilize, but also their self-perception and identities as employees. Given that people spend considerably more time in the workplace than in formal educational settings, researchers have been keen to explore the ways in which learning is organized and how it impacts on employees' work-related performance and identities. Of particular interest to researchers of work-related learning is the way in which employees not only acquire work-related skills and knowledge, but also become integrated as competent and valued members of the workforce.

A number of key scholars in this field (see, in particular, Lave and Wenger 1991; Wenger 1998; Billett 2002; Billett et al. 2007) have demonstrated how work-related learning involves significant processes of socialization and identity formation in relation to both the specifics of individuals' jobs and their wider place in an organization. The identities that individuals form through their working life mediate not only the way in which they come to understand themselves as an employee, but also their legitimacy and acceptance as members of a work organization. This is often largely facilitated and affirmed by significant others in the workplace, not least colleagues and managers. Moreover, a workplace's organizational culture and form, in terms of its particular practices and characteristics, is also likely to influence the nature and quality of workplace learning.

The theme of work-related learning, sometimes also referred to as workplace or work-based learning, is significant to discussions of the education–work interaction. In exploring how, and through what contexts, people acquire work-related knowledge and skills, we can get a better understanding of some of the key educational and pedagogic processes that may influence their experiences and outcomes when in the workforce. These processes are largely ongoing and form a strong element to individuals' lived experiences of work.

The significance of work-related learning is typically framed within the wider organizational and human resource development imperative for upskilling, continued professional development and workforce productivity (Easterby-Smith et al. 2000). Productive and effective organizational outcomes are often seen as a direct consequence of the nature and quality of learning within organizations. It is increasingly seen as vital for work organizations to manage the quality of employees' learning, as well as the opportunities open to employees to engage in continuous learning. It is also acknowledged that workplace learning has a dual purpose that is mutually beneficial: at one level it helps to enhance workplace productivity and output, while also helping individual employees develop their work-related knowledge and skills, thereby assisting their own career development (Boud and Garrick 1999).

The increasing significance attributed to workplace learning relates to the overall recasting of contemporary workplaces as 'learning organizations' (Watkins and Marsick 1993). A key feature of learning organizations is the abundance of learning opportunities provided for employees within more reflexive, open and facilitative environments. If workplaces aspire towards being learning organizations, they need to actively promote learning and harness positive relationships both among employees and between managers/supervisors and employees. This is further predicated on the view that workplace culture and its management are crucial in facilitating employees' potential, and increasing the emphasis within human resource development that 'people are our best assets'. The idea that learning is a potentially productive good that can enhance organizations' outputs, means that workplaces increasingly need to pay attention to how workplace learning occurs and ways in which it can be enriched (Garavan 2005).

There is no common agreement among researchers as to what precisely constitutes workplace learning. As Boud and Garrick (1999) have argued, there are a variety of ways in which workplace learning can be conceptualized, largely depending on the different types of activities people are engaged in and the specific context in which their learning is taking place. This can may entail learning that is related to work but which does not take place within the work environment, for example, off-the-job training. It may also, for instance, involve a highly structured training programme within a very specific work setting whereby the learning is directed ostensibly to a specific work problem. It could further constitute fairly unstructured and unplanned learning that occurs almost semi-consciously in the day-to-day informal activities of the work setting.

In all cases, some element of work-related learning is taking place but with different intentions and outcomes. However, the context is nonetheless significant, as this will affect what is being learnt and the types of skills, knowledge and understandings that are achieved through the process. There has been much debate over the extent to which work-related learning outside the actual and specific context of a workplace can add value to an employee's work. It has sometimes been argued that the educational context is too divorced from the realities of working life, even though it is recognized that crucial work-related knowledge and understanding can still be transferred outside the work setting.

Researchers have also pointed to the distinction that has been drawn between formal and informal forms of work-related learning (Colley et al. 2003; Malcolm et al. 2003). Formal learning is that which is often planned, predefined and located within very specific domains and often with very explicit and intentional sets of learning objectives. Formal learning is also fairly context-specific and based on the conscious intentions of both teacher and learner that some kind of learning, and learning outcome, will occur. It is related to a specific problem or objective that the learning is intended to address.

Informal learning, on the other hand, is that which is largely unplanned, and which tends to be contained within the interactive spaces of workplaces, including the relationships between employees. Here, learning is more likely to occur unintentionally and implicitly, but nonetheless in a potentially powerful way that might impact on an employee's development. For instance, someone may unintentionally acquire significant work-related knowledge through continued informal interaction with a more experienced colleague who transfers knowledge about particular work practices and structures. However, as Malcolm et al. (2003) discuss, these two forms of learning are often interlinked and complementary: sometimes individuals may learn informally from others in highly structured contexts as well as picking up explicit knowledge in less structured settings.

A number of significant theories have been developed around workplace learning, and these have also highlighted the significance of workplace dynamics and interactions between individuals. Hager (2004) has discussed the gradual shift in paradigms of workplace learning from what he terms as a 'learning as acquisition' to a 'learning as participation' paradigm. The learning as acquisition approach traditionally presents learning as a solitary, cognitive activity based on the receipt and internalization of externally presented information. This tends to focus predominately on the individual learner and the way in which they acquire work-related knowledge and apply that to their work activities. Furthermore, it assumes that work-related learning is largely formally channelled. By contrast, the 'learning as participation' paradigm sees learning as being largely derived from people's active involvement in the learning process and the lived experience this involves. Instead of viewing learning as a solitary and passive experience, this approach highlights the essentially social and participative nature of learning; individuals learn more effectively when they are active participants in the learning process. Their learning is intimately based on their experiences in social environments and the interactions this inevitably entails.

In exploring some of the interrelated themes of work-related learning, Fenwick (2008) highlights the presence of a number of core recurrent themes in research in this area. One particular theme is that of workplace learning as an essentially participative, collective and practice-based activity and not simply something that occurs at an individual level. Workplace learning research has often demonstrated the significance of actions, interactions and interpersonal relations for the establishment of workers' identities and competences. Thus, while cognitive processes are significant in the overall assimilation of significant work-related knowledge and skills, these are largely the by-product of wider social and interactive spaces of the work context. The participative and interactive nature of work-related learning means that learning is essentially embedded in sets of relationships with other actors – namely, colleagues, trainers and managers.

The work of the learning theorists Lave and Wenger has made a significant contribution to understanding the interrelationship between the learning process, employee integration and identity formation (Lave and Wenger 1991; see also Wenger 1998). This has been illustrated through their work on situated or participative learning. A central tenet of this approach is that learning is generated through the social interaction between different members within a learning setting, which influences the degree to which learners develop a sense of competence and their own capacities as learners. They apply the metaphor of *membership* in their analysis of situated learning.

As with most forms of membership, aspiring members need to acquire and abide by certain rules in order to be accepted as legitimate and respected members of that group. For meaningful learning to take place, individuals need to be purposefully integrated as legitimate members of what they call *communities of practice*. For instance, one of the challenges for a novice, inexperienced learner is to move from the periphery of a workplace to a more central location where they have acquired more expert status. They will then have a stronger overall platform from which to act more autonomously, confidently and competently. In order to achieve this transition, not only will they have needed to have acquired skills for competent performance in that setting, but also a coherent identity that gives them a meaningful role to play. Lave and Wenger demonstrate that this often occurs through the more informal setting of the workplace and the interaction between novices and more experienced 'old timers' who are able to pass on their knowledge and skills. Consequently, novices are able to operate successfully within their community of practice, which, through the process of transference and socialization, has recycled its own rules and practices.

The significance of this concept lies in its illustration of the highly situated and embedded practice of learning, located in people's ongoing day-to-day working experiences. It highlights that much workplace learning is based on acquiring insights and understanding of the rules and practices of immediate cultures. These cultures further mediate the development not only of specific skills, but also one's acceptability as an organizational member. Moreover, given the highly situated and contextualized nature of workplace learning, what might be seen as trivial and incidental to people's working life may, in fact, be influential if it plays some part in the formation of their identities and reinforces their place within a community of practice (Billett et al. 2007).

Research has also shown that work-related skills and competences tend to build up cumulatively and through a systematic build-up of knowledge, most of which is likely to be tacit in nature (Eraut 1994, 2007). Eraut has illustrated the significance of continued professional knowledge and expertize formation in a learning journey that involves the building up of key technical, inter-professional and organizational knowledge. His research shows how professional learning involves the acquisition and deployment of formal and informal knowledge through professionals' emerging organizational membership, including relationships with significant others. This is further linked to early professionals' agency and emergent identities as employees seeking to adapt to continued organizational challenges.

A range of research on workplace learning has also highlighted the significance of the nature and form of workplace cultures in shaping individuals' propensities for engaging in learning and other forms of professional development. Thus, how organizations are structured and the different ways in which work activities are designed and allocated may well have a significant bearing on the nature and quality of work-based learning.

Ashton and Sung (2002) have illustrated the dominant features of what they term 'learning supportive' work cultures, namely, those workplaces that tend to facilitate more positive and supportive environments for learning. Significant to learning supportive cultures are good trust relations between employees and where employees are continually supported, trusted and valued.

Learning-supportive cultures tend to be driven by values and beliefs around the importance of knowledge acquisition and sharing, the recognition of human capability and purposeful attitudes towards innovation and change. In terms of work practices, learning-supportive cultures tend to include measures such as job rotation, delegated decision making and cross-functional interaction and the overall expansion of employees' work remit. Moreover, employees are encouraged to participate in decision making and develop their professional knowledge through participation in training. Of course, while some organizations conform more closely to this model, others may continue to draw upon cultural practices that limit employees' scope for autonomy and responsibility.

Investigating learning through apprenticeships, Fuller and Unwin (2003, 2004) developed the concept of 'expansive' and 'restrictive' learning environments. The difference between these two learning environments is essentially based on the level of employee involvement and the ways in which trainees are utilized and positioned within organizations. In expansive learning environments, opportunities for learning and continued development are relatively high and employees/trainees are actively encouraged to undertake a variety of tasks, further their knowledge, pursue further training and acquire additional qualifications. This tends to operate in cultures where trainees are actively encouraged to see themselves as active lifelong learners as well as valued and esteemed organizational members. Furthermore, in such learning environments, employees are more active participants in the wider organizational community. As a consequence, their skills and experiences are valued more highly and they are more likely to become fully integrated in their work cultures. They are actively encouraged to work autonomously and exercise high levels of discretion and responsibility. By contrast, restrictive learning environments tend to constrain trainees' involvement. As such, they are likely to feel less integrated in the workplace and feel less like legitimate members of a community. Moreover, opportunities for training and professional development are limited and short-term employee goals are given more emphasis.

Large-scale research on learning in the workplace has further illustrated how processes of workplace learning operate across multiple domains and within different occupational levels (Felstead et al. 2009). These researchers also demonstrated the significance of context in mediating workplace learning, largely as a consequence of the specific nature of the work and the social relations inherent in what they refer to as different 'productive systems'. This mainly refers to the wider span of social relations that occurs from most stages of the work process, from production to service delivery, and where employees fall within these relations. The level to which employees can feel integrated and valued, as well as able to pursue opportunities for continued work-related learning, is very much contingent on their anticipated role within the work production process. Moreover, this will shape the level of discretion and autonomy individuals feel that they have within the work process – for example, as found in the above research, qualified engineers who were actively made to feel as if their input and professional development were a fundamental part of company strategy and direction.

Chapter summary

This chapter has considered the wider social dimensions that frame people's learning experiences, illustrating how learning is a largely socially and culturally mediated process. It is significantly shaped by the contexts in which people learn and the wider social and cultural contexts of individuals' lives. Somewhat inevitably, individuals follow different learning trajectories and make many different choices around future learning. For some, these learning trajectories may be smooth and form a relatively coherent pattern. Increasingly, however, trajectories may be fluid and non-linear, and more individuals may re-enter formal education and training at later stages of their lives.

We have seen how identity is a significant dimension in the learning process as it frames people's perceptions of themselves as learners and their wider attitude and orientations to formal education. Learning is a highly subjective and value-driven process and, as such, people's educational choices and pathways will be driven by this. The relative level of engagement and detachment people have towards formal learning undoubtedly has a strong bearing on their propensity to engage in further education and training. Thus, learner identities are important in shaping people's engagement with the process of 'lifelong learning', and they may well explain why some individuals progress almost seamlessly through education while some exit as soon as they can. Learner identities, however, can be recursive and reform through people's evolving engagement with the educational system. Moreover, they are also highly derived from people's wider cultural experiences and identities, not least their class, gender and ethnicity.

We have also seen how learning is far from confined to formal education; individuals' work-related skills and knowledge are also largely acquired through their actual lived experiences of work. The workplace is a significant source of learning, and we have seen how much of this also has a strong social dimension. This is largely based on the interactions between work members within specific organizational contexts and workplace communities. It further variably impacts on the extent to which people acquire work-related knowledge and skills and become integrated into the workplace.

CHAPTER SEVEN

Managing transitions from education to work

This chapter explores how transitions from education to work have been understood, and how this process has transformed over time. The extensive range of academic research in the field of education to work transitions has highlighted how these transitions have become increasingly complex, uneven and unpredictable (Furlong and Cartmel 2007; Ball et al. 2000; Brooks 2009). Traditional patterns of movement from school to work have transformed quite considerably over the past several decades. Increasingly, individuals – whether they are young school-leavers, graduates, mature learners or people making midlife changes – have now to actively manage their movements across different institutional settings. For some, this involves navigating through a complex labyrinth of options and potential pathways. The choices people make on leaving different forms of education are also likely to be shaped significantly by their educational biographies and learner identities formed during education. People's educational biographies may invariably frame available options, future goals and wider sets of attitudes towards the labour market. They are also related to individuals' wider class and gender experiences.

The transition from education to work, and the shifting sands of many young people's choices and pathways, is closely linked to the changing educational and labour market landscape. At one level, the transition process has become increasingly fluid and unpredictable in the contemporary economic context. This has invariably meant that the traditional institutionally mapped pathways that individuals might have conventionally followed have given way to more complex, protracted and fractured transitional experiences. This is perhaps most manifest in young people's increasingly delayed entry to the labour market, itself the by-product of the breakdown of traditional pathways and employment channels that directed young people's school to work transitions. This has been the case for both school-leavers and university graduates, who have been witness to transformations of the forms of employment associated with their credentials and educational profiles.

It has therefore become increasingly less common for young people to embark upon linear and straightforward pathways from school, and other forms of post-compulsory education, to the job market. The sometimes predetermined and anticipated trajectory towards particular jobs and associated lifestyles has given way to more fractured transitional narratives in the late modern context. During periods of more clearly defined and segmented labour market contexts, schools, colleges and universities functioned more clearly in terms of what Raffe (2008) has termed a 'transition institution': they effectively acted as bridges to anticipated future employment, routing and equipping individuals for fairly specific forms of employment. Ordinarily, a young person might have left school with adequate qualifications to attain a semi-skilled job, or to carry on to further education for additional education and training in order to achieve a more professionally orientated job. However, a combination of structural changes in the labour market, educational policy shifts and broader demographic changes among young people has significantly disrupted this process.

The theme of identity and personal agency underscores much of what has been written about and researched in the field of education to work transitions in recent times. Increasingly prominent in the study of transitions to work has been the exploration of individuals' choice making and the formation of labour market identities (Stokes and Wyn 2007; Banks et al. 1992). Stokes and Wyn (2007) have argued that individuals' emerging identities around specific areas of work tend to be formed through their ongoing experiences of their educational, social and employment worlds. Young people's subjectivities tend to be rich, multiple and derived from a wide range of influences and social relationships set within the ongoing contexts of their lives. Significantly, the kinds of self-perceptions and self-definitions individuals begin to form are likely to project onto their anticipated and desired location in the job market. Indeed, over time, analysis has moved towards a more fine-grained and nuanced understanding of young people's lived experiences, their personal action frames and increasingly reflexive understandings of their own educational and anticipated job market situations.

This theme of young people's active negotiation of transitions and future work identities very much chimes with the reflexive modernization notions of individualization and detraditionalization. Young people are no longer carried by traditional structures and fixed narratives based on pre-given social and economic conditions. Roberts (1995) and Evans (2007) have argued that, at a time when individuals' transitions and pathways have become increasingly complex, multifarious and unpredictable, they have also become increasingly individualized. This has effectively forced individuals to face up to the new challenges and realities of an uncertain jobs market, and to actively work out what their potential options might be. It has become increasingly imperative for individuals to proactively manage their transitions and the shaping of their future work trajectories. The patterned and stable biographical continuities that people might experience in traditional and industrialized contexts have given way to altogether more fluid and fluctuating trajectories. At the same time, transitions from education to working life are highly significant periods given that the choices that people make at such key 'turning points' can have a profound bearing on the course of their future lives.

The construction of work- and career-related identities significantly underpins young people's future action orientations and the ways they personally and actively mediate the wider economic context. Heinz (2009) illustrates that the changing routes and trajectories that young people embark upon in changing labour market contexts necessitates a new level of agency and self-reflection in negotiating increasingly complex and potentially fractured career narratives. As Heinz (2009) argues, individuals' biographies now play a substantial role in fashioning their future trajectories; in essence, individuals increasingly need to socialize themselves in preparation for the potentially multiple and complex future life goals that they set. He argues that: 'the transition from school to work has become a turning point in young adults' life course because whatever pathway they choose they are confronted with uncertain outcomes' (Heinz 2009, p. 397). Future labour market identities and their formation are not only a process that young people negotiate, but also a resource they can draw upon for facilitating access to employment. However, people's agency is invariably wedded to structures, not least the shifting socio-economic context. Therefore, when exploring issues around individuals' agency, biography and emerging identities, it is important not to underplay the importance of social structure, as this potentially influences the actions that people undertake.

Sociologists such as du Bois Reymond (2004) and Furlong and Cartmel (1997, 2007) have discussed the repatterning of people's transition activities in terms of a gradual shift from 'normal' biographies towards 'choice' biographies. Normal biographies tend to be characterized by relatively clear and predictable pathways that are largely referenced against an individual's class and gender profile. They are also based on conventional pathways through fairly established educational and training routes, leading to fairly specific and long-lasting forms of work. Such biographical development was particularly commonplace among young people in the middle part of the last century, many of whom targeted fixed labour markets that corresponded to their class backgrounds and gender.

By contrast, choice biographies are more complex and encompass a greater variety of pathways and future options that are far less predictable, patterned and based on stable modes of progression. Furthermore, the linkages between young people's educational experiences, profiles and achievements, and their orientations and outcomes in the job market have weakened somewhat. In short, individuals' educational biographies are more fractured and less likely to unfold in a linear way. This, nonetheless, presents greater challenges and risks as, increasingly, young people have to take responsibility for their future outcomes and successfully navigate their way through more diverse pathways.

To a large extent, this requires significantly higher levels of identity work: young people need to work out what they want from future employment, how to realize their goals and how to position themselves more actively in the changing job market. Yet, somewhat paradoxically, this is occurring at a time when their educational experiences and the climate of labour market risk and uncertainty provide them with potentially weaker labour market identities. Both Du Bois Reymond and Furlong and Cartmel highlight the reflexive and individualized dimension to the transitions process, based increasingly on the continual weighing up of options and use of personal agency and resources. However, they also stress that choice biographies do not necessarily represent free-reign choice and an unbounded self-determinism on the part of individuals. While late modernity and the new economy have generally weakened the grip of class in determining job market orientation and outcomes, many young people's choice and outcomes are still reproduced through class and gender. They also point out that, while choice biographies have become more prevalent, some young people still embark upon fairly patterned and predictable pathways, sometimes for lengthy durations of their working lives.

Research and theorizing in the area of education to work transition tends, therefore, to highlight a balance between agency and structure in the ways in which young people's transition activities play out. While transitions have an increasingly individualized and reflective nature, they are never entirely disconnected from individuals' wider educational, class-cultural and gender profiles. The wide body of literature on transitions from education to work has often demonstrated the complex interactions between individuals' job market goals and motivations and the wider educational, economic and sociocultural contexts that frame these. Individuals transiting to the job market are subject to influences that operate at many different levels.

In his review of changing youth employment, Roberts (2009) has argued that there are a range of 'push' and 'pull' factors shaping young people's choices around future employment, both of which are likely to fall outside their immediate volition. The former tend to be associated with young people's cultural profiles, including their family background and class-cultural make-ups. The latter is more related to the nature of the labour market, the wider economic climate and shifting employer demands and expectations of school-leavers' and graduates' educational profiles. Both these factors are significant in the way in which young people carve out various routes from education to the labour market; they tend to set the parameters and rules through which young people navigate their way to various forms of employment.

Perhaps one of the most significant influences in shaping transitional experience and outcomes is the availability, real or perceived, of relevant opportunities in any given time and location. Roberts has developed the concept of 'opportunity structures' in terms of the ways in which young people's work-related orientations and outlooks are typically framed, and the potential job market options and outcomes that are perceived as available and achievable. Opportunity structures are likely to be shaped by broader labour market dimensions and trends, including the supply and demand of specific work and changing employer requirements. They are also shaped by changes in educational provision, in particular the expansion of post-compulsory and higher education. Perhaps most significantly, they are also shaped by individuals' sociocultural experiences and positioning, which crucially frames the perceived availability and feasibility of future options.

It is clear that opportunity structures have transformed over time, although the extent to which the expansion of education and vocational provision has led to enriched job market outcomes for increasing amounts of learners has been contested. Roberts illustrates that, for all of the changes that have occurred over time, patterns of social mobility have remained constant over the past several decades. Relatedly, access to particular types of qualifications, educational institutions and future employment still very much appear to be class determined.

Changing identities and the transition from education to the labour market

Transitions, social reproduction and the 'youth labour market'

Early analysis of young people's relationship to schooling tended to examine the way in which their experiences of education served to reproduce future labour market orientations and destinations. This typically demonstrated the role of schooling as a vehicle for reproducing class-based attitudes and orientations to paid employment, and for channelling learners into specific segments of the labour market. This was seen to play a significant role in both occupational socialization and occupational placement: it affirmed pre-existing values and attitudes to education, which in turn set a compass towards specific forms of labour. Through formal schooling, young people developed a sense of their place in the labour market and the overall direction of their future working lives. This tended to reflect the types of job and related job market outcomes they subsequently experienced.

The concept of 'anticipatory socialization' has been developed by Bates (1984) to illustrate this process; in effect, schooling helps socialize young people in the types of values and attitudes towards particular types of employment. These attitudes and values are perhaps more significant than the direct skills acquired through schooling, given that they serve to frame the direction in which young people are headed in their quest for different forms of work. Heinz (1991) similarly refers to 'learning socialization' in terms of formal schooling's role in transferring values and attitudes towards future employment. This means that individuals become more orientated towards particular forms of future work more than others. Socialization through formal education helps produce learner identities that orientate individuals towards particular forms of learning and curricula. This, in turn, orientates them towards particular future job-related goals and aspirations. Some of these jobs will be more dependent on continued educational participation than others. Learning socialization therefore provides individuals with particular ideas about themselves as future employees and what they can bring to the job market.

Classic early studies on the transition to work illustrated how the transition from education to work was traditionally stable and predefined (Roberts 1968; Ashton and Field 1976). Moreover, this research showed that young people made labour market choices within reasonably clear and well-defined parameters. Such choices were closely linked to young people's educational profiles, which were also strongly informed by their social class and familial backgrounds. Perhaps significant here is the wider context, and related opportunity structures, through which choices and transitions were made. In the early research of Roberts and Ashton and Field, transitions took place in what could be seen as a more clearly defined 'youth labour market' that reflected the general features of employment in the 1960s and 1970s. This labour market context allowed for the absorption of a large cohort of young people armed with the requisite levels of education to meet the demands of low, semi-skilled and semi-professional work.

A dominant characteristic of the labour market during this period was the relatively full employment for young people within a context of stable, industrialized labour markets during the post-war period. It was also a segmented labour market with a clearer overall division between skilled, semi-skilled and professional/management-level forms of work. Young people therefore tended to move towards labour markets that corresponded to their educational profiles and achievements, and this would invariably form the basis for their longer-term career expectations and aspirations. In the industrialized urban areas of the Midlands and North of England where this research was conducted, young people could expect to find work almost immediately upon leaving school and in areas of employment that were largely commensurate with their expectations and level of educational achievement. Furthermore, they would anticipate their longer-term working lives to be played out in these particular jobs, and from which they could anchor other aspects of their lives such as family and lifestyle. The transition to adulthood was, as such, a fairly speedy and straightforward one.

The research conducted by Ashton and Field (1976) showed that young people's transition experiences tended to be relatively patterned, predefined and channelled towards specific labour markets. They developed an influential typology to depict these pathways, illustrating the types of further educational and/or job choices that young people tended to gravitate towards. The first group, the *careerless*, were characterized by low educational achievement and limited employment horizons, and whose wider self-perceptions were as low achievers. Such youth gravitated towards low-skilled, 'dead-end' work that, while offering little in the way of longer-term career prospects and intrinsic fulfilment, at least provided them with immediate earnings and the achievement of an adult identity. The second group, those with *short-term careers*, held generally more ambitious career aspirations, based on somewhat more successful and positive educational experiences. These students tended to use what qualifications they achieved to secure semi-skilled, technical and administrative work, although their career trajectories tended to be confined to specific jobs and skills sets that required some intensive training.

The experiences of the first two groups were somewhat different to those in the final category, the *extended careers*, as this group had experienced more marked educational success and made strong links between academic achievement and career prospects. These young people and their families tended to invest more in education as a route towards securing favourable future employment. This was often reinforced by the sense that they were destined for professional, managerial and other highly skilled forms of work. This is reflected in their educational pathways, which tended to span further education and also university. In the latter case, they would form what was a relatively elite band of academic achievers, comprising of traditional middle-class students and a minority of working-class educational high-flyers. However, given that university participation during this period was still relatively confined to an elite core of academic achievers, it was not considered an option for many young people. Moreover, many of these young people anticipated little need to extend their studies beyond what was required for their targeted employment, which was skilled, professional and management-level work. If jobs were available for them, there would be little need to participate in education beyond what the job market expected from them.

The rich ethnographic work of Paul Willis (1977), conducted at a similar time to the above research, explored the ways in which processes of class formation and social reproduction during formal education fed into young people's subsequent labour market outlooks and experiences. Like the Ashton and Field research, this study was set in the context of heavy industrialization and at a time when young people made relatively patterned transitions from schooling to paid employment. This study illustrated the way in which class- and gender-based orientations towards particular forms of work, in this case low-skilled, 'shop floor' labour, were reproduced through compulsory schooling.

Following a group of educationally alienated and disaffected male pupils, Willis' study demonstrated that rather than simply accepting their fate as educational failures, these young men instead looked to assert their identities through a range of countercultural activities. It showed how their resistance to school via the assertion of their masculinity further reproduced the types of labour market dispositions and attitudes that would ultimately seal their fate as low-skilled, low-paid, future workers. In resisting their formal schooling, they had socialized themselves as relatively lowly occupants within the division of labour. As with Ashton and Field's *careerless* learners, Willis' 'lads' rejected educational success as a means of achieving the kinds of desired and anticipated identities their class backgrounds had set them up for. In the context of highly industrialized and manual forms of labour, these young men would, nevertheless, be provided with a good platform from which they could play out their gender and class-based roles and identities.

The theme of class socialization and reproduction is very evident in much of this early research. Young people's educational experiences and identities are shown to be informed by significant aspects of their class and family background, which were shown to have a forceful role in shaping their self-images and self-perceptions. Moreover, such outlooks clearly impacted on both their formal educational achievements and aspirations, which, in turn, tended to reinforce their immediate and longer-term career outlooks. In these studies, young people are clearly making strong links between their educational experiences and anticipated labour market experiences. These studies clearly demonstrated how this process is intimately linked to young people's class and family background, which reinforces their self-perceptions and self-images as learners and future employees. To this extent, they have demonstrated the link between social class (and gender), learner identity and future work orientations.

However, as Roberts (1995) has argued, social reproduction approaches have tended to treat identities in an overly collective fashion as if young people's whole personal frame of reference is intractably fashioned by their class profile and affiliations. Social class is the glue that sets attitudes and values towards schooling and future work. Consequently, individuals' educational pathways and outcomes are firmly referenced against their class location. Young people inhabit what might be seen as 'block identities', whereby they develop collective frames of references and their outlooks are wedded to the attitudinal and value systems set by their class. Willis' lads perform set rituals and anti-school practices that are a direct by-product of their class-based socialization and attitude formation.

This interpretation has been criticized for overlooking the nuances and variations in young people's attitudes to education and future employment. Research by Brown (1987) and Jenkins (1983) showed that many young, working-class pupils' goals for future paid employment were more complex and differentiated. Many young people's approaches to both their education and future employment prospect take neither the form of an outright rejection nor an active acceptance of the values and ethos of formal education. Doing enough to 'get by' in order to access targeted employment is what has traditionally tended to inform the goals and aspirations of many 'ordinary' young people's post-school orientations.

Perhaps a more marked limitation in earlier approaches to education to work transitions is in the representation of relatively smooth and seamless education–work movements. During the period when social reproduction theories were most influential, the transition from education to work was based on a generally stronger coupling between young people's experiences of schooling and their activities and outcomes in their future employment. As such, the transition from school to work was more direct: young people's experiences of education prepared them more readily for their anticipated future labour market trajectories. School-leavers, more so than now, could anticipate clearer linkages between their schooling and future employment paths, and therefore develop straightforward measures to achieve their employment goals.

However, the characterization of the school to work transition during the more buoyant youth labour market has tended to downplay the many challenging realities faced by young people seeking to integrate into the job market during this supposedly 'golden age' era (Goodwin and O'Connor 2005, 2009). As Goodwin and O'Connor highlight, school-leavers nonetheless faced many challenges in securing work at a time of assumed job stability and still had to negotiate access to their target employment. This was reinforced by additional challenges in establishing an adult identity and meeting the day-to-day demands of learning new skills and proving their organizational worth. Many were further confronted by routine, low-skilled work and locked into mainly unfulfilling employment. Similarly, some young people continued to be marginalized from labour market opportunities and embarked on very fragmented and uncertain pathways. Such realities perhaps challenge the more nostalgic depictions of a settled and secure youth who simply used education as a stepping stone towards more meaningful labour market activities and adult-based roles.

Transitions and socio-economic change: The decline of the youth job market

Another significant factor driving the shifting conceptual focus is that of social and economic change. The economic restructuring at the start of the 1980s had a profoundly destabilizing impact on young people's transitions to paid employment, significantly destabilizing what was once a more stable and cohesive youth labour market. This also served to diminish the overall opportunity structures awaiting young people as they made the transition from education to work. The emergence of large-scale youth unemployment was clearly linked to the gradual erosion of industrialized forms of labour that had traditionally anchored their longer-term employment trajectories (Ashton et al. 1990; Roberts 1995).

With the decline in traditional forms of work that young people sought and anticipated entering, their routes to employment became altogether more fractured. Traditional pathways were increasingly closed off, forcing young people to make alternative sets of choices over the direction of their future working lives. Furthermore, these changes also reshaped the role of education in regulating young people's access to future employment. The once clearer link between education and future employment outcomes had become significantly ruptured by labour market change. Individuals leaving schools increasingly had to use education as a way of building up additional human capital and acquiring new vocational skills and credentials to give themselves a better chance of securing increasingly scarce employment.

A range of research charted the experiences of young people in these changing conditions and their attempts to make sense of increasingly problematic youth labour market conditions (Jenkins 1983; Brown 1987; Ainley 1998; Bates 1991). What these studies showed was that many young people entering the labour market in the 1980s were forced to reappraise their longer-term employment goals and the connection between their schooling and their job prospects. For some school-leavers, this entailed an undesired compulsion to undertake further education and training in order to 'stay ahead', while delaying adulthood (Brown 1987). For other school-leavers, this situation brought new demands for upskilling or changing the direction of their anticipated and (for some) very fixed work orientations. Brown's (1987) research on school-leavers during the collapse of the youth labour market and the rise in youth unemployment highlighted the growing complexities in young people's approaches to their working futures. Many young people who might have perceived further study in training beyond 16 as inconceivable, now had to weigh up the options in an expanding vocational educational market.

Critiquing the narrow 'training without jobs' vocationalism of the 1980s, this research illustrated that young people endeavoured to do what they could to maximize their chances of finding what they perceived to be respectable and meaningful work. Of course, many of these individuals got drawn into the vocational qualification market as a compensation for the scarcer employment opportunities they faced on leaving formal education. Embarking on emerging vocational qualifications, such as youth training credits, provided many of these people with a sense of purpose and a step towards getting a foot on the employment ladder. However, the longer-term efficacy of short-term vocational fixes in the absence of longer-term, secure and meaningful employment was seriously exposed in such research: many of the young people in this research experienced highly variable and contingent forms of training and transient work experiences that had minimal impact on their sustainable employment opportunities.

Ainley (1988) examined similar patterns among young people engaging in vocational training schemes, which, following the 1988 Educational Reform Act, had expanded hugely in the UK. Indeed, transformation in the youth labour market has corresponded with the massive upsurge in new forms of vocational qualifications and pathways. However, the extent to which this has helped facilitate access to desired forms of work has been extensively critiqued by research on youth employment. The dominant policy response of promoting vocational educational qualifications and skills has been seen as amounting to little more than a compensation for the types of work that these individuals would have hitherto attained. Such work would have provided ample opportunities in the first instance for these young people to acquire the types of vocational skills they would have needed to progress in their jobs. Yet, increasing orientation towards vocational education has been one particular feature of young people's post-school transitions.

Education to work transitions in late modernity: Individualization, choice and mapping uncertain futures

The changing labour market for young people has had a significant bearing upon both the condition of youth and the ways in which they embark on the transition process. For increasing amounts of young people, their 'youth' has been extended, along with a delay in acquiring the types of roles and activities linked to adulthood (Cote and Bynner 2008). There is now a widespread expectation of a significantly delayed entry into working life. As Cote and Bynner (2008) have discussed, a consequence of economic and social change is that many young people have had to reframe their perceptions and expectations around their labour market futures. Relatedly, there has been an extension to educational careers as more young people look to equip themselves better for future work opportunities. This, in turn, has further disrupted traditional modes of identity formation towards work and adulthood. For instance, the identities that might be developed around being a paid employee, union member and parent fairly soon after formal education have been significantly reformed in the current context. As young people are confronted with greater choices during and after formal education, they are also confronted with greater challenges. Managing these has become an altogether more salient issue.

Increasingly, research on transitions from education to work has tended to pay closer attention to the ways in which individuals make choices and decisions about further education and employment. The influential research by Hodkinson et al. (1996) (see also Hodkinson and Sparkes 1997;

Hodkinson 2004) has brought into sharper focus the interaction between young people's employment-related aspirations and their educational and cultural experiences. This research illustrates that, for many young people, paid employment has become just one component of their future life goals and planning. However, Hodkinson et al. (1996) argue that the end of formal education represents a key 'turning point' which young people need to negotiate carefully and with some degree of planning. Yet, they also emphasize that young people's decision making around future education or work is neither exclusively class-determined nor highly individualistic and autonomous. Instead, young people often exercise degrees of agency based on personally developed goals and aspirations, which still operate within the parameters of their available resources and potential options.

The notion of 'pragmatically rational choice' is developed by these authors to depict young people's decision making. Choices are pragmatic in that they tend to be both realistic and directed towards the fulfilment of goals relating to the person's interest and abilities and which they anticipate being potentially able to fulfil. As Hodkinson et al. illustrate, choices tend to be based on people's subjective perception of themselves and intimately linked to their emerging identities. But, they are also framed by objective conditions in the educational and employment market to which they are also responsive, and which set the boundaries to their choice making. So, while choices tend to be intuitive and have an affective underpinning, they are also shaped by wider external conditions that operate of the person's immediate volition, but which form a strong contextual backdrop.

This research has been strongly influenced by Bourdieu's theorizing, particularly in terms of the *dispositions* young people develop, how they are *positioned* within the wider labour market field and what they *possess* in terms of educational, cognitive and cultural resources. This tends to be derived from the individual's class and family background and significantly guides their options and decision making. Young people's educational and cultural identities tend to overlap significantly, providing particular resources and dispositions that guide them towards or away from particular future work-related options. To this extent, they are likely to be aware of the relative levels of cultural and social capital and resources they possess and that this will have a bearing on their access to different positional fields in an increasingly competitive jobs market. Furthermore, through their educational and cultural socialization, young people develop core dispositions, or what Bourdieu terms *habitus*, and these are also likely to play a significant role in shaping their future education and work-related outlooks.

Dispositions tend to be based on deeply formed sets of attitudes and ways of thinking and feeling which intuitively guide people through the social world, compelling them to act in particular ways. They are also likely to orientate individuals towards particular areas of social and economic life, including particular jobs and career avenues. Hodkinson et al. show that young people's emerging dispositions ultimately frame what they refer to as 'horizons for action' – that is, the perceived scope for undertaking certain forms of future education, training and employment. Thus, dispositions based on intuitive, tacit and often affective values and outlooks are likely to constrain or enable decisions and behaviours towards the job market. They account for why some people choose certain options over others and tend to avoid particular types of job markets altogether.

Hodkinson et al. cite many examples where young people's choices have been informed by wider culturally derived dispositions. This includes working-class students avoiding the middle-class fields, such as particular courses, higher institutions and particular 'professional' occupations, or simply jobs that fall well outside their particular ways of being and acting. This clearly extends to gendered dimensions of choices and why some females and males avoid labour markets and job areas that are perceived to be discordant with their own gender dispositions and profile. Colley et al.'s (2003) research on vocational training, clearly illustrated the ways in which grounded and embodied dispositions through class and gender tended intuitively to frame and guide vocational learners' early work socialization.

What is clear from much research is that the choices young people make between 14 and 16 have a significant bearing on their potential future educational pathways and trajectories. As Lumby and Foskett (2005) argue, these choices tend to set the course for young people's directions through further education and training, as well as paid employment. Thus, while there may be increasing flexibility for people to move between modes of education and training, including returning at later stages, choices at this period nonetheless have a potentially profound bearing on future outlooks and outcomes. The particular modes of learning and assessment that young people are exposed to through different forms of provision are likely to reinforce their self-perceptions of where they sit within both the educational and the wider labour market fields. As we have seen earlier, pathways towards academic and vocational routes tend to be fairly set: young people may not readily move between these pathways, instead following one particular mode of provision.

Research by Foskett and Hemsley-Brown (2001) and Foskett et al. (2004) has also demonstrated how young people's choice and transition behaviour tends to operate at the interface between broader macro-level, socio-economic dynamics and micro-level, individual preference and orientations. Like the Hodkinson et al. approach, their research illustrates the key interaction between contextual dimensions outside the individual's immediate experience and individuals' emergent identities and aspirations. The contextual milieu is multilayered. It encompasses not only the wider labour market context, but also the institutional context in which the person is educated, such as their particular schooling. It also incorporates the more immediate context of their family life, including their class background and influences, as well as relationships with peers. Young people are fully in tune with these contexts and are continually internalizing signals relating to opportunities, challenges and potential constraints. At the same time, young people are developing self-perceptions and self-images and are beginning to work out how they might position future options in relation to other lifestyle- and peer-related goals and interests.

Foskett et al.'s research shows that, in between the contextual milieu and the individual making choices, there is a range of 'choice influencers', including key players within the person's immediate environment. These include, for example, teachers, advisors, parents and peers. These researchers highlight that young people's choices and transitions tend to entail highly interactive and dynamic processes. These are based largely on their ongoing engagement with the social and institutional fields they move within. The choices young people make therefore express the ideas and understanding that are fed to them from their wider environment as much as their own immediate frames of reference and self-perceptions. The two are largely conjoined and are also mediated by significant others. This approach again emphasizes how the choice process is based on a large degree of goal direction and sense making on the part of individuals. But, it is careful to illustrate how this is not exclusively based on pure rationality and unfettered agency, and is instead mediated by many contextual variables. Choices are complex, sometimes transitory, but there are, nonetheless, likely to be strong forces of influence on the process.

The contextual mediation of choices and decision making has also been illustrated through research on young people's post-16 choices, including their decisions to participate in higher education. While there has been much policy interested in widening the participation in higher education, policymakers have not always given sufficient consideration to the key determinants of choice towards higher education. At one level, for many higher education learners, the choice to participate in university forms part of a clear learning trajectory from school, to college, to university. And as Foskett et al. (2004) demonstrate, for many prospective university students, this has tended to be formed at relatively early stages in their learning careers and often actively affirmed by teachers and parents. However, there continues to be a core of non-traditional learners, including those from lower socio-economic backgrounds and mature students, for whom such a process is not so clear and automatic. It may continue to be the case that many prospective students are often uncertain about whether to participate in higher education, often intuitively inferring that it is not in keeping with their existing educational and cultural profiles. The potential risks and difficulties associated with 'investing' in higher education also tend to be felt more keenly by such students.

Recent research on decision making towards higher education has illustrated the often embedded and socially mediated channels through which choices and decisions take place. At one level, there is a strong class-cultural dimension at work in this process and research shows the ways in which, for instance, middle-class families are skilled at deciphering the higher education market and the variable levels of cultural distinction within it (Ball et al. 2001; Reay et al. 2006). The question for increasing amounts of middle-class families is not so much about whether to encourage their children to participate, but which university to attend. However, there are, nevertheless, increasing amounts of students who might not have previously considered attending university, including students whose parents have not attended.

Research by Fuller et al. (2011) has demonstrated how the decision-making process is significantly bound up in the wider social relationships of the learner. The perceived levels of support a prospective learner receives from peers, family members and other actors within the learner's immediate milieu are crucial in framing the perceived feasibility, desirability and efficacy of participating in higher education.

Thus, decision making around post-compulsory and higher education appears to be largely influenced by the social capital possessed by individuals in terms of their social networks, ties and access to available knowledge and resources. These play a significant role in driving decisions. Key reference points are important in guiding what are often expected and anticipated courses of action. This extends to people's decisions not to participate. A prevailing indifference, uncertainty or apathy may well reflect and be reinforced by the attitudes of significant others within an individual's network of influence.

Transitions and the changing meaning of work for young people

A prominent theme in contemporary research on young people's transitions from education to work is the particular meaning that young people ascribe to work and careers, and the extent to which they fits with other aspects of their identities. We can see that the transition process has become more complex over time, and this has also entailed a reframing of young people's expectations towards work and careers. Traditional sociological inquiry on youth has often reported the significance that young people attach to work, both in terms of its legitimation of adult identity and the way in which work potentially provides a platform for self-expression. This was clearly evident in earlier transition studies, particularly during the buoyant youth labour market. However, the changing social contexts in which young people find themselves at significant turning points have certain implications for the ways in which they begin to align their goals and aspirations towards the labour market. The current generation of contemporary young people has been bestowed a range of labels, ranging from 'hedonistic youth', 'generation X' (in the UK 'Thatcher's children' and, increasingly, 'Blair's children') and 'new millennials'. What these labels tend to depict are changing attitudes and conditions of youth, predicated on largely consumerist values and a stronger preoccupation with lifestyle goals.

A theme in more recent research has been the plural and multiple identities that young people form during the middle part of adolescence. For increasing amounts of young people, the post-school choices they make are as much influenced by other identity dimensions around friendship, consumption, lifestyle and social life as they are by their economic role and standing. Research by Ball et al. (2000) shows that young people's horizons tend to encompass a broader range of life experiences, lifestyle choices and personal goals, and this is often set against a backdrop of a pervasive consumer culture and digital technology. At one level, this reflects growing ambivalence towards the job market, with far less expectations of securing long-term and stable employment from which they might build a coherent work narrative. At another level, it may also reflect young people's propensities towards finding forms of self-expression and peer acceptance at a period of increased uncertainty and risks. Lifestyle interests that have little connection with the job market therefore present opportunities for creative and expressive outlets, sometimes substituting that which might occur in paid labour.

The research carried out by Ball et al. reported some of the alternative means through which young people attempted to acquire social status and acceptability among peers – often as a way of asserting some kind of autonomy and control when job market prospects were perceived to be in decline. There also tended to be implicit acknowledgement among the young people in their study that the job market was only one outlet for offering self-expression, and for a disenfranchised element within their sample, this was perceived to be very minimal. Thus, for increasing numbers of young people, continued participation in post-compulsory education and training is a way of delaying entry into the job market and the grind of initial employment, while also allowing time to survey options and continue to pursue other lifestyle interests.

The increasingly disparate educational and labour market trajectories experienced by young people are perhaps mirrored in the different ways in which young people position their educational experiences towards future employment. For some young people, particularly those from traditional academic backgrounds, choices towards further educational participation are likely to be based on somewhat clearer labour market goals. Expectations for rewarding and fulfilling work more commonly underscore their choices and the labour market is seen to offer greater opportunities, both materially and personally. Others clearly have more disjointed trajectories and their educational and training experiences are largely marginal to other identity projects and goals. Yet, there is also a core group of young people who look to develop specific vocational and job-related skills in order to pursue particular types of jobs.

Such themes are evident in other research on young people's transitions from education to paid employment. Furlong and colleagues' research (2005) has clearly demonstrated that many young people leave school with much less fixed and clear ideas about how they will manage their transition into the labour market. Using longitudinal data from a youth cohort in west Scotland, they also found significant variability in the nature of school-leavers' transitions. While a proportion of the cohort experienced some stable and linear progression, it was common for the immediate post-school transitions to be fairly non-linear and risky. Significant amounts of school-leavers appeared to be experiencing what they called 'chaotic' transitions, marked by unemployment, financial insecurity and problematic forms of social exclusion. Even among those young people who expect and seek out continued education and training, there was not always a clear sense as to how this would precisely map onto their longer-term futures. Such pressures were found to be particularly intense for young people lacking formal qualifications and skills and who were likely to endure discernible labour market uncertainty and dislocation. The initial process of finding regular patterns of employment for all types of school-leavers and graduates therefore tends to be characterized by precariousness and uncertainty, even though more stable patterns of work tended to follow for some individuals. Such research tends to challenge the prevailing assumption that additional educational choices and pathways have led to greater empowerment among young people. Instead, the 'tyranny of choices' facing young people has generated ambiguities among both learners and employers over the value of various qualifications.

Bradley and Devadsson's (2008) research, set within a relatively buoyant urban context, has vividly illustrated the increasingly precarious contexts surrounding young people's transitions to work. Their research reported that young people making the initial transition to paid employment anticipated having to endure extensive challenges and potential upheavals, even among those who had made a relatively smooth transition through education. Relatedly, the young people in their study had internalized discourses around adaptability and flexibility, acknowledging both that their employment paths were unlikely to be certain and that they would need to develop strategies to militate against these challenges. For the majority of their sample, long-term and guaranteed employment was perceived as increasingly unfeasible: potential precariousness and continued job mobility were conditions that needed to be actively embraced. Within this changing context, they have to make more purposeful and active choices, often in the form of an 'internalized flexibility' that many had subscribed to.

This research has brought into play the considerable role of agency in terms of the way in which individuals draw upon personal and biographical resources to navigate their way through a more uncertain labour market. It is clear from such research that many individuals are aware that they have to invest more in their future work and 'give more' of themselves if they are to succeed. This is particularly the case for individuals who experience more fractured career histories and whose work is located in flexible and precarious labour markets. Several groups within Bradley and Devadsson's research, identified as *Shifters and Switchers*, were particularly prone to mobility and contingent job market situations. Some of these situations were voluntarily initiated and embraced by these individuals through excitement, challenge and change; others of which were out of individuals' hands due to the ever-shifting labour market circumstances they inhabited. At the same time, certain individuals still appear to be attracted to relatively secure employment, looking to minimize risks by following what they hope and perceive to be more structured and longer-term trajectories. In nearly all cases in their research, attitudes of resourcefulness and adaptability underpinned the new generation of workers' career outlooks. As such, many expect continuous change and movement, as well as the need to manage their work and learning profiles through varied work experiences and forms of continued learning.

Brooks (2009) has argued that an increasing feature of young people's transitions to the labour market is the new forms of strategies that they are developing in order to align themselves to shifting job market demands. Young people's delayed entry to the job market, and potential fluctuations within it, have increasingly needed to be compensated for by alternative forms of engagement and activity. The delay to being formally and directly involved in full-time, regularized employment following formal schooling has increasingly given way to new 'informal spaces' within the transition process. Within such spaces, there are increasing imperatives and potential opportunities for young people who have come to realize that they have to proactively manage their transition and the future outcomes that rest on it. It has therefore become more common for the post-school transition to be characterized by other life course pursuits, including gap years, voluntary work and part-time employment. Such pursuits are increasingly framed as a significant extension of their transition to the formal labour market and a crucial part of their ongoing lifelong and informal learning. It is acknowledge by many young people that these help facilitate new forms of social, cultural and personal capital that are likely to have a strong bearing on their access to particular jobs.

Chapter summary

This chapter has considered the changing nature of transitions from education to work and how this has been affected by the expansion of post-compulsory education and the changing 14–19 provision, both strongly linked to the changing labour market context for young people. We have seen how the expanded opportunities that young people have on leaving school are also matched by new forms of challenge and risk. The relatively smoother pathways that young people made from school to work increasingly complex. For increasing amounts of young people, this has involved an extension of youth and a delay in finding longer-term employment.

There is clearly a theme relating to social equality and exclusion in such research, showing that some young people continue to be marginalized from wider educational and employment opportunities. The wider cultural dynamics of class and gender appear to underpin post-school choices and the kinds of educational and labour market horizons that young people form. Research has also illustrated the way in which this is set within the wider life course of young people as they continually negotiate social identities, some of which might be more closely linked to future employment than others. Far from young people's trajectories being patterned within a relatively linear, stable progression from school to work, they instead encompass a range of critical 'turning points' that individuals have to make sense of and negotiate.

CHAPTER EIGHT

Transforming educational institutions for economic gain

In this chapter, we explore the government-driven effort to transform educational institutions to meet the changing demands of the economy. It first considers the sustained emphasis placed on education meeting economic goals, as well as some of the features of what might be described as a new 'economization' of education. It will show that the increasing economization of education at all levels is having far-reaching consequences for educational institutions as they become repositioned within the changing political and socio-economic environment. This is very much manifest in a range of state-directed measures aimed at aligning the educational system more closely to the needs of the economy. In many ways, economizing pressures have reshaped the institutional fabric of many educational institutions, redefining their perceived goals and purposes, along with what they are seen 'to provide'. This has also had a further significant bearing on the work and identities of educational professionals who have been caught up in these changes.

We build on some of the themes explored in Chapter 4, namely, the increasing emphasis on raising human capital and strengthening the productive capacity of the workforce. As we have shown throughout this book, national governments have strongly emphasized the role of education as a supply-side booster of future human resources. Educational institutions are therefore seen to have a major role and responsibility in raising the overall levels of human capital of the workforce for a competitive global economy. As a consequence, economic progress is seen to be largely determined by the extent to which the educational system can facilitate changing economic demands and equip the labour force with the requisite skills and knowledge to meet these demands. It has become seen as imperative that educational institutions develop modes of provision and practice that accord with these demands. In response to such imperatives, governments have been eager to pursue a range of policy directives geared towards transforming the structures and practices of educational institutions so that they are more responsive to economic goals. Consequently, schools and post-compulsory institutions have been subject to a range of wider policy-based pressures that have penetrated through to their internal practices and cultures.

This chapter first explores some of the dominant features and themes in the economization of education. It then considers the shifting context for this movement and some of the wider socio-economic changes that have given rise to it. It then explores some of the main government responses to perceived economic pressures and, in particular, some of the key policy directives that have been deployed by the government. It will show that these policies are not necessarily likely to have the desired effect of facilitating economic development, as they place heavy emphasis on meeting short-term, measurable goals and 'outputs'. Such goals themselves may not necessarily be in tune with wider economic challenges and, further, may actually denigrate some key educational processes that may better facilitate this. It then examines how economization has impacted on the work of educational professionals and some of the main effects on educational professionals' working lives and identities. It will illustrate how continued policy pressures have had a number of mixed effects on the practices, professional make-up and identities of educational professionals, particularly in terms of how they attempt to align themselves to a shifting policy landscape. The concepts of managerialism and leadership have assumed significance in the new reform settlement, and so this chapter will also explore some of these issues.

Towards a new economization of education

The shifting economic context

In earlier chapters, we have examined the shifting social and economic context around education, noting that key structural changes had significantly transformed the perceived value and purpose of education. One of the main challenges presented by economic globalization, and the associated shifts towards more knowledge-intensive labour, has been to equip the labour force with the requisite skills and capabilities to meet these challenges. Economies whose educational systems are based on the reproduction of an elite cadre of skilled workers are at risk of undermining the diffusion of wider skills and human talent into emerging areas of growth (Brown and Lauder 1992). As these authors point out, educational systems that effectively develop the workforce's 'collective intelligence' and nurture the wider pool of available talent will be more able to facilitate economic demands in the long term.

The concept of the knowledge-based economy has carried much significance in discussions on the role of education for wider economic development. Given that one of the principle characteristics of the knowledge-based economy is the large-scale exploitation and utility of knowledge across a wider spectrum of the labour market, it has become imperative that future prospective knowledge workers are provided with the appropriate tools to operate. Accordingly, education is seen to play a crucial role in enhancing the productive capacities of a changing labour force, whether in terms of raising their skills, instilling new productive dispositions or promoting new innovatory and enterprising propensities.

The knowledge economy might at one level, and as Robertson (2009) suggests, be taken as a new 'master narrative', or a new discursive imaginary that has been used to promote a broader set of overarching goals for contemporary educational systems. As such, the discourse becomes an almost totalizing feature of official policy framings on the role and potential economic value of educational systems. Moreover, educational systems are seen as fundamental in augmenting what Western governments have often referred to as the 'four pillars' of the knowledge economy, namely, innovation and enterprise, technological application, human capital and supportive institutional cultures that nurture knowledge (see World Bank 2003). And while it is continually acknowledged in official discourses that educational systems can contribute substantially to these different domains of the knowledge economy, there has been persistent questioning of its existing capacity to do so. This invariably spills over into questions about the ways in which educational systems can be designed and organized in order to best serve the changing demands of the new knowledge-based economy.

A major consequence of these changes has been a tightening of the link between educational systems and forms of advanced capitalist production. For much of the middle part of the twentieth century, education was increasingly seen as playing a significant role in economic development. By the end of that century and into the new millennium, it has become perceived as a *central* driver. This development is reflected in governments' thinking and strategizing about how to harness educational systems to meet challenges posed by economic change and new forms of global economic pressure. Governments have often taken it as axiomatic that future economic development is contingent upon the development of responsive and fit-for-purpose educational institutions that can meet global economic demands. In short, education is seen as a panacea to fulfilling the goals of the economy.

In their seminal work on the rise of vocational imperatives in education, Grubb and Lazerson (2004, 2006) refer to this mission as the 'educational gospel'. The faith placed by governments in education as an emancipating force for social and economic change has almost taken the form of a secular religion. This, the authors go on to argue, is clearly manifest in the many rhetorical pronouncements used by governments in advocating the role of education for economic ends. As they argue:

> In many countries an amazingly similar rhetoric has developed, one that stresses the failures of schools and universities and proceeds to reform them with more economic goals. We call this the Education Gospel because it has become an article of faith. Starting with a critique of schooling, it brings glad tidings about the potential of educational expansion and reform, leading to social and individual salvation. (Grubb and Lazerson 2006, p. 295)

What is interesting here is that, quite paradoxically, education is seen as both the problem and the solution to the wider needs of the economy. There has perhaps been a marked tendency for governments to point the blame for economic failure at educational institutions for pursuing the wrong practices and approaches. Schools and universities have been typically criticized for failing to produce future employees who are adequately equipped to meet the demands of the economy. The problem is therefore not necessarily attributed to government policy, or the way in which reforms may have constrained educational institutions' capacity to innovate or design forms of provision that might serve wider economic goals. Yet, the antipathy projected towards educational institutions for failing to respond to economic demands is matched with an equal faith in their capacity fundamentally to transform economic fortunes. Largely underpinning the 'educational gospel's' agenda is a concerted attempt on the part of government to transform educational systems to meet perceived economic ends. The question then is: in what ways have governments attempted to harness educational institutions to this end? Moreover, to what extent do they actually serve to enhance and fulfil economic goals?

Features of the economization of education

A number of key features stand out in the economization movement in education, and these can be seen to be the dominant elements or motifs that have come to characterize it. Many of these features overlap quite significantly, and in many cases tend to feed into each other.

Economization of education tends to be represented through the following main elements:

- A dominant ideological creed that tends to subsume educational goals and values under a broader utilitarian rationale that is preoccupied with economic development ahead of other goals that may be less economically tangible and useful.

- The anticipated role of education in enhancing economic output and efficiency under the broader remit of human capital development, workforce productivity and new innovation.

- A discursive framing of wider educational goals that accord with perceived economic demands, namely, the challenges of a 'globally competitive' and 'knowledge-driven' economy. These tend to frame educational goals in a strongly technicist way that is accompanied by a range of terms such as 'skills', 'employability' and 'outcomes'.

- An increasing vocationalization of educational provisions, often in the form of provision and learning that is perceived to have more immediate labour market value.

- New policy mechanisms designed to induce greater potential economic efficiency and outputs from educational institutions, in the form of various policy tools and levers (namely, performance management, curricula guidelines and league tables).

- The increasing marketization and commoditization of education, entailing the recasting of educational institutions as providers, and learners and parents as educational 'consumers'. This is underpinned by the principles of choice, competition and privatization within educational services.

Economization at one level may be seen as an *ideology* that propagates a number of core beliefs and value systems about how education should operate, as well as a *process* that is manifest in sets of practices and institutional arrangements that support these dominant goals. Like most ideological movements, economization can be seen as encompassing a set of overarching beliefs and value systems around how institutions and social life should be organized. In this particular case, there is a dominant belief that education should be organized in such a way that is both modelled upon the economic system that operates outside it, while also potentially feeding into it.

As an ideological movement that has gained significant momentum over time, the economization of education has further been legitimized and entrenched through a range of policy directives and discourses which reflect the dominant principles of this ideology. In this case, the organizing principle for education systems is that of economic gain through servicing the needs of a fast-changing and ever-demanding capitalist system. Economic goals and values are therefore given primacy over more 'softer', more traditional values around education as a 'public good', citizenship and the pursuit of social justice and opportunity.

The economization ideology that has been propagated by national governments is accompanied by a set of values and ideals about how education should best be organized and whose interests it should service. In this case, all roads lead towards the economy and its changing imperatives, not least the changing needs of industry. Hence, there is a very strong emphasis on fostering a successful, productive and harmonious relationship between the supply-side of the labour market, namely, educational institutions, and demands within the labour process. A dominant motif here is that of human capital development in terms of the overall enhancement of skills and the productive potential of the workforce. A key role of education is the development of human capital, or at least the correct forms of human capital, that will generate economic gain through the overall enrichment of the supply of skilled and useful labour entering the labour force. In effect, education is cast as a 'hand-maiden' in fulfilling wider economic imperatives whereby it can help facilitate new growth and development in an economy ever-reliant on human capabilities. The equation of education with human capital and future workforce development is therefore a key economizing theme and one that has been actively pursued by governments.

A look at most government educational policy over the past 30 years reveals the way in which policy has framed and positioned education as a driver for economic growth and key for national competitiveness. A strong discursive theme has been on the crucial need for more centrally positioned educational systems within the wider economy. This is clearly evident in prominent policy rhetoric and discussion about the role of education in meeting the demands of a fast-changing economy (OECD 2000). This concern is often intimately linked to related discourses around the knowledge-driven economy and the transformation in global relations in the supply and development of capital. Globalization and the gradual move towards a global knowledge infrastructure have resulted in new competitive imperatives to which national states and their educational institutions have to be fully responsive. Education plays a fundamental role in fulfilling these competitive challenges by enhancing areas of provision that are in accordance with these shifting demands. Thus, in the words of this World Bank report on emerging economies:

> One of the clues in support of the conclusion that education contributes to growth is that countries with higher levels of economic growth have labor forces with higher levels of formal schooling. Beyond such a macroeconomic approach to the relation between education and economic growth, the new growth theories assert that developing nations have a better chance of catching up with more advanced economies when they have a stock of labor with the necessary skills to develop new technologies themselves adopt and use foreign technology. (World Bank, *The Road not Travelled*, p. 23)

Robertson (2005) has illustrated how much of the policy discourse on economic competitiveness tends to work from the basis that educational provision should be more carefully attuned to meeting new economic conditions. The role of education in cultivating future potential 'knowledge workers' tends to carry particular weight. Moreover, knowledge workers are best developed through educational systems that are increasingly adaptive and flexible in terms of what they provide learners. The knowledge economy demands future employees who not only manage knowledge, but who also have the appropriate dispositions and mindsets to make value-added inputs in knowledge-intensive labour markets. In effect, educational systems need to instil the tools for lifelong learning in individuals, equipping them with the appropriate intellectual resources and dispositions.

The OECD (2000) and the World Bank (2003) have presented a highly aspirational vision of the need for a paradigm shift in the way in which learning and teaching is organized in educational institutions. They call for a move away from the traditional 'status quo' model of learning towards one that is much more learner centred. Educational institutions should effectively become 'learning organizations' whose key function is to produce proactive and engaged lifelong learners who can learn independently and across multiple contexts through their life course. This it is argued is not achievable through traditional models of learning, which have tended to reproduce uncreative and passive learners whose abilities are not in tune with the new fluid, post-industrial context in which they will be operating.

However, such aspirations do not rest easily with other more dominant policy framings that are more explicitly instrumental in their approach to how educational institutions should be equipping individuals. Here, much significance is placed on the operational and performance-based capacities of future workers. This is typically combined with a strong preoccupation with outcomes, output and throughput. Strongly woven into the outcome/output-based approaches to educational development are related economistic conceptions around 'skill', 'employability', 'competences' and 'human capital'. But these notions do not necessarily rest comfortably with a learning-centred educational model, given that they actually place little emphasis on the processes of learning and how properly to engage learners.

What the future employee can do, how well they can operate, what they can apply and how much they can contribute to the workforce has increasingly dominated public policy debates around education. In effect, 'skills', 'employability' and 'competence' become shorthand for the types of adaptable and economically useful future workers that education systems should be producing. In many ways, the preoccupation with outputs and outcomes reflect the ideological shift towards economic instrumentalism and the repositioning of education firmly within economic relations and imperatives. The end goals of education are to enhance economic output and the means of achieving this is through the enhancement of the productive capacities and attributes of future employees.

Policy responses to economization

We can see that official policy discourses have very much propagated the notion of education as a catalyst for economic renewal. But given the continued importance placed on the economic potential of education, how has this agenda been pursued by governments and to what effect? There has been a prevailing view among political economists and educationalists that the economization creed has resulted in a policy agenda that has had the opposite effect of enhancing the educational system's overall economic value. Accordingly, the drive to make educational systems more economically efficient has hampered the development of practices and pedagogical methods that may have better facilitated this goal.

Much of the problem, as Wolf (2002) argues, is that national governments have tended to become too preoccupied with ends instead of means. This is essentially manifested in an overriding concern with quantity, outputs and contestable notions of 'standards', ahead of educational quality, process and the wider learner experience. A new performance-based policy climate has prevailed that is heavily geared towards strengthening schools' and universities' efficiency and effectiveness. Wolf has challenged the prevailing agenda not only on the basis that it exaggerates the linkage between education and economic growth, but also that it tends to inculcate a policy agenda that is, paradoxically, inimical to facilitating the potential of the future workforce. A standards-driven educational agenda means that formal educational provision has become standardized; all attention and resources are effectively channelled towards meeting crude outcomes and targets. As such, these tend to have little to do with the enrichment of learners' educational experiences.

Lauder et al. (2006) adopt a similar critique in their concept of the 'state theory of learning'. This concept offers an analysis of the dominant policy mechanisms that governments have pursued to facilitate economic outcomes, as well as the principles behind these mechanisms. The state theory of learning is predicated on the notion that improved educational outcomes can be achieved through strong levels of state intervention in the form of policy directives that are purportedly designed favourably to enhance learners' future economic potential. In effect, the state has a strong intervening role in establishing policy objectives and agendas that are designed to meet wider economic imperatives.

The underlying rationale here is that the state must coordinate educational systems so that they can enable individuals to become fully 'employable' and economically efficient. The state has reframed its role in developing people's overall employability through the pursuit of provisions that may achieve this desired end. At one level, there has been a state-driven commitment towards promoting learning and its continuous engagement through the life course, as this is seen as a crucial means through which individuals can enhance their economic value and raise their overall employability. Hence, there has been widespread encouragement for individuals to extend their schooling beyond compulsory age and, where possible, embark upon higher education. The more people learn, the more economic potential they possess when entering the job market. But it is, nevertheless, the individual who must capitalize on these opportunities and ensure that their educational experiences equip them favourably for the job market.

A discernible feature of the state theory of learning is the level of top-down policy prescription to which educational institutions are subject. This is principally manifested in the plethora of policy directives that they must follow and actively implement in order to ensure that their educational outputs are in line with stipulated government objectives. As Lauder et al. point out, the prescriptive element of much state educational policy is most evident in new modes of curricula, assessment and pedagogical delivery that have tended to be stringently imposed by central governments.

The emphasis behind many of these policy directives has been towards meeting specific targets, performance benchmarks and learning outcomes that, if achieved, reflect well on the future potential of the learner. The outputs that schools generate in terms of examination results, league table position and inspection ratings are seen to represent the success of an educational institution in producing successful learners who are fit-for-purpose. Yet, sceptics question whether these 'outcomes' actually feed into the wider economic system in any meaningful or productive way. If anything, they could be taken to represent a conveyor-belt approach to teaching and learning, whereby educational outcomes take primacy over the enrichment of learners' experiences.

Broadfoot and Pollard (2000) have also critiqued the new *learning for assessment* drive within UK schools, particular in the context of performance-driven learning climates. They contrast the 'liberal progressive model' of education, which is child centred and based on teacher autonomy, with the 'performance model', which is predicated on the production of 'successful' learners who have gone through the various assessment hoops and hurdles. This, argue these authors, is at odds with the wider goals of 'lifelong learning' and probably accounts for why many learners feel disengaged from formal learning from a relatively early age.

The New Labour administration was a clear exponent of this approach, under the wider remit of 'standards-driven' reforms and national target setting (Docking 2001; Whitty 2008). Clear examples of this are found in the widespread use of assessment, the tightening of curriculum guidelines and the use of performance management techniques – all of which are designed to improve the standards and learning outcomes of students. In the UK, in particular, there has been a growing preoccupation with measuring educational 'performance'. Such measurement has been chiefly through the construction of quantifiable indicators of schools' and teachers' individual outputs and performances. This has been largely designed to measure how effectively their practices are aligned to wider externally set indicators and benchmarks.

Critics of this approach, such as Philips and Harper-Jones (2003) and Ainscow et al. (2006), have argued that this represents a highly technicist, regimented and instrumental approach to learning. Its main preoccupation is with producing outputs that are in line with specified targets and directives, but which are of little intrinsic educational value. They also argue that this is ultimately to the detriment of teaching and learning as the effectiveness of a school or a teacher is inferred through the fulfilling of objective measurement criteria rather than their actual skill and capacity for enriching learning. Less tangible educational processes and outcomes are invariably downplayed.

The state theory of learning therefore indicates a major fault line running through much government policy approaches to education, and highlights how much of it is grounded in high levels of government control and the streamlining of educational practices. In turn, it doesn't adequately address the more pressing matters of how best to transform young people's learning experience and help produce positive learner identities that may equip learners for productive labour market futures. Furthermore, this approach is likely to place educational institutions under greater scrutiny and generate a low-trust relationship between the state and educational institutions, as well as between professionals working within them.

In a similar critique of state educational policy, Ball (2008) has explored the reworking of institutional practice and relations through the policy levers that have been put in place by governments. Many of these policy pressures impacting on educational institutions have fallen under the wider government political project of 'modernizing' and 'personalizing' public services, making them more responsive to wider economic and consumer demands (Clarke et al. 2007). Thus, modernization and personalization have been dominant mantras associated with service reform and improvement and the alignment of public service institutions to shifting socio-economic imperatives. Modernized services were seen by the New Labour government as enhancing the quality and output to what they deliver, in turn enriching the experiences of the end user. Modernized services fit-for-purpose and their delivery is in line with the expectation of a wider range of external stakeholders, be they parents, students, employers and policymakers.

A significant part of the reform modernization agenda has been the application of what Ball terms 'policy technologies', which are described as the dominant 'organizational protocols' through which educational institutions have become restructured. Policy technologies are the institutional mechanisms, practices and procedures that are designed to effect change and reform within services. As Ball describes:

> The policy technologies of education are generic in two senses: as part of a global convergence in reform strategies. . . and as deployed across the

public sector as a whole. . . . These technologies are devices for changing the meaning and practice of social relationships. They provide a new language, a new set of incentives and disciplines and a new set of roles, positions and identities within which what it means to be a teacher, a student/learner a patient are all changed. (Ball 2008, p. 42)

Policy technologies have been actively pursued by governments that see the transformation of educational institutions as resting on the reworking of key structures and practice in order to deliver better overall economic responsiveness and output. Ball has identified three dominant policy technologies, namely, marketization, managerialism and performance management. These, in turn, are accompanied by a range of institutional practices and behaviours that have gradually begun to reshape how institutions operate and define their goals.

Moreover, these policy technologies have become embedded in the organizational fabric of educational institutions, compelling organizations and the key actors within them to behave in particular ways. For instance, the policy technology of marketization inculcates values around competition, reputation enhancement and serving institutional interests. Likewise, managerialism has generated an increasingly corporate and efficiency-driven climate that is underpinned by value orientations around productivity, targets, performance enhancement and institutional efficacy.

Economization, markets and marketization

A key motif in the wider economization of education has been the emergence of educational markets, with the associated drive for educational institutions to operate more on the lines of private sector organizations. The transformation of schools into quasi-markets was a flagship educational policy of the UK Conservative administration of the 1980s, with the overall goal of making educational institutions more responsive, efficient and outcome focused. However, unlike markets in the private sector, educational institutions would not become true markets given that the state remains the primary funder of institutions and distributor of resources, and the primary goal of education is not necessarily to generate profit or enhance shareholder value (Le Grand and Bartlett 1993).

However, in their drive to model educational institutions on private sector organizations and to reshape their overall practices, governments over the past three decades have placed considerable emphasis on educational markets as a mechanism for gaining better educational outcomes. The rise of markets in education can further be seen as a strong element of the economization ideology; not only do markets embody the principles and values of profit-orientated organizations, but they are also designed to move the educational system towards wider economic goals and values.

There is clearly a strong ideological underpinning to the spread of markets in education, based on the political ideology of neo-liberalism and its associated concepts of public choice and deregulation (Hayek 1973; Friedman 1980). At the heart of neo-liberalism is the idea that traditional public institutions should be liberalized in such a way that they can operate like private institutions. Like private institutions, they can also serve their own interests and manage their own affairs. For this to happen, public institutions need to be afforded greater individual autonomy and independent powers in order to be freed-up from the constraining powers of the state (Olssen 2004). Neo-liberalism calls for the devolvement of power away from the state to the individual institutions so that they, and the individuals within them, can operate as autonomous entities and control their own destinies.

In many ways, the ideology of neo-liberalism is at odds with another ideology that most twentieth-century, post-war public policy had been based upon, namely, welfarism (Tomlinson 2005). Neo-liberalism challenges the traditional welfare model of public organization, as it is seen as constraining the economic potential of educational institutions by putting too much emphasis on state planning and control. Similarly, the welfare approach is seen to be exclusively focused on the pursuit of equity and social justice ahead of economic pursuits, and for stipulating common and universal practices.

Neo-liberal ideology tends to conceive individuals as self-interested and self-optimizing, and who therefore should be allowed to exercise as much possible freedom in all areas of public life. Moreover, for individuals to pursue their private goals within the public sphere, public institutions need to be transformed in ways that facilitate their freedom to do so. This can only be realized if there is a contraction of the state and an expansion of the market, as it is through markets that individuals can genuinely fulfil their private goals.

The transformation of educational institutions into markets is therefore a key process through which the ideological project of neo-liberalism can be fulfilled. Perhaps two of the most prominent principles associated with the market movement are those of 'choice' and 'competition'. Neo-liberalism has been closely associated with the concept of public choice (Buchanan 2003). Thus, key advocates of public choice, such as the economic theorist Buchanan, argue that public institutions such as schools will be at their most effective if they provide greater levels of choice to an ever-discerning and discriminating public. If the public is allowed to exercise choice in education in more or less the same ways as consumers in a private market can exercise so-called consumer sovereignty over what products and services they wish to consume, then this will encourage educational institutions to raise their overall profile and game.

Choice is facilitated within a market model if there is a fundamental shift from provider to consumer and greater scope for public organizations to differentiate themselves in terms of the product or service they can offer to potential customers. Through generating a mixed and differentiated market, greater flexibility is established within the system. This also means that greater flexibility is afforded to customers, which, in the case of schools, are the pupil and parent. Most crucially, choice within education promotes competition. If schools, colleges and universities are encouraged to compete with each other for additional resources via potential customers, then they will inevitably raise the standards of what they offer. In effect, the marketization of education with its dominant principles of choice, competition and market responsiveness is seen as a crucial vehicle for raising educational standards and improving educational outcomes.

There have been a key set of policies associated with the market-driven reform of education. The most prominent of these have been school choice, formula funding, devolved management and outsourcing of educational services to private providers. These followed the 1988 Education Act in the UK, which was largely designed to allow schools to operate in a mixed marked economy of different educational providers. Parents were encouraged to exercise greater choice over where to send their child to be educated and schools were also obliged to provide 'market' information about their performance through the publication of league tables.

While the wider goal of raising educational standards may be an underlying rationale for the marketization of education, it has also been seen as a key means of fulfilling the neo-liberal project of public service reform (Whitty 1989; Ball 1994). Believing that the private sector was the true model around which education should be organized, the Conservative government was keen to dismantle existing educational structures and move towards a market agenda.

Supporters of market-based approaches in education view markets as being neutral and providing access to better opportunities than they would under the universal, 'comprehensive' welfare structure. Markets are also seen as a driver of education standards through institutions becoming more responsive. The winners are the individual learners and their parents, who not only enjoy a broader range of choice and potentially better forms of provision, but also experience improved educational standards. Educational institutions respond positively to the need to position themselves favourably in a system that allocates resources and distributes rewards on the basis of institutions' overall market strength. In addition, markets limit state jurisdiction over individual institutions, allowing greater powers to be devolved to them. This, in turn, means that individual institutions, and the managers and professionals within them, have greater freedoms and individual authority over how to manage their own organizations.

Markets in education have also received a wide range of criticisms. These have largely centred on the inequalities that educational markets engender, in terms of the different educational and cultural resources that families bring to education. As research by Ball (2003) and Gewirtz et al. (1995) clearly illustrates, education consumers enter the educational market with different sets of profiles and aspirations, all of which are likely to frame their capacity to act as rational and proactive market actors. Social class is invariably a strong mediating factor in how families both understand and approach the market, given that this is so fundamentally linked to the pre-existing educational profiles and resources that people have at their disposal. As these researchers have clearly illustrated, middle-class parents are able to decode the rules of the market more effectively in ways that give them a market advantage. This is not only based on a wider engagement with the national and local educational context (and market situation), but also by engaging in much more strategic behaviour in order to achieve access to desired schools. This ultimately skews the market in favour of those who have the resources and propensity to work the market to their advantage.

The market-driven agenda has continued over the past two decades under successive governments. Whitty's (2008) analysis of educational policy trajectories since the late 1980s shows that the spirit of marketization has permeated educational policy, albeit under somewhat different guises. The Labour government proclaimed a 'standards not structures' agenda. At the same time, they were fully committed to diversifying the state school sector through a combination of market plurality and promoting stronger links between educational institutions and private sector companies. This was particularly manifest in their specialist schools and academies programmes that were developed to encourage greater commercial involvement in state schools. Yet, in many ways, the New Labour policy framework tended to entail a double-edged sword of market diversity and strong levels of centralized planning and coordination – the latter being based on prescriptive policy directives and high levels of performance accountability.

The fusing of strong levels of centralization and market competition and responsiveness has, in turn, generated a range of challenges for schools and colleges. Whitty argues that, rather than being incompatible, these two approaches are being interlinked in the overall drive to ratchet up standards and educational outputs. Thus, schools' overall success in fulfilling centralized government targets in terms of performance outputs, most notably exam results, invariably conveys potentially significant market signals to ever-discerning parent-customers. Stevenson (2011) also discusses the legacy that the marketization agenda from the 1980s continues to exercise, as evinced in many of the coalition government's policies. Core marketization principles have continued to dominate the government's agenda for schools, not least allowing schools to run as autonomous entities, with strong levels of devolved management and a greater role for *for-profit* providers.

Economization and professional identities

Having outlined some of the dominant, government-driven initiatives to restructure educational systems and practices, we turn our attention to the impacts that these have had on educational professionals and their professional practices and identities. It is clear that the new economization of education and its accompanying sets of reform imperatives have brought new forms of accountability and regulation to professionals' work. As reform pressures mount and educational professionals' roles continue to diversify and intensify, increasing expectations are placed on them to fulfil a wider host of external demands and goals. At the same time, the educator's role in facilitating positive educational outcomes and improving the fortunes of learners has been continually emphasized by governments (DFES 2006; DfE 2011). In recent times, there has clearly been much government-led emphasis on the professional standards, and standing, of educational professionals and the need to generate renewed purpose and value within the profession.

However, there may well be a resultant tension between new forms of policy-driven pressures and external regulation over educational professions and their assumed position as autonomous agents of change. Whitty (2000) has discussed how, at one level, educational professionals are characterized as skilled, informed and self-directed, yet at another level, policy pressures have reduced their role and status to more technocratic functions and operations. Any decline in educators' professional power and autonomy is likely to significantly delimit their capacity to facilitate positive learning experiences and outcomes. As Reay (2006), in her analysis of teachers' roles in mediating class relations in schools, points out:

> There has been a paradoxical process of, on the one hand, surveillance and prescription in which teachers have been reduced to technicians and divested of much of their earlier scope for autonomy and initiative in relation to pedagogy and curriculum, and on the other investing them with impossible powers of transforming educational systems into success without any of the knowledge and understanding that is necessary before they can even begin to make a small headway into an enormous problem. (Reay 2006, p. 292)

A range of academics, including Bottery and Wright (2000) and Ozga (2000), have observed the reconfiguring of educational professionals' work within the wider processes of economic and policy-driven change. Both have argued that educational professionals' work has become increasingly realigned towards helping mobilize the government's agenda for enhanced economic output and delivery. The educator has been recast as a key player in helping make educational institutions more responsive to changing economic imperatives.

There may be competing interpretations, however, in terms of whether this either represents a re-professionalization or de-professionalization of educators' work. The former would imply a renewal of professionals' agency and responsiveness, whereby their work is valued for its wider social and economic contributions through which they are provided with more autonomy. As such, professional educators will be in receipt of greater professional standing and capacity, as well as stronger overall jurisdiction over the direction of their work. The latter, on the other hand, is likely to signal an overall denigration of educators' conditions of work and its overall social value. Both Bottery and Wright (2000) and Fielding (2001) argue that, in the context of greater state control over professional work through strong accountability regimes, heavy regulation and audit, educators have increasingly witnessed a gradual decline in their levels of professional power and jurisdiction.

It is clear that educational professionals have been subject to substantial policy pressures over time, all of which have had a significant bearing upon the shaping of their professional identities. Hargreaves (2000) has described the gradual decline of the post-war, welfare state educational professional who was largely independent, self-regulating and able to exercise high levels of personal jurisdiction over the conditions of their work. Over time, and particularly with the emergence of centralized curricula control and the increase in assessment and external audit, educational professionals have been subject to heightened levels of accountability and external control over their performance and outputs. The introduction of the national curriculum, and its accompanying pressures to achieve specified outcomes, constrained what and how teachers taught and conducted their work. This, in turn, challenged some of their traditional autonomy. However, as Hargreaves points out, while this has delimited aspects of professionals' independence, it also potentially helped to collectivize aspects of professional practice in terms of allowing for new forms of professional dialogue that the 'siloed' post-war professional was unable to achieve.

The changing policy landscape and its attendant pressures linked to the policy technologies of markets, managerialism and performance management has invariably affected the working conditions of many educational professionals. This is likely to extend to the ways in which they perceive the conditions of their work, how they are positioned within their organizations and the level of autonomy they feel they are able to exercise. The shift, therefore, from relatively loosely regulated professional environments to those of managed markets, where performance output is central, undoubtedly has far-reaching ramifications for professional work and identity formation. Gewirtz et al. (2009) have discussed the reversal of influence among educational professionals, whereby most educational professionals have increasingly become the subjects of policy rather than the shapers of it. They see the shifting policy and ideological context to professionals' work as significant, arguing that

> Under the influence of neo-liberal ideologies – with their privileging of cost-containment and productivity goals – this period has seen an increase in central regulation of the work of teachers and an increased role of quasi-market centred on the ideas of choice and competition. As the

influence of these alternative modes of coordination has increased, so, in many national setting, the scope for professional influence on policy and practice has diminished. (Gewirtz et al. 2009, p. 5)

This raises some significant questions around the reshaping of professionals' identities. It would appear that the conditions that may have traditionally anchored educators' professional subjectivity have been reconfigured through a shifting policy landscape. Day et al. (2006) discuss how teaching professionals have built their identities around relative autonomy and their capacity to exercise professional jurisdiction over their professional activities. This is also highly value driven and linked closely to the ideals, professional principles and ideological leanings of the professional. Many continue to value being part of a professional community within a specific educational context. However, educators' professional identities are broad and multifaceted, as well as being highly contingent on their institutions and wider policy climate.

What such research shows is that educational professionals are eager to safeguard their professional lives, and make active, albeit sometimes unconscious, attempts to preserve professional autonomy. Hoyle and Wallace (2009) discuss the propensities that professionals have towards an *informed professionalism*, mainly in terms of the capacity to exercise some degree of professional judgement and values. As these authors point out, at one level, educational professionals' capacity to exhibit these features has been severely compromised by the sheer pace and volume of reform and all the ambiguity and endemic change that this constitutes. At another level, professionals, more than ever, need to exercise greater levels of contextual sensitivity in interpreting and working with the policy landscape, as well as developing a meaningful and beneficial professional responsiveness towards its multiple challenges.

The professional and the new performative subject

A clear theme in the changing nature of educational professionalism has been the increasing pressures being placed on educational professionals to meet ever-increasing and multifarious government demands. It would appear that the changing policy context for schools has placed sharper attention on the performance of the educational professional, as well as their capacity to bring about desired educational outcomes. In one sense, this places significant responsibility on professionals not only to manage their work outputs, but also the nature of their professional and pedagogic practices. The wider state-directed pressures on schools and colleges have necessitated new forms of professional alignment and responsiveness. Indeed, educational professionals not only have to actively interpret and implement a fast-changing policy landscape, but also ensure that learners are equipped with the necessary tools to operate in the labour market.

We have seen that this has been interpreted as representing a decline in professional control and autonomy. The relatively high level of professional discretion and jurisdiction once enjoyed by educational professionals has been replaced by a much more compliant and subservient approach. Avis (2009) has interpreted the decline in professional control and autonomy as representing a growing proletarianization, deskilling and crisis of legitimacy among a profession whose working conditions have also intensified. An all-pervasive, top-down and compliance-based policy culture has tended to streamline educational professionals' behaviours. It has further served to undermine a more bottom-up, informed professionalism that is based on deeply held professional values. This represents something of a shift in power away from professional educators to those who have increasingly come to exercise influence over educational practices, namely, policymakers, managers and external auditors.

The concept of *performativity* has been used to capture the changing conditions of educational professionals' work, as well as those working in other professional areas. In their discussions of the changing conditions of professional work, Dent and Whitehead (2002) have identified the shift towards performativity as a key feature in the shaping of professionals' subjectivity and values. In many ways, performativity captures the retooling of professionals' values and behaviours. This is manifest in the shift away from intuitive and professionally derived judgements towards quantifiable measurements over 'outputs' and conformance to externally imposed expectations. Performativity therefore entails a change in both values and practices. The values attached to professionals' work increasingly rest more on the fulfilment of measurable performance criteria, including key benchmarks and performance indicators, than on factors to do with their professional skills and collegiality. Put crudely, if professionals' work and output can't be measured, and to the requisite level that has been predetermined externally, then it isn't necessarily to be valued.

Performativity goes a step further than mere performance, as it is not just about measurable outcomes, but also transformations in professionals' identities and relationships. Performativity signals a reworking of professional work behaviours and the nature of professional relationships. Traditional forms of professional judgement become supplanted by more stringent forms of measurable accountability and performance control. In heavily performative professional climates, the former are perceived as unreliable in the face of the challenges confronting educational systems. In some cases, professionally derived values and judgements may be seen as a hindrance to successful educational 'outcomes' if they are at odds with wider policy and economically driven goals. Thus, Philips and Harper-Jones (2003) define performativity as:

> The belief that standards of "quality" exist and can be measured, that institutional quality can be assessed by reference to performance

indicators, that league tables will drive up performance, and that assessment is a "neutral" measuring instrument that can be refined technically still further. (Philips and Harper-Jones 2003, p. 130)

In such a definition, educational quality is something that can be quantifiably measured and validated, and the drive towards meeting these measures has come to dominate educators' working life. This has been strongly echoed by Ball (2003, 2008), who has described performativity as a 'system of terror' – that is, an all-consuming condition that has shifted professionals' behaviours and outlooks. This entails the continued scrutiny and surveillance of teaching professionals, whose activities are increasingly bound by government imperatives and their measurable fulfilment. These are often linked closely to the new policy technologies that have been pursued by central government, not least those of performance management and accountability. In effect, the professional is subject to far tighter external regulatory regimes that not only exercise considerable control over their work and outputs, but also the way in which they conduct their professional activities. Consequently, professionals' work has become mapped against highly stringent and codified systems of performance measurement that result in high levels of professional risk-inhibition and conformity.

These performative pressures ultimately impact on professionals' values and identities. Performativity may have led professionals' behaviours to be based more upon an instrumental 'what works' ethos, ahead of more principled, professionally informed values over what might be intrinsically beneficial for learners. Thus, the 'ethical retooling' of educators' professional subjectivity engenders a significant reshaping of professional goals and orientations, which have increasingly become conditioned towards fulfilling new performative demands. How educators define their role and undertake their practices is increasingly shaped by the capacity to fulfil, and fare favourably on, various externally imposed criteria; not least examination performance and success in external audits.

The reframing of professional values is further likely to affect an educator's sense of what is professionally relevant and worth pursuing. Ball argues that performativity is ultimately based on the pursuit of perverse incentives, whereby second-order professional concerns take precedence over more salient educationally orientated ones. One particular manifestation of this is 'teaching for the test', rather than attempting fully to engage learners or develop innovative practice that may entail risks.

As a condition of professional life, performativity is potentially disempowering and destabilizing for professionals as their agency becomes substantially constrained. Indeed, research has shown that the prevailing climate of new public management, and its related micro-management tools, has intensified the emotional labour among teaching professionals (Jenkins and Conley 2007). As these researchers illustrate, the performative pressures within educational institutions are often set within a challenging climate of audit, surveillance, clientistic relationships and stringent managerial control. This has sometimes led to problems such as burnout, stress, low morale and high turnover among teachers, as well as perceptions among teachers that their core role has become reduced to technocratic functions.

However, other research has shown that the impacts of wider policy-based changes are experienced differently by educators. This is likely to be influenced by the different contexts they work within and the different make-up and values of the professional. Such factors may affect how they make sense of and respond to these various performance-related demands. As Gleeson and Shain (1999) and Stronach et al. (2002) show in their research on teachers' responses to managerialism, many professionals still demonstrate an allegiance to long-standing professional values and practices. Some professionals are able to win 'earned autonomy' through their standing and esteem as educators, which may enable them to resist the excesses of performative pressures. Moreover, some professionals are adept at strategically aligning themselves to new performance-based pressures and demands while also looking to pursue deeply held professional goals. Such research very much demonstrates the resilience and robustness of professional cultures and practices, as well as the relative levels of agency that educators continue to possess. It also highlights the scope that professionals and managers have for adapting aspects of government policy to suit their own institutional contexts.

While new performative and performance-based pressures may lead to a more cynical 'resigned compliance' among a growing body of teaching professionals who perceive their autonomy to be increasingly constrained, such pressures may also be actively embraced by some professionals who are skilled at playing the game (Farrell and Morris 2004). In some cases, the changing professional climate also provides opportunities for professionals to occupy new identity positions as aspiring managers, or as new entrepreneurial strategists and shape-shifters (Avis 1999).

Clearly, the changing climate of continued policy pressures and performance-based governance has placed significant pressures on educational professionals. In many cases, this is likely to have reshaped many aspects of their values, identities and professional practices. Performative pressures and challenges pervade much of the professional landscape, although the impacts of these are experienced differently by professionals. It is clear that many professionals have been 'held to account' in fulfilling the demands and expectations of governments. At the same time, many continue to value professional autonomy and agency even though some of these have become compromised through a more stringent policy climate.

New managerialism and leadership

A clear policy theme in the drive to make educational systems more efficient and economically driven is that of *managerialism*. Managerialism has been conceptualized as both a practice and an ideology, and its underlying rationale is to enhance educational institutions' outputs through effective and robust forms of management control. Managers and leaders in public organizations are highly instrumental in effecting and implementing changes that enhance their service delivery and output. Thus, managerialism has been seen as a key institutional instrument or technology that enhances the performance capacity and responsiveness of organizations and the professionals working within them. It may also be seen to represent the incorporation of practices, principles and ethics from the private and commercial sector into state organizations, such as schools, social services and hospitals (Rainey 2003; Pollitt 2007).

The spread of managerialism in public services such as education at one level to represent a state-directed effort to bring key institutional actors 'on board' with increasing government expectations and demands. In many ways, educational managers and leaders are significant conduits in the link between wider government reform pressures and the responsiveness of organizations and their professionals. The rise of managerialism has also been interpreted as a significant way of rupturing traditional forms of influence and control by professional groups such as teachers. Clarke and Newman (2000) discuss the move towards managerialism as part of a gradual dismantling of state professionals' authority and control, which governments have viewed as an obstruction to reform progress. The earlier post-war settlement of 'bureau-technical' professional control came to be seen as inimical to change and modernization. Professionals were seen as having too much power in safeguarding their own 'professional interests', sometimes to the detriment of their organizations. As such, professional monopoly made government intervention difficult to achieve as professionals were seen to be able to easily pursue their own agendas.

Deem and Brehony (2005) discuss how the ideology of managerialism is largely predicated on the notion that public institutions' improvement and success can be achieved through the pursuit and implementation of effective systems of internal management. As part of this ideology, considerable significance is attached to managers' and leaders' work in helping to reshape existing organizational structures and practices in ways that enhance their outputs. This is linked to the prevailing view among policymakers that educational institutions have traditionally operated in ways that necessitate stronger forms of management-level intervention and control. Managerialism is therefore geared towards bringing organizational practices in line with shifting imperatives and demands, as well as the reshaping of organizational practices. Thus, at one level, managerialism might be seen as a kind of 'management by excess': anything that can be potentially managed within the organization, should be managed. A consequence of managerialism is that more power is given to managers within organizations and less to professionals: it is managers who have increasingly assumed the mantel of key organizational strategists, decision makers and policy implementers (Ball 1994, 2008).

Grey (1999) has conceptualized the rise of the managerial class in terms of the increasing identification that professionals have with managerialism. The notion that 'we're all managers now' perhaps captures the rise of the new occupational category, and the fact that increasing numbers of professionals and administrators are embracing more managerial activities. The rise of managerialism in education inevitably places considerable responsibility onto educational managers and leaders to effectively pursue and implement change. Educational managers very much sit at the interface between the wider policy reform environment and the professional environment that they manage and influence. Yet these two fields may not always be in harmony.

Educational managers are therefore positioned within a wide range of stakeholder agendas and demands, including those of policymakers, clients, commercial agents and their own organizational members. As Preedy et al. (2011) argue, educational managers often have to manage competing stakeholder demands, as well as being highly adept at reading and responding to the ever-changing external environment. This external environment is not only the national policy context, but also, increasingly, the globalized and internationalized educational market environment. The management of change and the proactive response to external challenges appears to be increasingly central to the work of educational managers. Managers also have to find a balance between raising educational standards and attainment while also responding to the diverse needs of young people and their well-being.

In more recent times, there has been something of a shift in emphasis from 'management' to 'leadership', reflecting a change in the ways in which organizational governance has been conceived. Whereas 'management' depicts a more command-and-control mode of organizational control and coordination, 'leadership' is seen as a more facilitative, enabling and positive way of motivating the organization's members (Harris and Lambert 2003). Effective management may therefore rest more on more transactional processes in terms of the rational and operational execution of organizational objectives. Effective leadership, on the other hand, is seen to be more associated with the establishment of organizational visions, values and positive cultures that lead to long-term change and improvement. In more optimistic interpretations, leadership is seen to help generate more receptive and high-trust organizational cultures that are committed to service improvement. Newman (2005) discusses the gradual repositioning of public service managers as transformational 'change agents' who have been charged with the task of rejuvenating the structures, goals and values of professional organizations for the wider public good. Indeed, central to this vision is the work of proactive, enabling and 'charismatic' leaders who can, in almost entrepreneurial fashion, shape-shift their organizations.

In many ways, there are likely to be significant overlaps between management and leadership as modes of organizational control. Bush

(2008) discusses how some of the differences may be meaningful while others are likely to be largely semantic. There are likely to be significant overlaps between management and leadership and in many ways they are conjoined: effective leaders often need to be effective managers and combine operational skills and savvy with the 'softer' elements of people-management and strategic vision. However, perhaps what differentiates managers from leaders is the demonstration of core attitudes and behaviours such as the ability to influence, inspire and motivate. In the context of increasing external challenges and pressures, such behaviours may become more and more significant in order for institutions to be effectively aligned to the shifting policy landscape.

There is no doubt that the wider environment surrounding schools, colleges and universities has become more complex and challenging in the context of various political and socio-economic challenges and pressures. The role of managers and leaders is now seen as central to meeting these challenges. When viewed critically, managerialism is seen as a form of organizational control that places power in the hands of organizational elites, while challenging the authority of the many professionals. The more recent research on leadership illustrates, however, that in the changing educational environment, managers may need to be more creative and flexible in achieving consent and fulfilling multiple and competing agendas. The success of managers and leaders may, as Hoyle and Wallace (2005) argue, rest on their ability to cope with and respond to the inherent ambiguity and complexity of reform changes. Moreover, school managers and leaders often need to find creative ways of mediating the shifting policy environment, and in ways that best serve their organizations.

Chapter summary

The drive to align educational systems more closely to the wider economy has been a prominent theme in much educational policy in recent times. Underscored by a strong utilitarian and human capital rationale, this approach to educational provision has been a response to the anticipated need to make educational systems more efficient, economically responsive and competitive. Yet, we have also seen, this is largely driven by the ideological movement of neo-liberalism with its core principles of market responsiveness and plurality, competition, consumer sovereignty and devolved institutional autonomy. Educational institutions across all levels have increasingly become attuned to these principles and have had to shape their practices around them. A key consequence of the 'economization' of education is that attendant pressures have arisen for educational systems to meet the needs of the economy, however broadly defined. Yet, the extent to which this can and should be an educational aim has been much contested.

We have also seen how economization has resulted in a policy agenda that has looked to enhance the practices and outputs of educational institutions. The overriding goal here is to generate educational outcomes that fit with governments' notion of what constitutes effective educational provision and what might facilitate the production of fit-for-purpose future workers. There has been much centralized pressure on educational institutions in the form of intensive policy directives with which institutions must abide. Critical interpretations of this agenda see it as having the opposite effect in constraining schools', colleges' and universities' capacity to be economically responsive and innovative. Moreover, the economization agenda has fed through into the professional landscape in terms of the expectations and responsibilities placed on educational professionals and managers.

CHAPTER NINE

Higher education, social change and shifting identities

This chapter examines some of the impacts that the wider processes of social and economic change, discussed throughout this book, have had upon higher education. As an institution, higher education has been subject to considerable changes, both in terms of its institutional form and character and its relationship with wider society and the economy. These changes have largely stemmed from a number of far-reaching policy reforms of higher education, themselves linked to broader macro-level changes through globalization and the knowledge society. Consequently, there has been something of an overall repositioning of universities within wider social and economic life, as well as changing conceptions of its overall social and economic role.

The relationship between higher education, the state and the economy has been reconfigured over time. This has resulted in increasing pressures on higher education institutions (hereafter HEIs) to coordinate their activities in ways that best suit new national economic imperatives. Questions continue to be asked over its capacity to meet the changing needs of the economy, as well as its organizational efficiency and responsiveness to changing social and economic demands. At the same time, considerable importance has been attached to higher education and it has come to be seen a core social institution that forms the bedrock of the knowledge society. This chapter will explore wider changes and, in particular, the changing interaction between higher education and the labour market. It considers what these changes entail for the overall identities of universities, the professionals working in them and, most importantly, students and graduates.

Once relatively autonomous institutions that existed within their own 'bounded spaces' (Henkel 2000), universities have become increasingly subject to new public demands. One of these has been the increased demand for higher education, and its related credentials, by larger numbers of students and their families. In recent decades, students have been increasingly drawn from a broader and more heterogeneous demographic field, including those who hitherto might not have participated in higher education. The once traditional elite cadre of academically high-achieving, white, middle-class students that represented universities for much of the twentieth century has given way to a more academically and socially diverse student population. For an increasingly large number of students, participation in university is not necessarily the typical rite of passage from relatively smooth and successful forms of earlier education (Leathwood and Connell 2003). Furthermore, contemporary students in higher education are likely to hold different views and expectations of the purpose of their university experience and its potential bearing on their future lives.

In an account of the social changes impacting on universities, Brennan (2008) points to a number of significant changes to higher education over time. Of particular significance has been the globalization and massification of the system, the standardization of provision and practice, its increasing centrality to the development of the knowledge-driven society and economy, and the recasting of universities as service providers in a more market-based system. He also highlights successive governments' preoccupation with the continued dual private and public benefits from universities. Higher education may bring private benefits in the form of better pay and job opportunities as individuals achieve higher levels of qualification that employers may value. The benefits may also be public in the form of a better qualified and more productive workforce, potentially leading to future economic growth. Public benefits may also go beyond economic productivity and feed into areas of civic and public life, positively shaping social and community relations. It is therefore clear that there are strong expectations – be they from individual students, policymakers and employers – that universities will meet a wide range of demands. Universities are increasingly expected to be crucial players in the social and economic sphere and to tailor their activities to desired social and economic ends.

HEIs have witnessed considerable demands from national governments, in part as a response to wider economic and industry-driven concerns over their outputs. A number of authors, such as Kogan and Hanney (2000), have discussed the overall shift from the relative institutional and academic freedoms and privileges enjoyed by universities and academics towards tighter external governance of the system. While universities might have traditionally enjoyed relative autonomy in how they managed their own institutional affairs, they have now become subject to greater scrutiny and auditing by central government. This again tends to reflect the general economic repositioning and framing of universities, and the continued pressure on them to pursue research and teaching activities that will potentially be of wider economic value. But it also, reflects a changing political attitude towards higher education since the late 1970s, which has come increasingly to view universities as publicly accountable institutions that need to rationalize and justify their share of public expenditure (Henkel and Little 1999).

A consequence of these pressures is that HEIs have experienced tighter regulatory control and governance and have been subject to a more rigorous measure of their output and its quality (Harvey 2005). Deem et al. (2007) illustrate how 'new managerialism' has been as pervasive in higher education as in other public sector organizations; universities have been held increasingly to account over their structures, practices and outputs. Such pressures have had a profound bearing on social relations within universities and on the nature of academic work and relationships. This has become more strongly regulated along managerialist lines. As these authors further argue, the growing corporate climate in universities has coincided with the gradual privatization of the sector. This is evident in the contraction of public funding and the growing financial contributions made by students. As increasingly 'part-public' institutions, universities have also looked to open themselves up to the commercial sector and leverage far more in the way of private financial input. These themes have been endorsed by governments and form a clear agenda in the Browne review of higher education (DfE 2010), which also advocated the raising of student financial contributions in light of declining public expenditure for higher education.

The shift from elite to mass higher education

The higher education system has evolved dramatically during the course of the past century, and most significantly from the middle to the latter part of the twentieth century. Put simply, higher education has transformed from an elite system that recruited around 5 per cent of 18–21 year olds in the 1960s, to a mass system where around 45 per cent of this age group participate (Trow 2006). This overall trajectory must be seen in the context of broader social-economic, political and demographic shifts that have taken place over the course of the past century. Thus, while at one level the move towards mass higher education can be seen as a policy-driven response to changing economic demands, it also reflects other changes that have influenced new demands for higher education. These include the general expansion of the post-compulsory sector, the changing youth employment landscape, the expansion of the middle classes and occupational changes in professional work. Such shifts have generated new levels of social demand for higher education as participation is seen as a route to better social and economic opportunities.

The trajectory from elite to mass higher education has reflected some significant shifts in the interrelationship between higher education and society, as well as some significant policy landmarks. In particular, the overtly elitist higher education model of the late nineteenth and early twentieth-century has given way to a more open and inclusive system that has generally promoted better access. In their earlier elite phase, universities were explicitly exclusive institutions that were geared towards the reproduction of an aristocratic elite. Halsey (1993) has discussed the 'inegalitarianism' that drove elite higher education, particularly around its hoarding and conferment of middle-class privileges and the system's incapacity to embrace anything approaching social diversity. The onset of advanced industrialism and the expansion of the professional classes saw a gradual rise in participation, together with the establishment of new civic universities; however, for much of the early-to-middle part of the twentieth century, a university education remained confined to a small segment of society (Trow 2006). Thus, in terms of social equality, elite higher education tended to reinforce social divisions and relative access to social and economic opportunities. Participation in elite higher education could be seen to constitute an established process of cultural reproduction that confirmed middle-class status and privileges (Bourdieu and Passeron 1979).

Over time, the manifest elitism of higher education was challenged, particularly with the advent of a growing post-war social democratic political consensus that promoted new forms of social inclusion and opportunity. One of the cornerstones in the movement towards mass higher education was the Committee of Higher Education's (1963) policy framework in the early 1960s, more commonly referred to as the 'Robbins Report'. At the time of this report, only 6 per cent of young people participated in higher education. Its key recommendations included: instruction in skills suitable for work; the promotion of the general powers of the mind; the advancement of learning; and the transmission of common culture and common standards of citizenry. Crucially, the report advocated the opening up of the system to wider groups of academically able students who could benefit from higher learning, but who had hitherto been denied access. Higher education gradually became reframed as a public good. This, in turn, heralded a gradual expansion of student numbers, along with the creation of new universities and polytechnic colleges throughout the UK. A steady rate of expansion continued over time, reinforced by increased social demand for higher education among the expanding professional classes.

A further significant shift occurred in the early 1990s with the unification of universities with polytechnic colleges. This resulted in the formal rebranding of polytechnics as 'universities' in their own right, and they were also given the power to award degree qualifications. As the system expanded in the early and middle part of the 1990s, there were renewed concerns about the continued relative under-representation of lower socio-economic groups. This also coincided with a concern about the financial sustainability of higher education, as well as the need to strengthen links between universities and the economy. The Dearing Report (NCHIE 1997) addressed the issue of higher education funding and student access, as well as the importance for universities to develop more economically focused aims and practices. The report highlighted HEIs' increasing financial burdens and the need for greater financial contributions from individual students. The Labour administration was further committed to increasing participation in the UK, but towards the end of its office, it began placing less emphasis on meeting its 50 per cent target of 18–21 years olds participating in higher education. The following coalition government also made a commitment to capping student numbers in the context of diminished public funding, but have sought to put new demands on the more elite universities to recruit students from under-represented socio-economic backgrounds (DfE 2011).

The move towards mass higher education has largely been celebrated as a triumph for social inclusiveness, and for helping to break down barriers to a previously exclusive system. Its development has therefore been lauded for facilitating greater social and economic opportunities among students from lower socio-economic backgrounds. However, as Leathwood (2006) points out, there are still existing social disparities in the participation rates between different socio-economic groups. To this extent, access to participation in higher education is not necessarily a neutral process that is detached from wider socio-economic processes.

The socio-economic inequalities that exist in wider society are likely to impact profoundly on learners' earlier educational experiences and achievements, which, in turn, are likely to determine individuals' propensity to participate in higher education. This tends to be supported by figures on the differential levels of participation among different socio-economic groups. For instance, participation figures clearly show that, while the absolute numbers of students from a lower socio-economic background have increased, there are still marked differences in participation between socio-economic groups (DfE 2011).

A range of research has shown that earlier educational experiences and horizons still strongly influence decisions to participate in higher education, and that for a significant core of individuals from lower socio-economic backgrounds, it clearly does not figure on their aspirational radar (Archer et al. 2003; Reay et al. 2006). Furthermore, as research by Fuller et al. (2011) shows, prospective students' decisions are often embedded in wider networks of familial, peer and community influence and support. These tend to frame the possibility, and likely benefits, of embarking on higher education. It appears, therefore, that the main beneficiaries of higher education are still predominately those from higher socio-economic groups who have been primed for higher education from the early stages of their educational lives. The expansion of higher education has been driven mainly by increased middle-class demand; and while access has improved for lower socio-economic groups, their participation is still much lower in comparison.

The diversity of the university sector within mass higher education has often been highlighted, together with the high levels of differentiation between different HEIs. Discussing the continued evolution of the higher education system, Scott (2005) argues that the development of higher education has not necessarily followed a straightforward trajectory over time. In countries such as the UK, the transition from elite to mass higher education has not happened incrementally, but instead has occurred in response to changing political and social demands. A key drive in the movement to mass higher education in most advanced political economies has been the advancement of a post-industrial economy where production and exploitation of knowledge have become paramount. Universities have increasingly been seen to be at the core of this development through the types of activities they engage in. Yet, there is still some degree of ambiguity over the ways in which different institutions fit within this picture. As Scott illustrates, the expansion of higher education has largely reinforced institutional differences and internal differentiation within the sector: elite and mass higher education tend to coexist in a market-orientated and hierarchical system driven by reputation and institutional prestige. Thus, some institutions are still modelled on the time-honoured principles of academic elitism and exclusiveness, while others have had to mould alternative identities that have not always favoured their institutional identity.

The emergence of institutional differentiation is perhaps reflected in the different types of activities that different universities are engaged in, their various modes of programme and provision, and the varying profiles of student within them. The higher education White Paper of 2003 explicitly acknowledged the differentiation of universities and called for universities to develop distinctive institutional missions and goals in accordance with their particular profiles. Underpinning this was a further acknowledgement of the divisions between 'teaching' and 'research' institutions, which itself tends to reflect the relative status of different universities. Not only do more 'teaching-led', 'post-1992' institutions tend to have a wider profile of student, often from less traditional backgrounds, but also a wider range of more applied, vocational provisions. At the same time, the more prestigious, research-driven institutions have been encouraged to embark on world-leading research, which normally entails public research funds being selectively channelled towards them. The White Paper was seen by some as serving to reinforce institutional divisions and hierarchies, particularly through advocating the selective channelling of research funding to top-ranked institutions (Jones and Thomas 2005).

The extent to which the plurality and diversity of contemporary mass higher education has resulted in greater parity has often been questioned. A prevailing view has been that the types of programme and provision in new universities have not been given the same level of credence as more traditional universities. As Ainley (1994) argues, new universities have often been perceived as having lower pedagogic and cultural esteem than their more elite counterparts, even though they have been presented as providing the types of vocationally relevant and 'skills-rich' provision that employers say they value. In some cases, less prestigious institutions have tried to model themselves on their more elite counterparts in a process of 'academic drift', even though they were originally conceived on far different grounds.

Globalization, marketization and the new commoditization of universities

The move towards mass systems of higher education across the globe again reflects new forms of pressures to meet changing economic demands, manifest in governments' continued framing of universities as key drivers within a competitive, yet uncertain, global economy. The economic challenges surrounding higher education are not only in the form of restructured labour markets and changing employer demands, but also a fast-changing global environment that has seen the emergence of new global players within emerging economies (Enders and Fulton 2002; King 2004). Universities across the globe have expanded significantly, not least in Asian economies such as China and India, and so has the skills infrastructure within these economies. This presents significant challenges to individual national systems, and the different institutions within them, in terms of responding effectively to the increasingly internationalized higher education market.

The focus on universities' role in aiding national prosperity has also broadened to a focus on responding to increasing challenges from global labour markets and educational systems. The increasingly global interconnectedness of institutional and cultural practices is clearly manifest in higher education. At a global level, not only are universities sharing practices, but they are also competing for resources. Marginson and Van der Wende (2007) have discussed the various dimensions of the globalization of higher education. One of these is the cross-border fluidity between different HEIs, mainly in terms of the flow of knowledge, academic production and collaboration, policy initiatives and institutional activity. The flow of students across national higher education systems is itself reflective of the ways in which HEIs have embraced new international markets. Correspondingly, modes of provision have become increasingly standardized across national systems. Thus, there has been a general convergence in practice across national higher education systems, meaning that HEIs have increasingly harmonized practices in terms of their activities and wider institutional goals. In Europe, for example, the influential Bologna process set out to develop new coordinating policies across EU member states, particularly around institutional governance and student provision. For instance, a key principle behind developing standardized modular and degree programmes was that students could be more mobile and universities could accommodate a wider international student base (Teichler 2004).

Marginson (2008) has also highlighted the inequalities inherent in global higher education, given that HEIs both within and between national systems operate on a largely uneven playing field. Some national systems, and the institutions located within them, are able to broker far stronger levels of influence in the global higher education arena. This is most evident in the increasing institutional hierarchies that have been formed within national and international higher education systems, as evident in the formation of international higher education league tables. This again places new performative pressures on individual HEIs in order for them to be positioned favourably in the new global higher education competitions for resources, students, top academics and, more so, sources of revenue. In effect, national universities have had to become increasingly aware of where they sit within a wider international market context that continually reinforces where institutions are globally 'positioned'. In particular, policymakers and senior managers in higher education increasingly have to mediate these changes and find flexible ways of adapting new global demands to their own specific contexts (Maringe and Foskett 2010). Part of this may involve trying to leverage greater partnership between universities and reaching out to potential student bases across emerging economies.

The increasing global pressures on universities are further reflected in governments' approaches towards the output and intellectual produce that universities generate. In the UK, there has been an explicit emphasis on attuning universities' activities towards the needs of the economy, namely, through high-calibre and appropriately 'skilled' graduates and 'high impact' and innovative forms of research (DFES 2003; DIUS 2008). It has become increasingly common for governments to frame the output value of universities in largely instrumental terms. This again often tends to be set within globalizing discourses in terms of the need for universities to produce the kinds of intellectual capital that will provide national advantages in the global wars for knowledge and innovation. Thus, as drivers of the knowledge-based economy, there are renewed government expectations that universities become 'world leading' rather than 'world following', continually looking to enhance their research and knowledge infrastructures. The emergence of new global elite university players in East Asia, who are increasingly at the forefront of leading-edge research, has very much heightened these demands.

At a more conceptual level, this shifting emphasis reflects a reconceptualizing of the way in which 'knowledge' is understood. The influential work of Gibbons et al. (1994) posits a shift from what might traditionally be seen as Mode 1 knowledge to more applied and context-based Mode 2 knowledge. Universities have been traditionally associated with the first knowledge mode, namely, that which is theoretically abstract and based on disciplinary scholarship and 'pure research'. The emphasis here is mainly on knowledge for 'knowledge's sake' and advancing scholarship for its own intrinsic purposes. Academic output is therefore directed towards the wider academic field and given legitimacy through its value within the wider academic community. Mode 2 knowledge, however, is that which has applied relevance and which can traverse beyond the academic community into numerous spheres of public and commercial life. This type of knowledge is therefore potentially more fluid and adaptable to continued social and economic change; it is knowledge that has a more immediate social and economic 'impact' and can move beyond the confines of the institutions in which it is produced.

The shift from Mode 1 to Mode 2 knowledge production in universities may not be as pronounced as many commentators have described. Much research continues to be pure and based on abstract, theoretical and propositional knowledge. Similarly, truly applied research is likely to be the domain of specific research communities and disciplines that have closer connections to industry, commercial organizations and the wider public. A clear example of this is biomedical research, much of which has strong commercial backing. Nevertheless, the theme of relevance and 'impact' has permeated much discourse on academic scholarship and output, mainly in terms of how it can potentially impact on public and commercial life. The majority of public-funding bodies are keen for research to broaden its wider social and economic impacts, and demonstrate how it will be of broader public benefit.

The increasing commoditization of higher education has not been without its criticisms. Taken together, many of the changes in universities have been seen by some commentators to represent a new ideological creed that is strongly utilitarian in its agenda. Critics of this agenda have warned that universities' end goals have become almost singularly orientated towards economic enhancement and efficiency. Lynch (2006) has discussed some of the more corrosive effects of the neo-liberal agenda on universities, in terms of institutional and the practices and the nature of academic scholarship. She sees the neo-liberal agenda, and its accompanying discourses around privatization, marketization and commoditization, as having penetrated well into the institutional fabric of universities.

A consequence of the neo-liberal agenda in higher education is that HEIs have increasingly to re-image themselves, their goals and practices towards profit enhancement and maximizing positional value and status within a new competitive order. The growing corporate alliance between universities and business has been actively pursued by governments looking to exploit the potential economic trade-off of university knowledge. This inevitably places pressures on universities to engage in the 'right' kinds of knowledge production and scholarship. Knowledge then becomes valued on the basis of its commodity value or utility in fulfilling economic imperatives. Other knowledge that does not have such a role becomes increasingly valueless.

In a similar vein, Barnett (2003) has offered a powerful critique of the new ideological shifts in higher education, particularly in terms of how they engender new value systems and institutional practices that are inimical to the wider intellectual project of universities. Moreover, ideological movements, such as managerialism, entrepreneurialism and competition, have become highly prominent in the drive to make universities more accountable and responsive to their external environment. Significantly, these ideologies have altered universities' overall perspective of where they belong in the wider world. This invokes Harbermas' notion of life-world colonization, which this author has discussed earlier (Barnett 1993). Thus, the value systems and modes of being that traditionally enabled universities to operate as distinct social systems have been overridden by a new set of agendas and imperatives that have challenged the legitimacy of traditional university values and practices. These have largely been derived from the world of commerce and industry, and have been enthusiastically endorsed by policymakers. Furthermore, the values of critical detachment have become superseded by instrumental, short-term goals that potentially undermine traditional modes of being within the university.

For authors such as Barnett and Lynch, ideological shifts towards economization are likely to permeate all aspects of university life, from governance, inter-colleague relationships and scholarship, through to teaching and learning. Operational knowledge based on the instrumental production and acquisition of relevant and applicable knowledge therefore replaces reflective knowledge that is harder to codify and classify. This is also linked to the increasing move towards vocationalization in the university curriculum, with its strong emphasis on 'competency' and 'skills'-based teaching and learning. Relatedly, there is a concern that higher education learning, traditionally orientated to higher-order pursuits and intellectual development, is becoming reduced to the level of training. The value of university learning is increasingly centred on what students and graduates 'can do' in the labour market, rather than on the cultivation of intellectual and citizenship-related dispositions.

Changing academic work and identities

The changing policy and socio-economic context surrounding universities has brought inevitable changes and pressures on the nature of academics' work, including the ways in which they are positioned within this shifting environment. There has been a traditional notion of academics as socially detached and independent specialists who have enjoyed high levels of institutional autonomy. However, increasingly, contemporary academics have been recast as fully accountable professionals who are subject to ever-growing external and internal demands (Kogan and Hanney 2000; Henkel 2000; Reed 2002). Academic professionals have, in turn, had to attune their activities to changing institutional imperatives. Moreover, their work has become subject to stronger levels of regulation and monitoring, designed to ensure that their outputs are aligned to the new institutional climate that includes much greater managerial- and student-level demands. This also entails stronger levels of regulation, often involving compliance to a wide range of institutionally imposed performance indicators and benchmarks (Cave et al. 1997). This is likely to have further implications for how academics perceive their role and attempt to align their practices to the changing institutional landscape. Brennan et al. (2007) have discussed how the contemporary academic profession has increasingly organized itself around the core agendas of 'relevance', 'output' and 'impact'. The move towards accountability, transparency and efficiency appears to be framing how academics understand and organize their work.

A number of reports over time have called for much higher levels of audit and scrutiny over the efficiency, economic value and level of service quality achieved by HEIs (e.g. CVCP 1985; NCHIE 1997). Significant here is a need for improvements in the ways that universities are organized and managed in order that they optimize their economic efficiency. Stronger levels of managerial control are seen as an effective means of inducing the desired performance outputs that are in keeping with the increasing economic imperatives and pressures on HEIs. Research on the impacts of managerialism in universities (Deem et al. 2007; Deem and Brehony 2005) has shown that academics perceive themselves to be under increasing scrutiny from managers, often with accompanying concerns over their value and legitimacy as academics. At the same time, they have also witnessed an intensification of their work and attendant pressures to fulfil an ever-increasing range of managerially imposed tasks and duties. This has largely been reinforced by the growing privatization of universities through student fees and greater student expectations in the current higher education market.

It is also clear from such research that greater numbers of academics are taking on hybrid roles as academic managers, whose roles encompass both traditional academic activities and substantial administrative ones (Henkel 2000). Winter's (2009) research illustrates how academics making the transition to management are not only attracted to the status and added academic capital it offers, but also the opportunities for pursuing strategic change. Many are aware of the high levels of status and responsibility it carries, even though some are more attached to their traditional academic roots than others. Research by Wallace et al. (2011) has reported that academic managers are also likely to perceive themselves as playing crucial roles in helping to align professional colleagues' work towards the new institutional challenges and priorities now facing HEIs. Moreover, senior academic managers have been shown to perceive themselves as key institutional actors in facilitating widespread sector-based and institutional-level changes, as well as being a significant link between government policy and the wider academic community.

The academic labour market has been shown to operate within a clearly defined field of power that reflects differences in status, power and prestige (Bourdieu 1988). Academics continue to be positioned in terms of their relative levels of institutional capital, autonomy and status in what has been shown to be a clearly stratified academic labour market (Musselin 2005; Locke and Teichler 2007). However, the changing external environment has somewhat redrawn the way in which academics themselves are positioned within this environment. The shift from collegial to managerial modes of internal governance has altered the 'rules' through which academics are able to acquire academic capital in order to enhance their positional status with the wider academic field (Halsey 1992). The new institutional climate of accountability and performance management has compelled academic professionals to rethink strategies for their own career enhancement and how to enhance their institutional capital. As Henkel's research on academic careers has illustrated, those academics who are adept at fulfilling new performative imperatives, in terms of research, teaching and other administrative output, have been favourably rewarded within the new institutional climate.

For some academics, the increasing alignment of universities to the commercial sector has allowed them to embrace new identities and practices that have a more entrepreneurial and utilitarian dimension than the traditional ones of pure scholarship (Slaughter and Lesley 1997; Jary and Parker 1998). In some cases, independent and pure scholarship has been replaced by what Slaughter and Lesley (1997) describe as a new form of 'academic capitalism'. Academic capitalists are orientated towards exploiting the commercial potential of their knowledge production and finding possible economic trade-off from what they produce in universities. Such shifts carry implications for the way in which academic cultures, professionalism and work-related identities are articulated and developed. As such, knowledge production takes on a far more utilitarian dimension and the academic is imbued with more entrepreneurial values and outlooks.

Research has shown the ways in which the various policy drifts associated with marketization, commoditization and managerialism have affected academics' self-perceptions and values around their work (Trowler 1998; Jary and Parker 1998; Henkel 2000, 2005). Both Trowler's and Henkel's research in a range of HEIs has illustrated academics' increasing attempts to align their practices to meet new institutional pressures and demands; not only those from managers, auditors and government intermediaries, but also from colleagues and students. In turn, many have become much more strategic and instrumental in the development of their career profiles and outputs. As Trowler's research shows, contemporary academics have had to adopt more strategic approaches to their career development, including a more careful reading of the wider external policy environment. Academic managers, in particular, have had to carefully read the shifting policy agenda and find creative ways of appropriating this to their own institutional contexts. This has invariably refashioned many academics' identities and self-perceptions, and many have had to abandon traditional approaches to research and teaching as a response to increasing pressures.

Changes to academics' work have been interpreted with a strong degree of pessimism by some commentators (Davies and Petersen 2005; Sikes 2009). These authors have discussed the increasing standardization and routinization of the academic labour process and the attendant erosion of independent scholarly pursuit. Thus, the shifting institutional climate has helped produce new academic labour divisions between those who seek to resist new imperatives and those who abide by the increasingly economistic rules of the game. These critics also discuss the gradual submission of academics' work to an overarching neo-liberal agenda that is inherently at odds with the traditional goals and values of academic scholarship. Academic freedom has traditionally been linked to critical detachment and challenging dominant ideological agendas, yet these freedoms have been undermined by the increasing embrace of such agendas.

It is clear that all academics have been more keenly experiencing the various 'pressure points' from internal and external demands. This has been found to be especially evident among younger academic professionals who have not necessarily experienced the previous conditions of earlier generations of academics (Archer 2008). Archer's research clearly demonstrated how new academic professionals had actively internalized the wider neo-liberal and managerialist discourses around performance output and quality assurance. This was perceived not only as an inevitable reality in contemporary academic work, but also as something they needed to professionally align themselves towards. Indeed, all were critical of 'golden age' notions of unaccountable and cosseted institutional academic practices.

It was also evident that many of these younger academics were of the belief that a compromise was needed between fulfilling more managerialist agendas and pursuing academic projects that were of personal and intrinsic value to them. This research resonates with Henkel's (2000) earlier research, which showed that academics were keen to reconcile their personally held academic goals and values with the more pervasive short-term goals of managerial audit and accountability. Moreover, most academics were found to harbour strong allegiances to their native academic communities and disciplines around which their initial academic identities had been formed. The identities that academics look to develop and invest in still appear to be largely derived from the 'communitarian' spaces of their disciplines and substantive subject areas. Traditional ideals around scholarship and developing substantive academic interests, therefore, still appear to inform academics' motivations and values around their work. Nevertheless, this has become bounded by the changing policy climate.

In discussing the 'vexed' issue of academic identities, Clegg (2008) points to more optimistic ways forward in relation to the reshaping of academics' work. This may entail reconciling wider institutional challenges with the wider intellectual project they seek to pursue, and around defining the wider purpose of their work. The new performative and managerialist agenda does not necessarily have to represent a constraining challenge or threat among the academic community; indeed, many academics have been able to use it to their advantage. Clegg argues that while a significant number of academics may be critical of the new managerialism, and its related audit culture, this has not always constrained their scholarly pursuits. Many academics have experienced the development of hybrid roles; roles that encompass a range of different managerial-administrative, pedagogical and scholarly endeavours. Hybridity is perhaps part of the super-complex and post-modern world that universities increasingly inhabit, and to which academics need to respond. The key challenge for contemporary academics is perhaps being able to creatively mediate new policy pressures while still carving out personal spaces for academic freedom and autonomy. This may involve developing complementary interplays between the different facets of their academic make-up and identity.

Students, graduates and the changing higher education experience

A changing student experience of higher education

Wider socio-economic and institutional changes to higher education have clearly had a profound bearing on the experience of being a student in higher education. In the middle part of the twentieth century, the academic and cultural profile of students was more homogeneous. Many of these students' earlier educational experiences served to affirm what seemed to be an inevitable trajectory towards higher education and the professions. This was largely based on the formation of positive learner identities during formal education and the sense that they were part of a relatively small academic minority. While, as Silver and Silver (1997) point out, there has been a tendency to overly caricature previous generations of students in elite higher education, students in previous decades nevertheless tended to follow more established routes towards higher education. Ainley (1994) has discussed how the relatively elite and exclusive nature of higher education studentship at this time is likely to have framed students' university experiences as relatively distinct and forming something of an elite cognitive apprenticeship. Furthermore, the strong emphasis on acquiring academic knowledge to build intellectual capacities for professional and managerial jobs served to reinforce traditional students' self-perceptions of being part of a select academic and future occupational elite.

The expansion of the higher education sector in terms of the growth of institutions, new types of programmes and student numbers has challenged these traditional notions of studentship. Mass higher education encompasses a more heterogeneous mixture of 'new' learners and mode of study. Students' routes towards higher education, and their experiences in it, are no longer typical and widely shared (McNay 2006). However, mass higher education still contains a large proportion of 'traditional' students who share similar intellectual and cultural characteristics to previous generations. However, it has also increasingly opened up to new and diverse groups of students, including those from lower socio-economic backgrounds, mature students, part-time students and distance learners. Again, we can see that elements of elite and mass higher education coexist in the wider university system, as reflected in the contrasting profiles of students and the assortment of different HEIs. However, we have also seen that the main participants in higher education are those from higher socio-economic groups. It is evident that newer universities and those with lower entry requirements still attract a disproportionately higher share of students from lower socio-economic backgrounds, including students from ethnic backgrounds and mature students (Connor et al. 2001).

It would appear that social class continues to have a major bearing on shaping students' orientations to higher education, including their choice of university and general perspectives while participating in higher education. Research by Archer et al. (2003) and Reay et al. (2006) quite clearly demonstrates the link between students' class profiles and their choice of university. Their research has found that the pre-existing levels of social and cultural capital that prospective students have at their disposal is significant in informing the types of universities and courses that students choose. Significantly, prospective students were often very discerning over the class-cultural context and constitution of many universities, and the degree of cultural match between their own profiles and potential institutions.

Students' choices and attitudes towards university, therefore, appear to be socially patterned on the basis of their existing cultural resources and knowledge, and informed by implicit perceptions of what is 'right for them'. Inevitably, some students' university horizons may encompass a limited range of institutions, some of which may be of lower status and rank. Indeed, research by Vignoles et al. (2008) found that, even among higher-achieving students from lower socio-economic backgrounds, there may be a tendency to preclude a higher-status institution which was perceived not to correspond that comfortably with their existing educational experiences.

Irrespective of the continued social divisions in mass higher education, most contemporary students are likely to encounter new types of experiences and challenges that are different from previous generations. Brennan and Osborne (2008) have discussed the new forms of diversity that have come to characterize students' experiences of the mass higher education landscape. At one level, this may take the form of *institutional diversity* as reflected in the different cultures, missions, size and modes of study that operate in different institutional contexts. Some institutions, for example, also have a higher proportion of residential-based and commuting students, varying links to their wider community and sometimes based in markedly different geo-social locations. Mass higher education also encompasses what they see as a distinctive *horizontal diversity*, based on the factors relating to an institution's perceived reputation, historical legacy and success on a range of state-led measures, such as research and teaching outcomes. Such diversity is likely to strongly influence students' perceptions of where they sit in the wider higher education field and their wider experience of being a student.

There is also a range of other factors that mark the contemporary experience of higher education. Students increasingly learn in larger groups and with less one-to-one pastoral support as a consequence of the decline in the staff–student ratio. At the same time, there have been far-reaching developments in the structure of academic learning, not only in terms of academic programmes but also in the forms through which learning is conducted. Increasingly, students are able to exercise greater choice through the advent of modular programmes as well as through new modes of virtual learning and accessibility to a broader range of online resources. Similarly, there has been a rapid increase in different modes of provision, including an increase in part-time study, distance learning, foundation degree programmes and flexibility in delivery, not least through further education colleges. In the context of a more globalized system, HEIs have also opened themselves up to more international students and now have a much greater international feel to them.

It would appear, however, that the actual lived experience of university is far from uniform among students. Brennan et al. (2009) show through their research on the social dynamics of learning in higher education that students not only enter higher education with a broad range of motivations and learning profiles, but also have different experiences during higher education. It is clear that some students have more isolated, individualized experiences and may not feel fully part of their university community. This may be shaped by their specific institutional and disciplinary contexts, some of which may lend themselves to more collective and shared experiences. Their research, as well as others (Holdsworth 2006) also found that students tended to attribute high value to the social dimensions of university experience in terms of friendships, life skills and social development. This was often seen as being as important, if not more, than their academic development.

Non-traditional students in higher education, particularly mature students, have been shown to find difficulties in making the transition to higher education and adjusting the wider aspects of their lives, including family life, to their new situation as students (Crozier et al. 2008). Indeed, mature students may bring forward fractured learner identities based on previous levels of low academic achievement (Crossan et al. 2003). Research by Leathwood and O'Connell (2003) shows how the 'new' type of higher education student, including working-class and mature students, have been shown to experience various challenges, insecurities and 'struggles' in trying to adapt to a seemingly alien cultural world. For some 'new' students, adjustment to this new lifestyle is never quite achieved and the university experience remains a challenging one. For others, a sense of personal and cultural emancipation may occur as they begin to identify with and become absorbed in their new cultural environment.

Research on mature students' experiences of higher education has shown their experiences to be significantly varied and indicative of discernible differences in educational biography (James 1995; Waller 2006). As James argues, there has often been a tendency to depict all mature students into a single 'species' of student. Again, students' relative social-class profile is likely to frame how they adapt and fit into the academic and cultural environs of university, and many bring forward contrasting pre-existing profiles and identities.

One particular feature of the new higher education landscape is the growing financial pressures on students. Since the advent of tuition fees in the late 1990s and the more recent moves towards raising the level of graduate financial contribution with the lifting of fee levels, students have become more acutely aware of the immediate and future financial challenges they face. Callender's (2008) research has revealed the upsurge in students working part-time in order to meet the financial challenges of studying in university. This research has reported the challenges that students face in finding a balance between academic study and paid employment; in some cases, the latter significantly encroaches on students' study time and quality and their level of commitment to their formal studies. While students appear to be adopting pragmatic approaches to paid employment during higher education, sometimes couching it in terms of potential marketable work experience, it has also been shown to impede academic engagement. This may particularly be the case when such employment takes up a considerable period of a student's working week. Students with less familial resources and existing economic capital are also more likely to have to embark more extensively on paid employment during study.

Perhaps more than any other time, students in higher education have had to be more strategic and instrumental in their approach, given that there are stronger elements of risk and challenge to being a student and, subsequently, a graduate. The increased marketization and commoditization of higher education, and its reframing as a positional good, are likely to have a significant bearing on how students understand their participation in higher education (Morley 2003; Naidoo and Jamieson 2005). For some commentators and researchers, this signals increasingly consumerist approaches to learning on the part of students. The current higher education student may be more likely to see themselves as a consumer of a service or a product that is supplied within a mixed economy of provider institutions. As such, values towards higher education experience may increasingly be based on its perceived role in enhancing their future labour market outcomes. Consequently, students are not only likely to be more discerning about the nature and quality of provision they receive, but they may also demand new forms of pre-packaged, accessible and commoditized knowledge.

Naidoo and Jamieson (2005) have outlined the problems with consumerist approaches to higher education. They point to the short-termist, outcome-driven approach to learning that this promotes, particularly in terms of the devaluing of learning and the developmental aspect of independent study. Consumer-driven learning is principally about the acquisition and market exploitation of credentials rather than the advancement of cohesive learning dispositions. The quest to seek immediate market relevance from learning may, however, be to the detriment of students' personal and intellectual development. Consumerist learning may actually be corrosive to learning and foster attitudes that are at odds with the needs of a flexible, knowledge economy. These authors also argue that a consumerist agenda in higher education may further exacerbate the positional and status differences between HEIs. A new hierarchical division may emerge between traditional institutions that are insulated from consumerist struggles, based on existing prestige, and those who have to battle it out for a share of the new student market. The former are likely to continue to engage in a broad curriculum that is of benefit to learners whereas the latter increasingly engage in a short-term, pre-packaged curriculum that is of limited intrinsic value.

Higher education and the changing graduate labour market

The changing economic context around higher education has also had a considerable bearing on students' post-university experience and outcomes. Once depicted by Kelsall et al. (1972) as a 'social elite' who occupied the best social and economic positions, their place in the economy has become increasingly ambiguous. The relatively close coupling between higher education and the labour market during elite higher education has been significantly disrupted. This relationship is no longer characterized by elite graduates entering a limited preserve of elite management-level jobs within clearly defined corporate career structures (Brown and Hesketh 2004).

Harvey (2000) has highlighted how the interaction between higher education and the labour market has been reconfigured through a combination of corporate restructuring, including changing recruitment practices, and the sheer volume and diversity of graduates entering the labour market. The traditional consensus that universities regulated future occupational elites has, therefore, been challenged by organizational changes and the advancement of mass higher education. Consequently, graduates making the transition from university to the job market have had to reframe their employment expectations and approaches. An increasing emphasis by policymakers, employers and HEIs themselves has been on how *employable* graduates are when entering the labour market.

These changes have a significant bearing on the relationship between students' participation in higher education and their future labour market outcomes. A university education is now far less of a clear institutional passage towards specific types of 'graduate' jobs. This, in turn, has both reshaped graduates' access to professional and management-level jobs as well as the ways in which they understand their employment futures more generally. Traditional notions of *graduateness* were often associated with possession of relatively distinctive and elite credentials that were held in limited reserve. Yet, degree credentials are no longer taken as a clear marker of a particular academic and cultural identity that confers clear cultural and economic advantages onto its holders.

In the context of mass higher education, the process of acquiring a degree-level qualification is no longer something of a *status-confirmation* for middle-class achievements and qualities that have been validated and reproduced through elite forms of education (Bourdieu and Passerson 1979). In effect, degree-level credentials have become less of a 'badge of distinction' that confirm specific forms of cultural capital possessed by a relatively privileged few. In turn, they have increasingly lost their potency in shaping graduates' future employment outcomes and many students and graduates have become increasingly aware of this (Tomlinson 2008; Brooks and Everett 2009). It appears that, while many graduates see their investment in higher education as providing positional advantages in the job market, they are also aware of the need to add value to their educational and future employment profiles. Table 9.1 illustrates the shifting relationship between

Table 9.1 Shifting relationships between higher education and labour market

Mode of higher education	Relationship to labour market
Elite higher education	

• Middle-class participation
• Traditional 'academic' student
  ○ Participation as a form of cultural reproduction
• Liberal conception of learning
	• Traditional graduate careers
	  ○ Stable job markets/career structures
	• Graduate as social and occupational 'elite'
	• Loose integration of graduate knowledge in work organizations

Mass higher education	
• New heterogeneous student base • Participation an investment for economic ends • Preparation for labour market and vocational development • Credential inflation	• New diversity in graduate occupations • More flexible job market/ruptured career structures • Changing employer demands; move towards 'employability and 'marketability'Employability pressures and positional competition among graduates

higher education and the labour market in the transitions from elite to mass higher education.

The historical depiction of elite graduates entering elite jobs was clearly more relevant at a time when graduates formed a more distinctive social group and when they entered a clear 'graduate labour market'. In this context, a graduate career was shorthand for the sort of secure, high-status, well-paid and rewarding jobs found within various well-defined professional and management-level fields. It also implies a segmented labour market that draws upon the elite knowledge and skills of a particular group. Doctors, lawyers and civil servants, as well as a range of middle managers who were fast-tracked to senior positions, were all viewed as archetypes of the 'graduate career'. However, the idea of the 'graduate labour market' that graduates move seamlessly into has been significantly challenged through higher education-related and labour market shifts.

Writing in the early 1990s, Brown and Scase (1994) discussed the decline of the traditional 'bureaucratic career' that many graduates embarked upon for relatively lengthy periods of their working lives. This has been a consequence of far-reaching corporate restructuring, organizational redesign and shifting recruitment practices in an organizational context where patterns of career progression have been reshaped. The gradual restructuring of corporations away from bureaucratic to more flexible modes of organizational efficiency has had significant implications for the way in which organizations manage their human resources as well as the nature of managers' and professionals' career progression. Indeed, as Adamson et al. (1998) have argued, it is no longer the case that companies take a long-term approach to graduate-level careers, planning graduates' progression through well-defined career stages.

Purcell and Pitcher's (1998) and Elias and Purcell's (2004) research has illustrated the new diversity of graduate jobs and the broad range of occupational fields that graduates are likely to enter. At one level, this reflects different labour market outcomes and pathways, including those divided on gender lines. Their research also shows that graduates occupy a broad range of occupational fields, only some of which match the archetypal 'traditional' graduate profession. Increasingly, graduate occupations encompass an increasing amount of *new*, *modern* and *niche* forms of graduate employment, including graduate sales managers, marketers, PR officers and IT executives.

A key question that has occupied researchers in this area is the extent to which graduates are experiencing a fair return on their investment in higher education. Research has shown a mixed picture. At one level, longitudinal research has revealed positive overall returns among graduates (see Elias and Purcell 2004; Schomburg and Teichler 2006). Such research indicates that graduate earnings have remained stable over time and that the supply of graduates is matched by their economic demand. Graduates continue to enjoy a so-called 'graduate premium' over non-graduates, as reflected in both higher earnings and wider job market scope. It also illustrates graduates' relative utilization of the skills and credentials acquired through university and generally positive views on the role of higher education in facilitating access to jobs. This would also suggest that higher education is a worthwhile investment for graduates whose credentials are acknowledged and valued in the labour market.

However, other research has shown marked disparities between graduates in terms of their earnings, their access to particular jobs and the matching-up of their existing credentials and skills in the job market. The Brown and Hesketh (2004) research has highlighted discernible differences in graduates' experiences and outcomes, particularly within increasingly competitive and crowded labour markets. What is clear from such research is that not all graduates are likely to fare equally or favourably in high-stakes and tough-entry forms of employment and whose profiles do not match employers' increasing recruitment demands. This has been confirmed by other research (Lauder et al. 2005; Smetherham 2006), which highlights disparities in graduates' financial and job-related returns, the latter showing clear gender differences in earnings and opportunities. Significantly, there appear to be marked differences *among* graduates in their labour market returns. Research that has disaggregated graduates' employment returns has shown significant income disparities between top-, middle- and bottom-earning graduates (Green and Zhu 2010). Significantly, bottom-earning graduates may not necessarily fare better than many non-graduates and may find themselves struggling to attain equitable returns over time.

Graduates' returns, outcomes and experiences in the job market are also shown to be linked closely to key factors around class, gender and ethnicity. Furlong and Cartmel (2005) point to evidence of lower overall job market returns among students from lower socio-economic backgrounds, as well as overall patterns of social exclusion from the more elite and exclusively middle-class labour market. Conversely, Power and Whitty (2006) show continued patterns of sociocultural advantage among more privileged graduates, including those who have graduated from elite universities and attended prestigious schools. Such graduates were shown to command higher wage returns and access relatively high-profile and exclusive jobs. Moreover, they are clearly more able to exploit their existing social contacts and networks, generally approaching the job market with considerable confidence and personal resources.

Universities and employers

The various changes in the higher education–labour market relationship have not escaped the attention of policymakers and employers. At one level, higher education has continually been presented by policymakers as a significant investment in human capital that will yield longer-term benefits for individuals and the economy as a whole. This, in many ways, has driven the programme of university expansion. However, at another level, there are continued concerns that both universities and their graduates are falling short of labour market demands. Indeed, increasing pressures have been placed on universities to meet the needs of the labour market and nurture the types of skills that graduates need to draw upon in their future employment. In short, HEIs' activities have been seen to be not in tune with the flexible and fast-changing economic context in which graduates work.

Research on employers' perceptions of graduates' employability on leaving university again shows a variable and complex picture. Employers' perception of graduates has sometimes been characterized by discontent, as evident in a range of employer surveys over time (see the Association of Graduate Recruiters 2009; CBI 2011). The message tends to be fairly straightforward: graduates are not fully fit-for-purpose and there is a general mismatch between the skills they acquire through university and those required in the labour market. It has become very clear that employers demand more than the traditional academic skills associated with a degree, although precisely what skills is not always clear.

The nature of graduate skills, and their development and transfer in the labour market has been shown to be particularly problematic. Various researchers (Archer and Davison 2008; Mason et al. 2009) have shown that there is unlikely to be any clear compatibility between skills acquired in university and those required in the job market. This is partly due to the broad profile of skills that employers demand and the fact that skills are highly dependent on context. It would, therefore, appear that whatever skills are formally taught and practiced in an educational setting are not necessarily easily transferred into employment, irrespective of how seemingly closely matched and transferable such skills might appear to be.

Research over time has indicated that employers generally want graduates to demonstrate a wide range of 'attributes' relating to the various interpersonal, communicative, behavioural and decision-making dimensions of their jobs (Harvey et al. 1997; Hesketh 2000). These are likely to encompass attributes such as self-motivation, confidence, resilience and risk taking. Significantly, the various attributes that graduates bring to the labour market appear to reflect the value and potential impact they have within employer organizations. This may work across a wider range of domains, whether in terms of dealing with customers, managing teams, selling and marketing products or managing independent projects. This research, therefore, highlights that employers place considerable value and emphasis on graduates' behavioural and personal qualities. These have been taken to be as important, if not more, than their technical and academic skills.

The demonstration of soft skills and values, including commitment, motivation and self-efficacy therefore appears to be given significant weighting in the labour market, both in recruitment and beyond (York and Knight 2006). Research by Hinchliffe and Jolly (2011) on employers' values and demands clearly illustrates that many recruiters look to engage with the broader identities of graduates. Employers clearly expect graduates to be able to 'perform' successfully in the operational sense. But they also appear to want graduates' performance to be underpinned by broader personal and identity-related dispositions that positively reflect company goals and values. This research showed that graduate recruiters are particularly keen to examine the values, ethical awareness, political interests and intellectual make-up of the graduate. These tend to be referenced against the specific context of their organization and the values and modes of practice that are embedded in them. It may, therefore be imperative that graduates look to engage their prospective employees with wider facets of their identity and personal make-up.

Other research on graduate recruitment has illustrated the various cultural dynamics that underpin employer decisions to recruit graduates. Brown and Hesketh's (2004) research explored the various criteria that employers use to inform their recruitment decisions. In an increasingly competitive graduate labour market, graduate recruiters have extended the remit of their recruitment decision in the quest to win the 'war for talent'. This invariably means that some graduates will be at a greater advantage than others, often depending on the resources they possess. The above research has exposed some of the inequalities that exist among graduates around accessing desired forms of employment. This appears to be particularly the case in more elite organizations where the cultural profile of the graduate is likely to shape their outcomes in recruitment and beyond. Employers appear inclined to seek some kind of 'social fit' between the graduate and their organizations.

Significantly, their research illustrated that employers favour graduates who can project a dynamic set of 'employability narratives'. These narratives not only encompass their hard currencies in the form of academic credentials, but also a broad range of experiential, interpersonal and behavioural assets – what they term as graduates' 'personal capital'. To this extent, employers' recruitment decisions are not necessarily rational and objective, and instead often relate to deep-seated cultural biases towards particular 'types' of graduate. It therefore becomes increasingly imperative that graduates are able to decode employers' recruitment criteria and package their profiles towards this criteria.

However, when approaching the labour market, and particularly elite organizations, not all graduates have the resources – educational, cultural, experiential and interpersonal – to negotiate tough entry jobs. Moreover, in their search for the best pool of talent, employers' invariably bias towards graduates from more elite universities as these are seen to potentially add the most value to organizations and potentially take on the role of future organizational leaders and elites (Morley 2007).

The changing nature of the graduate labour market and employers' changing recruitment practices therefore presents significant challenges for students and graduates. These changes appear to have become internalized by contemporary students and graduates who are aware of the greater challenges they face. A number of features now appear to underpin contemporary graduates' perceptions of the labour market and the relationship between their participation in higher education and future labour market outcomes. Research has shown that contemporary graduates anticipate their labour market trajectories to follow less certain and more flexible pathways in the context of what is perceived to be a high-risk, hazardous and challenging labour market for the highly qualified (Tomlinson 2007; Moreau and Leathwood 2006). The traditional views of a stable, longer-term corporate career have increasingly given way to expectations of more piecemeal, protean career trajectories that entail marked disruption and mobility between jobs and across the job market. In short, graduates are aware of the need to more actively manage their future employability and career profiles.

In the context of significant levels of competition among the highly qualified, graduates also perceive a decline in the value of university credentials in shaping future employment opportunities and outcomes. They are aware that they are positioned in relative terms to other graduates with very similar academic profiles. Consequently, they perceive a need to add value to their credentials in order to achieve positional advantages in higher-stakes labour markets (Tomlinson 2007, 2008; Brooks and Everett 2009). Tomlinson's and Brooks and Everett's research showed that while graduates attribute value to the additional 'human capital' acquired through higher education, they nonetheless perceive this to play an increasingly limited part in their wider employability narratives. Instead, graduates are more likely to frame their employability around the accruement of additional value-added credentials that convey wider aspects of their profile and future marketability. As such, they have become increasingly concerned with enriching their experiences in order to construct and package an employability narrative that is attractive to potential employers. Part of this strategy involves engaging and undertaking wider experiences beyond their formal studies and acquiring additional facets to their profile that will allow them to 'stand apart' from other graduates. Graduates are also aware of the importance of soft skills and behavioural competences, particularly during recruitment.

The evidence, therefore, shows that graduates making the transition from higher education to work are sensitive to the challenges they face in integrating into the labour market and enriching their potential employability. It also shows that graduates approach their future employment, and the management of their employability, in different ways. The theme of identity is significant here. The types of identities that graduates develop around future work and careers appear to have a significant bearing on how they approach the job market and manage their own individual employability. In some cases, students whose life goals are more centred around work and careers invariably take a more proactive and strategic approach to the management of their employability.

Chapter summary

This chapter has explored the wider social and economic context surrounding higher education, and its impacts on institutions, academics, students and graduates. The shifting relationship between higher education, society, economy and state has given way to marked transformations in universities' perceived role and purpose. These transformations have reshaped HEIs and affected the work of the professionals working in them. Moreover, they have had profound impacts on students' experiences of higher education, the transition from higher education to work, as well as their wider outcomes in the labour market. The massification of higher education has been viewed as a key movement towards expanding opportunities and life chances to a greater number of people. The changing shape of higher education has clearly had a bearing on the lived experiences of students, many of whom have the challenge of balancing study with paid employment. The recoupling between mass higher education and an increasingly disparate labour market for the highly qualified has also presented new challenges for graduates making the transition to work.

In the context of a more market-driven and globally orientated system, HEIs have experienced more pressures from government and business to meet the needs of challenges set by the wider external environment. This, in turn, has entailed greater pressures on universities to engage in practices that may best serve social and economic needs. Within this context, universities have become increasingly accountable to the many stakeholders they serve and have had to adapt accordingly. All these changes have taken place in the context of renewed debates over the wider role of universities, particularly as they become increasingly privatized, and the extent to which their status as 'public goods' can be sustained in light of the many challenges they face.

CHAPTER TEN

Conclusions

This book has sought to map the complex and challenging terrain around which systems of education and work operate, and some of the key conceptual themes that have informed this area. As we have seen, there are many contrasting and sometimes opposing perspectives on how the relationships between education and work might be understood. Yet, the interaction between education and the economy is a complex one on a number of different levels. First is the precise way in which educational processes and outcomes feed into economic activities and outcomes at both a social and individual level. Second are the ways in which individuals negotiate this relationship and look to use their educational experiences and outcomes to shape future employment opportunities. Both these processes have become increasingly complicated through wider patterns of educational and economic change.

The wider context is very significant to these discussions, not least the challenges of economic globalization, the renewed role of national governments in coordinating education policy, and the advances in the information and 'knowledge-driven' society. All these entail potential opportunities, yet also considerable challenges for individuals and institutions. The changing political economy resulting from economic globalization has not only redrawn the traditional lines between labour markets and national states, but also the power balance between economic actors. The scale and pace of change in emerging economies, and the gradual enhancement of their skills and educational infrastructures, have profound implications for the future economic opportunities in many Western economies. It is also forcing Western nation states to begin formulating strategies about how to establish a positive economic platform within the new competitive political-economic order. Inevitably, attention has been focused on the reform of educational institutions as education continues to be positioned centrally in wider discourses of economic progress.

The move towards a post-industrial economy has also generated challenges for both educational systems and work organizations. This relates to the types of skills, knowledge and credentials that people draw upon within the work process, as well as the nature of their work experiences and career progression within more flexible labour market contexts. The increasing flexibilization of the labour process entails changes in how individuals think about and plan careers, and the role that continued education and 'lifelong learning' has in shaping opportunities. More emphasis has indeed been placed on the development and management of individual employability as careers become reframed as individualized life projects that have to be carefully managed. Lifelong learning is therefore an increasingly dominant motif in the changing context of work in terms of greater responsibilities for individuals to enrich their career profile and stock of human capital. Formal education is not a finite point in the acquisition of specific credentials that facilitate access to a specific job; instead, the development of one's career profile is increasingly an ongoing project that occurs at many different phases of the work cycle.

We have seen how the transition process from education to work has become more challenging and complex, in terms of not only navigating pathways from education into employment, but also accessing appropriate forms of work. Increasing numbers of school-leavers and university graduates have witnessed extensions to the period from when they leave school and university to establishing longer-terms careers. When they do enter the labour market, their futures are now likely to be played out in far less patterned ways and they continually have to manage the challenges of working in a flexible labour market context.

Debates around the changing nature of work relate strongly to another theme explored in this book – that of individualization. The individualization of experience, biography, life trajectory and working life has entailed greater responsibility for individuals to navigate their way through riskier and less certain labour market terrain. This has also taken place within a context of labour market contraction, risk and wide-scale organizational reconfiguration. Individualization as a process and experience necessitates new forms of self-responsibilization or, to invoke Foucault's (1986) conceptualizing, self-regulation, self-disciplining and autonomy. The self becomes a productive resource in shaping life opportunities, and people's capacity to negotiate economic challenges is increasingly contingent on the utility of personal resources and technologies. This clearly extends to the kinds of labour market resources, capitals and credentials that people bring forward to the labour market and how they work on these in order to optimize chances.

Wider macro-level changes have also corresponded with a pervasive ideological climate of neo-liberalism and, with it, substantial pressures for educational institutions. The attendant thrust towards marketization and institutional competition within many national educational systems has been matched by heightened pressures from nation states in coordinating educational policies designed to meet economic interests. The neo-liberal project, therefore, provokes the need for educational institutions and their key actors – professionals, managers and learners – to be both more enterprising and market orientated, while at the same time being more complicit with stringent forms of state regulation, assessment and accountability.

There are, however, some potential paradoxes in dominant policy orthodoxies; not least in the narrow technicist solutions that have been presented to meet wider economic challenges and the production of a fit-for-purpose future workforce. We have seen throughout this book that dominant policy orthodoxy has been on the supply-side development of educational systems to enhance workforce employability and productivity. This has not, however, necessarily resulted in significant structural and pedagogical reformations in ways that might bring about the kinds of 'creative destruction' (Schumpter 1976) needed to meet shifting economic paradigms. The increasing economization of education has, nonetheless, significantly reframed educational goals, purposes and values. Moreover, it has reshaped the experiences and values of learners and educational professionals. We have seen that the technocratic agenda has resulted in a recasting of professionals as operative commodity producers in the production of appropriately skilled workers.

The policy approach of human capital and employability tends to underplay many significant variables in how people's educational experiences and subsequent labour market experiences are mediated. While human capital models place much more emphasis on the so-called 'embodied human attributes' in terms of skills, knowledge and competences, they don't always consider other 'human' factors relating to individuals' agency. Human capital is a model of human production and output rather than one of reflexive and identity-driven action. The identities that people develop through their educational profiles and their wider cultural experiences are crucial in how people understand, and come to value, their participation in education. Moreover, it will affect how they approach the labour market, including the management of their employability.

Identities, therefore, connect many issues in the education–work dynamic, not least in terms of the way people approach learning and position it towards future work. Agency is a significant component of identity as it relates to the goals and values that individuals develop around their labour market future. At the same time, significant aspects of people's identities are socially reproduced through broader cultural experiences relating to class and gender, which, in turn, are strongly mediated through people's formal and informal education. This shapes agency in terms of the goals people set, the opportunities they anticipate and how adept they might be in negotiating access to different types of employment.

The changing relationship between education, state and the economy has been particularly manifest in higher education as this institution has witnessed marked changes since the latter part of the twentieth century. Successive governments have looked to harness higher education towards neo-liberal goals: higher education has gradually been repositioned as a key economic driver that produces globally commodified credentials. This, in turn, has significant implications for the goals and values of higher education. Many critics have argued that the reframing of higher education as a market commodity based on private investment within internally differentiated markets, has served to marginalize the traditional 'public good' values of universities. All roads have increasingly led to market competition, investment and employability, and at a time when state commitment to performance in higher education has declined. The global commodification of universities inevitably has implications for students and graduates as they are encouraged to view their learning as an investment and their credentials as marketable goods that have potentially significant economic purchase. However, a new consumer-driven approach to learning based on short-term forms of instrumental rationality is not necessarily in tune with the needs of a flexible economy, where productive and positive forms of continued learning are required.

The shift from elite to mass higher education perhaps represents more than a social-democratic consensus that has extended opportunities to a wider social demographic. It also represents increased social demand for university-level credentials and this itself maps onto changes in the class and occupational structures. Within the expanded middle classes, more and more individuals are investing economic and personal capital in higher education as a way of securing future rewards. The paradox is that while a higher education continues to be a route towards better employment opportunities, these opportunities have been pursued more vigorously by increasing numbers of individuals who might not have traditionally enjoyed these opportunities. Consequently, higher levels of competition, market congestion and inter-class conflict have ensued, set against a stratified and differentiated higher education structure. This clearly feeds through to the graduate labour market and the different ways in which graduates are managing their future employment expectations and goals.

BIBLIOGRAPHY

Abell, P. (1991) *Rational Choice Theory*. Aldershot: Brockfield.

Adamson, S. J., Doherty, N. and Viney, C. (1998) 'The Meanings of Career Revisited: implications for theory and practice', *British Journal of Management*, 9: 251–9.

Ainley, P. (1988) *From School to YTS: Education and training in England and Wales from 1944–1987*. Milton Keynes: Open University Press.

—(1993) *Class and Skill: changing divisions of knowledge and labour*. London: Cassell.

—(1994) *Degrees of Difference*. London: Lawrence Washart.

—(1999) *Towards a Learning or a Certified Society?* London: UCL Press.

Ainscow, M., Booth, T. and Dyson, A. (2006) *Improving Schools, Developing Inclusion*. London: Routledge.

Alheit, P. (2005) 'Stories and Structures: an essay on historical time, narrative and their hidden impact on adult learning', *Studies in the Education of Adults*, 37(2): 201–12.

Alvesson, M. (1998) 'Gender Relations and Identity at Work: a case study of masculinities and femininities in an advertising agency', *Human Relations*, 51(8): 969–1005.

Amin, A. (ed.) (1994) *Post-Fordism*. London: Routledge.

Antikainen, A., Houtsonen, J., Kauppila, J. and Houtelin, H. (1996) *Living in the Learning Society: life histories, identities and education*. London: Falmer.

Archer, M. (2007) *Making Our Way Through the World: human reflexivity and social mobility*. Cambridge: Cambridge University Press.

Archer, L. (2008) 'The New Neo-liberal Subjects? Young(er) academics' constructions of professional identity', *Journal of Education Policy*, 23(3): 265–85.

Archer, L. and Hutchings, M. (2000) 'Bettering Yourself'? Discourses of risk, cost and benefit in ethnically diverse, young, working class non-participants' construction of higher education, *British Journal of Sociology of Education*, 22(4): 555–75.

Archer, L. and Yamashita, H. (2003) 'Knowing their Limits: identities, inequalities and inner city school leavers' post-16 aspirations', *Journal of Educational Policy*, 18(1): 53–69.

Archer, W. and Davison, J. (2008) *Graduate Employability: the view of employers*. London: Council for Industry and Higher Education.

Archer, L., Hutchens, M. and Ross, A. (eds) (2003) *Higher Education and Social Class: issues of exclusion and inclusion*. London: Routledge.

Arnot, M. (2002) *Reproducing Gender? Essays on Educational Theory and Feminist Politics*. London: Routledge Falmer.

Arnot, M. and Miles, P. (2005) 'A Reconstruction of the Gender Agenda: the contradictory gender dimensions in New Labour's educational and economic policy', *Oxford Review of Education*, 31(1): 173–89.

Arnot, M. and Mac an Ghail, M. (eds) (2006) *The Routledge Falmer Reader in Gender and Education*. London: Routledge.

Arthur, M. and Rousseau, D. (2001) *The Boundaryless Career: a new employment principle for a new organizational era*. Oxford: Oxford University Press.

Ashton, D. and Sung, J. (2002) *Supporting Workplace Learning for High Performing Working*. Geneva: International Labour Office.

Ashton, D. N. and Field, D. (1976) *Young Workers*. London: Hutchinson.

Ashton, D. N. and Green, F. (1996) *Education, Training and the Global Economy*. Cheltenham: Edward Elgar.

Ashton, D, Maguire, M. and Spilsbury, M. (1990) *Restructuring the Labour Market: The Implications for Youth*. London: Macmillan.

Association of Graduate Recruiters (2009) *Graduate Recruiters' Survey*. Warwick: ARG.

Avis, J. (1999) 'Shifting Identities: new conditions of practice and the transformation of practice-teaching within the post-compulsory sector', *Journal of Vocational Education and Training*, 51(2): 245–64.

—(2009) *Education, Policy and Social Justice: learning and skills*. London: Continuum.

Avis, J., Bloomer, M., Esland, G., Gleeson, G. and Hodkinson, P. (1996) *Knowledge and Nationhood: education, politics and work*. London: Cassell.

Baker, D. P. (2009) 'The Educational Transformation of Work: towards a new synthesis', *Journal of Education and Work*, 22 (3): 163–191.

Ball, S. J. (1994) *Education Reform: a critical and post-structuralist perspective*. Buckingham: Open University Press.

—(2003) *Class Strategies and the Education Market: the middle classes and social advantage*. London: Routledge Falmer.

—(2008) *The Education Debate*. Bristol: Policy Press.

Ball, S. J., Maguire, M. and MacRea, S. (2000) *Choice, Pathways and Transitions: 16–19 education, training and (un)employment in one urban locale*. Swindon: ESRC.

Ball, S. J., Davies, J., David, M. and Reay, D. (2001) 'Classification' and Judgement': social class and the 'cognitive structures' of choice', *British Journal of Sociology of Education*, 23(1): 51–72.

Banks, M., Bates, I., Breakwell, G., Bynner, J., Emler, N., Jamieson, L. and Roberts, K. (1992) *Careers and Identities*. Milton Keynes: Open University Press.

Barnett, R. (1993) 'Knowledge, Higher Education and Society: a postmodern problem', *Oxford Review of Higher Education*, 19(1): 33–46.

—(1994) *The Limits of Competence*. Buckingham: Open University Press.

—(2003) *Beyond All Reason: living with ideology in universities*. Buckingham: Open University Press.

Barone, C. and Van de Werfhorst, H. G. (2011) 'Education, Cognitive Skills and Earnings in Comparative Perspective', *International Sociology*, 26(4): 483–502.

Bates, I. (1984) *Schooling for the Dole? The new Vocationalism*. London: McMillian.

Bauman, Z. (1998) *Work, Consumption and the New Poor*. Buckingham: Open University Press.

— (2000) *Liquid Modernity*. London: Wiley Blackwell.
— (2002) 'Individually, Together' (foreword) in U. Beck and E. Beck-Gernsheim, *Individualization*. London: Sage.
Beck, U. (1992) *Risk Society: Towards a new modernity*. London: Sage.
— (2000) 'Living Your Life in a Runaway World: individualisation, globalisation and politics', in A. Giddens and W. Hutton (eds) *On the Edge: living with global capitalism*. London: Jonathan Cape.
— (2000) *The Brave New World of Work*. Cambridge: Polity Press.
— (2004) *Ulrich Beck- Johannes Willms – Conversation with Ulrich Beck* (translated by M. Pollack). London: Polity Press.
Beck, U. and Beck-Gernsheim, E. (2002) *Individualization*. London: Sage.
Beck, U., Giddens, A. and Lash, S. (1994) *Reflexive Modernisation: politics, tradition and aesthetics in the modern social order*. Cambridge: Polity Press.
Beck, V., Fuller, A. and Unwin, L. (2006) 'Increasing Risk in the 'Scary' World of Work? Male and female resistance to crossing the gender lines in apprenticeships in England and Wales', *Journal of Education and Work*, 19(3): 271–89.
Becker, G. S. (1976) *Human Capital Theory: theoretical and empirical analysis with special reference to education* (1st edition). Chicago: University of Chicago Press.
— (1993) *Human Capital: theoretical and empirical analysis with special reference to education* (3rd edition). Chicago: University of Chicago Press.
Bell, D. (1973) *The Coming of the Post-industrial Society: a venture in social forecasting* (1st edition). New York: Basic Books.
— (1999) *The Coming of the Post-industrial Society: a venture in social forecasting* (2nd edition). New York: Basic Books.
Berg, I. (1970) *Education for Jobs: the great training robbery*. New York: Preager Publishers.
Bernstein B. (1996) *Pedagogy, Symbolic Control and Identity: theory, research, critique*. London: Taylor and Francis.
Beynon, H. (1972) *Working for Ford*. Wakefield: E.P. Publishing.
Bhagwati, J. (2007) *In Defence of Globalisation*. Oxford: Oxford University Press.
Billett, S. (2002) 'Critiquing Workplace Learning Discourse: participation and continuity at work', *Studies in the Education of Adults*, 34(1): 56–67.
Billett, S., Fenwick, T. and Somerville, M. (eds) (2007) *Work, Subjectivity and Learning: understanding learning through working life*. New York: Springer.
Bills, D. (1988) 'Credentials and Capacities: employers' perceptions of the acquisitions of skills', *Sociological Quarterly*, 31(1): 23–35.
Bills, D. B. (2003) 'Credentials, Signals, Screens and Jobs: explaining the relationship between schooling and job assignment', *Review of Educational Research*, 74(4): 441–9.
Bloomer, M. and Hodkinson, P. (2000) 'Learning Careers: continuity and change in young people's dispositions to learning', *British Educational Research Journal*, 26: 583–98.
Bolton, S. and Muzio, D. (2008) 'The Paradoxical Processes of Feminization: the case of established, aspiring and semi-professionals', *Work, Employment and Society*, 22(2): 281–99.
Bottery, M. and Wright, N. (2000) *Teachers and the State: towards a directed profession*. London: Routledge.

Boud, D. and Garrick, J. (eds) (1999) *Understanding Learning at Work*. New York: Routledge.

Bourdieu, P. (1977). *Outline of a Theory of Practice*. Cambridge: Cambridge University Press.

— (1988) *Homo Academicus*. Cambridge: Polity Press.

Bourdieu, P. and Passeron, J. C. (1977) *Reproduction in Education, Society and Culture*. London: Sage.

—(1979) *The Inheritors: French students and their relation with culture*. Chicago: Chicago University Press.

Bowles, S. and Gintis, H. (1976) *Schooling in Capitalist America: education reform for economic life*. London: Routledge & Keegan Paul.

Bradley, H. and Devadsson, R. (2008) 'Fractured Transitions: young adults' pathways into contemporary labour market', *Sociology*, 42(1): 119–36.

Bradley, H., Erickson, H., Stephenson, C. and Williams, S. (2000) *Myths at Work*. Oxford: Blackwell Publishers.

Braverman, H. (1974) *Labour and Monopoly Capitalism: the degradation of work in the twentieth century*. New York: Monthly Review Press.

Brennan, J. (2008) 'Higher Education and Social Change', *Higher Education*, 56(3): 381–93.

Brennan, J. and Osborne, M. (2008) 'Higher Education's Many Diversities: of students, institutions, experiences; and outcomes', *Research Papers in Education*, 23(2): 179–90.

Brennan, J., Locke, W. and Naidoo, R. (2007) 'United Kingdom: an increasingly differentiated profession' in W. Locke and U. Teichler (eds) *The Changing Conditions of Work and Careers in Selected Countries*. Kassell: International Centre for Higher Education Research.

Brennan, J., Edmunds, R., Houston, M., Jary, D., Lebeau, Y. Osborne, M. and Richardson, J. T. E. (2009) *Improving What Is Learnt at University*. London: Routledge.

Brine, J. (2006) 'Lifelong Learning and Knowledge Economy: those that know and those that don't – the discourse of the European Union', *British Educational Research Journal*, 32(5): 649–65.

Brint, S. (2001) 'Professionals and the "Knowledge Economy": rethinking the theory of post-industrial society', *Current Sociology*, 49(4), 101–32.

Broadfoot, P. and Pollard, A. (2000) 'The Changing Discourse of Assessment: the case of primary schools', in A. Filler (ed.) *Assessment: social practice and social product*. London: Routledge.

Brooks, R. (ed.) (2009) *Transitions From Education to Work: new perspectives from Europe and beyond*. Basingstoke: Palgrave.

Brooks, R. and Everett, G. (2009) 'Post-Graduate Reflections on the Value of a Degree', *British Educational Research Journal*, 35(3): 333–49.

Brown, D. K. (2001) 'The Social Sources of Educational Credentialism: status cultures, labour markets and organisations', *Sociology of Education*, 74: 19–34.

Brown, P. (1987) *Schooling Ordinary Kids*. London: Tavistock.

—(2000) 'The Globalisation of Positional Competition', *Sociology*, 34(4): 633–53.

—(2003) 'The Opportunity Trap: education and employment in a global economy'. *European Educational Research Journal*, 2(1): 141–79.

Brown, P. and Lauder, H. (eds) (1992) *Education for Economic Survival: from Fordism to Post-Fordism?* London: Routledge.

Brown, P. and Scase, R. (1994) *Higher Education and Corporate Realities: class, culture and the decline of graduate careers*. London: UCL Press.

Brown, P. and Hesketh, A. J. (2004) *The Mismanagment of Talent: employability and jobs in the knowledge economy*. Oxford: Oxford University Press.

Brown, P., Lauder, H. and Green, A. (2001) *High Skills: globalisation, competitiveness and skill formation*. Oxford: Oxford University Press.

Brown, P., Hesketh, A. J. and Williams, S. (2003) 'Employability in a Knowledge Driven Economy', *Journal of Education and Work*, 16(2): 107–26.

Brown, P., Lauder, H. and Ashton, D. N. (2011) *The Global Auction: the broken promises of education, jobs and incomes*. Oxford: Oxford University Press.

Buchanan, J. (2003) 'Cost and Choice', *The Encyclopaedia of Public Choice*, 2: 454–6.

Burroway, M. (1979) *Manufacturing Consent: changes in the labour process under monopoly capitalism*. Chicago: Chicago University Press.

Bush, T. (2008) 'From Management to Leadership: meaningful or semantic change?', *Educational Management, Administration and Leadership*, 36(2): 271–88.

Bynner, J. (1988) 'Education and the Family Components of Identity in the Transition from School to Work', *International Journal of Behavioural Development*, 22(1): 29–53.

Callender, C. (2008) 'The Impact of Part-Time Employment on Higher Education Students' Academic Attainment and Achievement', *Journal of Education Policy*, 23(4): 359–77.

Castells, M. (1997) *The Power of Identity*. Oxford: Blackwell.

—(2000) *The Rise of the Network Society*. Oxford: Blackwell.

— (2001) *The Rise of the Network Society: the information age: economy, society and culture*. London: Willey.

Cave, M., Hanney, S., Henkel, M. and Kogan, M. (1997) *The Use of Performance Indicators in Higher Education: the challenge of the quality movement*. London: Jessica Kingsley.

Child, J. and McGrath, R. G. (2001) 'Organizations Unfettered: organization forms in an information-intensive economy', *Academy of Management Journal*, 44: 1135–48.

Clarke, M. (2008) 'Understanding and Managing Employability in Changing Career Contexts', *Journal of European Industrial Training*, 32(4): 258–84.

Clarke, J., Newman, J. and McGlaughlin, E. (eds) (2000) *New Managerialism, New Welfare*. Buckingham: Open University.

Clarke, J., Newman, J., Smith, N., Vidler, E. and Westmarland, L. (2007) *Creating Citizen Consumers: changing publics and changing public services*. London: Sage.

Clegg, S. (2008) 'Academic Identities Under Threat?', *British Educational Research Journal*, 34(3): 329–45.

Coffield, F. (2000) 'Introduction: a critical analysis of the concept of a learning society', in F. Coffield (ed.) *Differing Vision of a Learning Society*. Bristol: Polity Press.

Colin, A. and Young. R. A. (2000) *The Future of Career*. Cambridge: Cambridge University Press.

Colley, H., James, D., Tedder, M. and Diment, K. (2003) 'Learning as Becoming in Vocational Education and Training: class, gender and the role of vocational habitus', *Journal of Vocational Education and Training*, 55: 471–96.

Collins, R. (1979) *The Credential Society: an historical sociology of education and stratification*. New York: Academic Press.

—(2000) 'Comparative and Historical Patterns of Education', in M. Hallinan (ed.) *Handbook of the Sociology of Education*. New York: Kluwer Academic Publishers.

Collinson, D. (2003) 'Identities and Insecurities: selves at work', *Organization*, 10(3): 527–47.

Committee of Vice-Chancellors and Principles (CVCP) (1985) *Report for the Steering Committee for Efficiency, Jarrett Report*. CVCP: London.

Confederation of Business Industry (2011) *Building for Growth: business priorities for education and skills*. CBI: London.

Conley, H. (2008) 'The Nightmare of Temporary Work: a reply to Fevre', *Work, Employment and Society*, 22(4): 731–6.

Connor, H., Dewson, S. and Tyers, C. (2001) *Social Class and Higher Education: issues affecting the decisions to participate by lower class students*. London: Department for Education and Employment.

Cote, J. and Bynner, J. (2008) 'Changes in the Transition to Adulthood in the UK and Canada: the role of structure and agency in emerging adulthood', *Journal of Youth Studies*, 11(3): 251–68.

Crompton, R. (ed.) (1999) *Restructuring Gender Relations: the decline of the male breadwinner*. Oxford: Oxford University Press.

Crossan, B., Field, J., Gallacher, J. and Merrill, B. (2003) 'Understanding Participation in Learning for Non-Traditional Students: learning careers and the construction of learner identities', *British Journal of Sociology of Education*, 24(1): 55–67.

Crozier, G., Reay, D., Clayton, J., Colliander, L. and Grinstead, J. (2008) 'Different Strokes for Different Folks: diverse students in diverse institutions – experiences of higher education', *Research Papers in Education*, 23(2): 167–77.

Dale, R. (2005) 'Globalisation, Knowledge Economy and Comparative Education', *Comparative Education*, 41(2): 117–49.

Davies, B. and Petersen, E. B. (2005) 'Neoliberal Discourse in the Academy: the forestalling of (collective) resistance', *Learning and Teaching in the Social Sciences*, 2(2): 77–98.

Davis, K. and Moore, W. E. (1945) 'Some Principles of Stratification', *American Sociological Review*, 10: 242–9.

Day, C., Kington, A., Stobart, G. and Sammons, P. (2006) 'The Personal and Professional Selves of Teachers: stable and unstable selves', *British Journal of Educational Research*, 32(4): 601–16.

Dearing, R. (1997) *The Dearing Report: Report for the National Committee of Inquiry into Higher Education: higher education in the learning society*. London: HMSO.

Deem, R. and Brehony, K. (2005) 'Management as Ideology: the case of New Managerialism in higher education', *Oxford Review of Education*, 31(2): 217–35.

Deem, R., Hillyard, S. and Reed, M. (2007) *Knowledge, Higher Education and the New Managerialism: the changing management of universities*. Oxford: Oxford University Press.

Dent, M. and Whithead, S. (2002) *Managing Professional Identities: knowledge, 'performativity' and the "new" professional*. London: Routledge.

Department for Business, Innovation and Skills (2009) *Higher Ambitions: the future of universities in a knowledge economy*. London: HMSO.

Department for Education (2010) *Securing a Sustainable Future for Higher Education (The Browne Review)*. London: HMSO.

—(2010) *The Importance of Teaching: schools white paper*. London: HMSO.

—(2011) *Putting Students are the Heart of the Higher Education System (Higher Education White Paper)*. London: HMSO.

— (2011) *The Wolf Review of Vocational Education*. London: HMSO.

Department for Education and Employment (1998) *The Learning Age*. London: HMOS.

— (2001) *Education into Employability: the role of the DfEE in the economy*. London: HMSO.

Department for Education and Science (1991) *Higher Education: a new framework*. London: HMSO.

Department for Education and Skills (2003) *The Future of Higher Education*. London: HMSO.

—(2006) *Leitch Review – Prosperity for All in the Global Economy: world class skills*. London: HMSO.

Department for Innovation and Universities (2008) *Innovation Nation*. London: HMSO.

Devine, F. (2005) 'The Cultural Turn: sociology and class analysis', in F. Devine, M. Savage, J. Scott and R. Crompton (eds) *Rethinking Class: identities, cultures and lifestyles*. London: Palgrave.

Docking, J. (2001) *New Labour's Policies for Schools: raising the standard?* London: David Fulton Publishers.

Doherty, M. (2009) 'When the Working Day Is Through: the end of work as identity', *Work, Employment and Society*, 23(1): 84–101.

Dore, R. (1976) *The Diploma Disease: education, qualification and development*. California: University of California Press.

Drucker, P. (1993) *The Post-capitalist Society*. New York: Harper Books.

Du Bois-Reymond, M. (2004) 'Youth – Learning – Europe. Menage a Trois?', *Young*, 12(3): 187–204.

Du Gay, P. (1996) *Consumption and Identity at Work*. London: Sage.

Durkheim, E. (1893) *The Division of Labour in Society*. New York: The Free Press.

Easterby-Smith, M., Crossan, M. and Nicolini, D. (2000) 'Organisational Learning: debates past, present and future', *Journal of Management Studies*, 37(6): 783–96.

Eccelston, K. (2002) *Learning Autonomy in Post-16 Education*. London: Routledge.

Eccelstone, K., Beista, G. and Hughes, M. (eds) (2009) *Lost and Found in Transition: change and becoming through education*. London: Routledge.

Edwards, R. and Nicoll, K. (2001) 'Researching the Rhetoric of Lifelong Learning', *Journal of Education Policy*, 16(2): 103–12.

Elias, P. and Purcell, K. (2004) *The Earnings of Graduates in Their Early Careers: Researching Graduates Seven Years on. Research Paper 1*, University of West England & Warwick University, Warwick Institute for Employment Research.

Enders, J. and Fulton, O. (eds) (2002) *Higher Education in a Globalising World*. Dordrecht: Kluwer Academic Publishers.

Entwistle, T., Marinetto, M. and Ashworth, R. (2007) 'Introduction: New Labour, the new public management and changing forms of human resource management', *The International Journal of Human Resource Management*, 18(9): 1569–74.

Equality and Human Rights Commission (2008) *Sex Discrimination and Gender Pay Gap, a Report by the EHRC*. Manchester: EHRC.

Eraut, M. (1994) *Developing Professional Knowledge and Competence*. London: Routledge Falmer.

—(2007) 'Learning from Other People in the Workplace', *Oxford Review of Education*, 33(4): 403–22.

Evans, K. (2002) 'Taking Control of their Own Lives? Agency in young adult transitions in England and West Germany', *Journal of Youth Studies*, 5(3): 245–69.

Evans, K. (2007) 'Concepts of Bounded Agency in Education, Work and the Personal Lives of Young People', *International Journal of Psychology*, 42(2): 85–93.

Evetts, J. (2008) 'Introduction – Professional Work in Europe: concepts, theories and methodologies', *European Societies*, 10(4): 525–44.

Exworthy, M. and Halford, S. (1999) *Professionals and the New Managerialism of the Public*.

Farrell, C. and Morris, J. (2004) 'Resigned Compliance: teacher attitudes towards performance-related pay in schools', *Educational Management, Administration and Leadership*, 32(1): 81–104.

Felstead, A., Gallie, D., Green, F. and Zhu, Y. (2007) *Skills at Work in Britain: from 1986–2006*. Centre for Skills, Knowledge and Organisational Performance, Oxford: SCOPE.

Felstead, A., Fuller, A., Jewson, N. and Unwin, L. (2009) *Improving Learning as Work*. London: Routledge.

Felstead, A., Fuller, A., Jewson, N., Unwin, U., Bishop, D. and Kakavelakis, K. (2009) 'Mind the Gap: personal and collective identities at work', *Studies in the Education of Adults*, 41(1): 6–20.

Fenwick, T. (2003) 'Flexibility and Individualisation in Adult Education Work: the case of portfolio educators', *Journal of Education and Work*, 16(2): 165–84.

—(2008) 'Workplace Learning: emerging themes and new perspectives', *New Directions in Adult and Continuing Education*, 119: 17–26.

Ferlie, E., Ashburner, L., Fitzgerald, L. and Pettigrew, A. (1996) *The New Public Management in Action*. Oxford: Oxford University Press.

Fevre, R. (2003) *The New Sociology of Economic Behaviour*. London and Thousand Oaks: Sage.

—(2007) 'Employment Insecurity and Social Theory: the power of nightmares', *Work, Employment and Society*, 2(3): 517–35.

Fevre, R. Rees, G. and Gorard, S. (1999) 'Some Sociological Alternatives to Human Capital Theory and their Implications for Research on Post-compulsory Education and Training', *Journal of Education and Work*, 12(2): 117–40.

Field, J. (2006) *Lifelong Learning and the New Educational Order*. Stock-on-Trent: Trentham Books.

Fielding, M. (ed.) (2001) *Taking Education Really Seriously*. London: Routledge.

Finegold, D. and Soskice, D. (1988) 'The Failure of Training in Britain: analysis and prescription', *Oxford Review of Economic Policy*, 4(3): 21–53.

Forrier, A. and Sels, L. (2003) 'The Concept of Employability: a complex mosaic', *International Journal of Human Resource Development and Management*, 3(2): 102–24.

Foskett, N. H. and Hemsley-Brown, J. V. (2001) *Choosing Futures: young people's decision-making in education, training and careers markets*. London: Routledge.

Foskett, N. H., Dyke, M. and Maringe, F. (2004) *The Influence of the School in the Decision to Participate in Post-16*. London: DFES.

Foucault, M. (1986) *Disciplinary Power and Subjection*. New York: New York University Press.

Francis, B. (2000) 'The Gendered Subject: students' subject preferences and discussions of subjects and ability', *Oxford Review of Education*, 26(1): 35–48.

Friedman, M. and Friedman, R. (1980) *Free to Choose*. New York: Harcourt, Brace and Jovanovich.

Fugate, M., Kinicki, A. J. and Ashforth, B. E. (2004) 'Employability: a psycho-social construct, its dimensions and applications', *Journal of Vocational Behavior*, 65(1): 14–38.

Fuller, A. and Unwin, L. (2003) 'Learning as Apprentices in the Contemporary UK Workplace: creating and managing expansive and restrictive participation', *Journal of Education and Work*, 16(4): 407–26.

—(2004) 'Expansive Learning Environment: integrating personal and organisational development', in H. Rainbird, A. Fuller and A. Munro (eds) *Workplace Learning in Context*. London: Routledge.

—(2011) 'Apprenticeship as an Evolving Model of Learning', *Vocational Education and Training*, 63(3): 261–7.

Fuller, A., Heath, S. and Johnston, B. (eds) (2011) *Rethinking Widening Participation in Higher Education: the role of social networks*. London: Routledge.

Furlong, A. and Cartmel, F. (1997) *Growing up in a Classless Society: individualisation and risk in late modernity*. Buckingham: Open University Press.

—(2005) *Graduates From Disadvantaged Backgrounds: early labour market experiences*. York: Joseph Rowntree Foundation.

—(2007) *Young People and Social Change: new perspectives*. Buckingham: Open University Press.

Furlong, A., Cartmel, F., Biggart, A., Sweeting, H. and West, P. (2005) 'Complex Transitions: linearity and labour market integration in the West of Scotland', in C. J. Pole, J. Pilcher and J. Williams (eds) *Young People's Transitions: becoming citizens*. Basingstoke: Palgrave.

Gallacher, J., Crossan, B., Field, J. and Merrill, B. (2002) 'Learning Careers and the Social Space: exploring the fragile identities of adult returners in the new Further Education', *International Journal of Lifelong Education*, 21(6): 493–509.

Gallie, D., Felstead, A. and Green, F. (2004) 'Changing Patterns of Task Discretion in Britain', *Work, Employment & Society*, 18(2): 243–66.

Garavan, T. (1999) 'Employability: the emerging new deal?', *Journal of European Industrial Training*, 23(1): 1–9.

—(2005) 'Organisational Restructuring and Downsizing: issues relating to learning, training and employability of survivors', *European Journal of Industrial Training*, 29(6): 488–508.

Gazier, B. (1999) *Employability: concepts and policies*, InforMisep Reports No. 67068. Birmingham: European Employment Observatory.

Gewirtz, S. and Cribb, A. (2009) *Understanding Education: a sociological perspective*. Cambridge: Polity.

Gerwirtz, S., Ball, S. J. and Bowe, R. (1995) *Markets, Choice and Equity in Education*. Buckingham: Open University Press.

Gewirtz, S., Mahony, P., Hextall, I. and Cribb, A. (2009) *Changing Teacher Professionalism: international trends, challenges and ways forward*. London: Routledge.

Gibbons, M., Limoges, C. and Nowontny, H. (1994) *The New Production of Knowledge*. London: Sage.

Giddens, A. (1984) *The Constitution of Society*. Cambridge: Polity Press.

Giddens, A. (1990) *The Consequences of Modernity*. Stanford: Stanford University Press.

—(1991) *Modernity and Self-identity*. Cambridge: Polity Press.

Giddens, G. (2002) *Runaway World: how globalisation is reshaping our lives*. London: Profile Books.

Gillborn, D. (1990) *'Race', Ethnicity and Education: teaching and learning in multi-ethnic schools*. London: Unwin Hyman.

Godin, B. (2006) 'The Knowledge-Based Economy: conceptual framework or buzzword', *The Journal of Technology Transfer*, 31(1): 17–30.

Goffman, I. (1959) *The Presentation of Self in Everyday Life*. New York: Doubleday.

Goldthorpe, J. (2003) 'The Myth of Education-Based Meritocracy', *New Economy*, 10(4): 234–9.

Goldthorpe, J. and Jackson, M. (2008) 'Education-Based Meritocracy: barriers to its realisation', in A. Lareau and D. Conley (eds) *Social Class – how does it work?* New York: Russell Sage Foundation.

Goldthrope, J. and Mills, C. (2008) 'Trends in Inter-Generational Class Mobility in Modern Britain: evidence from national surveys', 1972–2005, *National Institute for Economic Research*, 205(1): 83–100.

Goodwin, J. and O'Connor, H. (2005) 'Exploring Complex Transitions: looking back at the golden age of From School to Work', *Sociology*, 39(2): 201–20.

—(2009) 'Whatever Happened to the Young Workers?', *Journal of Education and Work*, 22(5): 417–31.

Gorard, S. and Rees, G. (2002) *Creating a Learning Society? Learning careers and policies for lifelong learning*. Bristol: Polity Press.

Gorard, S., Rees, G. and Salisbury, S. (2001) 'Investigating the Patterns of Differential Attainment of Boys and Girls at School', *British Journal of Educational Research*, 27(2): 125–39.

Grace, A. (2009) 'A Canadian View of Lifelong Learning Culture Through a Critical Lens', in J. Field, J. Gallacher and R. Ingram (eds) *Researching Transitions in Lifelong Learning*. London: Routledge.

Granovetter, M. (1985) 'Economic Action and Social Structure: the problem of embeddeness', *American Journal of Sociology*, 91(3): 481–510.

Green, A. (1997) *Education, Globalization and the National State*. London: McMillan.

—(2003) 'Is the UK Exceptionally Unequal?', *Forum*, 45(2): 67–70.

Green, F. (2006) *Demanding Work: the paradox of job quality in the affluent economy*. Princeton: Princeton University Press.

Green, F. and Zhu, Y. (2010) 'Over-Qualification, Job Satisfaction, and Increasing Dispersion in the Returns to Graduate Education', *Oxford Economic Papers*, 62(4): 740–63.

Grey, C. (1994) 'Career as a Projection of Self and Labour Process Discipline', *Sociology*, 28(5): 479–98.

—(1999) '"We Are All Managers Now; We Always Were": on the development and demise of management', *Journal of Management Studies*, 36(5): 561–85.

Griffin, K. (2003) 'Economic Globalisation and Institutions of Global Governance', *Development and Change*, 34(5): 789–808.

Grint, K. (2005) *The Sociology of Work* (3rd edition). Cambridge: Polity.

Grubb, W. N. and Lazerson, M. (2004) *The Education Gospel: the economic value of schooling*. Cambridge Mass: Harvard University Press.

—(2006) 'The Globalization of Rhetoric and Practice: the education gospel and vocationalism', in H. Lauder, P. Brown, A. H. Halsey and J. A. Dillabough (eds) *Education, Globalisation and Social Change*. Oxford: Oxford University Press.

Guile, D. and Young, M. (2001) 'Apprenticeships as a Conceptual Basis for a Social Theory of Learning', in C. Paechter (ed.) *Knowledge, Power and Learning*. Buckingham: Open University Press.

Hager, P. (2004) 'Conceptions and Learning and Understanding in the Workplace', *Studies in Continuing Education*, 26(1): 3–17.

Hakim, C. (2000) *Work-Lifestyle Choice in the 21st Century: preference theory*. Oxford: Oxford University Press.

Hall, P. A. and Soskice, D. W. (2001) *Varieties of Capitalism: the institutional foundations of comparative advantage*. Oxford: Oxford University Press.

Halsey, A. H. (1992) *The Decline of the Donnish Dominion*. Oxford: Oxford University.

—(1993) 'Trends in Access and Equity in Higher Education: Britain in international perspective', *Oxford Review of Education*, 19(2): 129–40.

Halsey, A. H., Floud, J. and Anderson, J. (1961) *Education, Economy and Society*. New York: Free Press.

Halsey, A. H., Heath, A. F. and Ridge, J. M. (1980) *Origins and Destinations: family, class and education in modern Britain*. Oxford: Oxford University Press.

Handy, C. (1995) *The Empty Raincoat: making sense of the future*. London: Arrow Business.

Hansen, H. (2011) 'Rethinking Certification Theory and the Educational Development of the United States and Germany', *Research in Social Stratification and Mobility*, 29: 31–55.

Harris, A. and Lambert, L. (2003) *Building Leadership Capacity for School Improvement*. Maidenhead: Open University Press.

Harvey, L. (2000) 'New Realities: the relationship between higher education and employment', *Tertiary Education and Management*, 6(1): 3–17.

—(2001) 'Defining and Measuring Employability', *Quality in Higher Education*, 7(2): 97–109.

—(2003) *Transitions from Higher Education to Work*. York: LTSN.

—(2005) 'A History and Critique of Quality in Higher Education', *Quality Assurance in Education*, 13(4): 263–76.

Hartley, R. (2009) *Simply Learning: improving the skills system in the UK*. London: Policy Exchange.

Harvey, L., Moon, S. and Geall, V. (1997) *Graduates' Work: organisational change and students' attributes.* Birmingham: QHE.

Hassard, J., McCann, L. and Morris, J. L. (2008) *Managing in the New Economy: restructuring white-collar work in the USA, UK and Japan.* Cambridge University Press.

Hayek, F. (1973) *Law, Legislation and Liberty.* London: Routledge and Keagan Paul.

Hayward, G. (2008) 'Degrees of Success: learners' transitions from vocational education and training to HE', *Widening Participation in Higher Education: a commentary by the Teaching and Learning Programme.* Swindon: Economic Council for Social and Economic Research.

Heinz, W. (ed.) (1991) *Theoretical Advances in Life-course Research: status passages and the life-course.* Weinheim: Deutscher Studienverlag.

Heinz, W. (2009) 'Structure and Agency in Transition Research', *Journal of Education and Work,* 22(5): 391–404.

Held, D. and McGrew, A. (2007) *Globalization Theory: approaches and controversies,* Oxford: Polity.

Hemsley-Brown, J. and Oplatka, I. (2006) 'Universities in a Competitive Global Marketplace: a systematic review of the literature on higher education marketing', *International Journal of Public Sector Management,* 19(4): 316–38.

Henkel, M. (2000) *Academic Identities and Policy Change in Higher Education.* London: Jessica Kingsley.

—(2005) 'Academic Identity and Autonomy in a Changing Policy Environment', *Higher Education,* 49(1): 155–76.

Henkel, M. and Little, B. (eds) (1999) *Changing Relationships Between Higher Education and the State.* London: Jessica Kingsley.

Hesketh, A. J. (2000) 'Recruiting a Graduate Elite? Employer perceptions of graduate employment and training', *Journal of Education and Work,* 13(3): 245–71.

Hickox, M. and Moore, R. (1992) 'Education and Post-fordism: a new correspondence?', in P. Brown and H. Lauder (eds), *Education for Economic Survival? From Fordism to Post-fordism.* London: Routledge.

Higher Education Funding Council for England (HEFCE) (2010) *Higher Education Funding For Academic Years 2009–10 and 2010–11 Including New Student Entrants.* HEFCE: Bristol.

Hillage, J. and Pollard, E. (1998) *Employability: developing a framework for policy analysis,* DfEE Research Briefing No. 85. London: DfEE.

Hinchliffe, G. and Jolly, A. (2011) 'Graduate Identity and Employability', *British Educational Research Journal,* 37(4): 563–84.

Hirsch, F. (1977) *The Social Limits to Growth.* London: Routledge.

Hodgson, A. and Spours, K. (2008) *Education and Training 14–19: curriculum, qualifications and organisation.* London: Sage.

Hodkinson, P. (2004) 'Career Decision-Making, Learning Careers and Career Progression', *Nuffield Review of 14–19 Education, Working Paper 12, February.* Oxford: Nuffield Foundation.

Hodkinson, P. and Sparkes, A. C. (1997) 'Careership: a sociological theory of career decision-making', *British Journal of Sociology of Education,* 18(1): 29–44.

Hodkinson, P., Biesta, G. and James, D. (2008) 'Understanding Learning Culturally: overcoming the dualism between social and individual views of learning', *Vocations and Learning*, 1(1): 27–47.

Hodkinson, P., Sparkes, A. and Hodkinson, H. (1996) *Triumphs and Tears: young people, markets and the transition from school to work*. London: David Fulton.

Holdsworth, C. (2006) 'Don't You Think You're Missing Out, Living at Home? Student experiences and residential transitions', *The Sociological Review*, 54(3): 495–519.

Holford, S. and Exworthy, M. (eds) (1999) *Professionals and the New Managerialism in the Public Sector*. Buckingham: Open University Press.

Hoyle, E. and Wallace, M. (2005) *Educational Leadership: ambiguity, professionals and managerialism*. London: Sage.

—(2009) 'Leadership for Professional Practice', in S. Gewirtz, P. Mahony, I. Hextall and A. Cribb (eds) *Changing Teacher Professionalism*. London: Routledge.

Hughes, C. (2004) 'New Times, New Learners, New Voices? Towards a contemporary social theory of learning', *British Journal of Sociology of Education*, 25(3): 395–408.

Hyland, T. and Johnson, S. (1998) 'Of Cabbages and Key Skills: exploding the mythology of core transferable skills in post-school education', *Journal of Further and Higher Education*, 22(2): 163–72.

Ingram, R., Field, J. and Gallacher, J. (2009) 'Learning Transitions: research, policy and practice', in J. Field, J. Gallacher and I. Ingram (eds) *Researching Transitions in Lifelong Learning*. London: Routledge.

Jackson, S. and Jamieson, A. (2009) 'Higher Education, Mature Students and Employment Goals: policies and practices in the UK', *Journal of Vocational Education and Training*, 61(4): 399–411.

Jackson, S., Malcolm, I. and Thomas, K. (eds) (2011) *Gendered Choices: learners, work, identities and lifelong learning*. London: Springer.

James, D. (1995) 'Mature Studentship in Higher Education: beyond a species approach', *British Journal of Sociology of Education*, 16(4): 451–66.

Jamieson, I., Miller, A. and Watts, A. G. (1988) *Mirrors of Work: work simulations in schools*. London: Falmer Press.

Jarvis, P. and Parker, S. (2005) *Human Learning: a wholistic look*. London: Routledge.

Jary, D. and Parker, M. (eds) (1998) *The New Higher Education: issues and directions for the post-Dearing university*. Stoke-on-Trent: Staffordshire University Press.

Jenkins, R. (1983) *Lads, Citizens and Ordinary Kids: working-class youth lifestyles in Belfast*. London: Keegan Paul.

—(1996) *Social Identity*. London: Routledge.

Jenkins, S. and Conley, H. (2007) 'Living with the Contradictions of Modernisation: emotional management and the teacher profession', *Public Administration*, 85(4): 979–1001.

Jones, R. and Thomas, L. (2005) 'The 2003 Government Higher Education White Paper: a critical assessment of its implications for the access and widening participation agenda', *Journal of Education Policy*, 25(5): 615–30.

Keep, E. (2009) 'The Limits of the Possible: shaping the learning and skills landscape through a shared policy narrative', *SKOPE Research Paper, No. 86. SKOPE*: Cardiff School of Social Sciences.

Keep, E. and Mayhew, K. (2004) 'The Economic and Distributional Implications of Current Policies on Higher Education', *Oxford Review of Economic Policy*, 20(2): 298–314.

—(2010) 'Moving Beyond Skills as Social and Economic Panacea', *Work, Employment and Society*, 24(3): 565–77.

Kelly, A. (2009) 'Globalisation and Education: a review of conflicting perspective on their effect on policy and professional practice in the UK', *Globalisation, Societies and Education*, 7(1): 51–68.

Kelsall, R. K., Poole, A. and Kuhn, A. (1972) *Graduates: The sociology of an elite.* London: Methuen.

King, R. (ed.) (2004) *The University in the Global Age.* London: Palgrave.

Klein, N. (2000) *No Logo.* London: Harper Perennial.

Kogan, M. and Hanney, S. (2000) *Reforming Higher Education.* London: Jessica Kingsley.

Lauder, H. and Egerton, M. and Brown, P. (2005) 'A Report on Graduate Earnings: theory and empirical analysis', *Report for the Independent Study into the Devolution of Student Support System and Tuition Fee Regime.* Cardiff: Welsh Assembly Government.

Lauder, H., Brown, P., Halsey, A. H. and Dillabough, J. A. (eds) (2006) 'Introduction: the prospects for education: individualisation, globalisation and social change', *Education, Globalisation and Social Change.* Oxford: Oxford University Press.

Lauder, H., Brown, P. and Ashton, D. (2008) 'Globalisation, Skill Formation and the Varieties of Capitalism Approach', *New Political Economy*, 13(1): 19–35.

Lave, J. and Wenger, E. (1991) *Situated Learning: legitimate peripheral participation.* Cambridge: Cambridge University Press.

Leadbetter, C. (2000) *Living On Thin Air.* London: Penguin.

—(2006) 'Accessing Higher Education: policy, practice and equity in widening participation', in P. McNay (ed.) *Beyond Mass Higher Education: building on experience.* Buckingham: Open University.

Leathwood, C. and O'Connell, P. (2003) 'It's a Struggle': the construction of the 'new student' in higher education, *Journal of Education Policy*, 18(6): 597–615.

Le Grand, J. and Bartlett, W. (eds) (1993) *Quasi-Markets and Social Policy.* London: McMillan.

Lloyd, C. and Payne, J. (2003) 'The Political Economy of Skill and the Limits of Educational Policy', *Journal of Education Policy*, 18(1): 85–107.

Locke, W. and Teichler, U. (eds) (2007) *The Changing Conditions of Work and Careers in Selected Countries.* Kassell: International Centre for Higher Education Research.

Lumby, J. and Foskett, N. (2005) *14–19 Education: policy, leadership and learning.* London: Sage.

Lynch, K. (2006) 'Neoliberlism and Marketization: implication for higher education', *European Educational Research Journal*, 5(1): 1–17.

Mac an Ghail, M. (1994) *The Making of Men: masculinities, sexuality and schooling.* Maidenhead: Open University Press.

Malcolm, J., Hodkinson, P. and Colley, H. (2003) 'The Inter-Relationship Between Formal and Informal Learning', *Journal of Workplace Learning*, 15(7): 313–18.

Marginson, S. (1999) 'After Globalisation: emerging politics of education', *Journal of Education Policy*, 14(1): 19–31.

—(2008) 'Global Field and Global Imaging: Bourdieu and worldwide education', *British Journal of Sociology of Education*, 29(3): 303–15.

Marginson, S. and Van der Wende, M. (2007) *Globalisation and Higher Education*. Twente: Centre for Higher Education Policy Studies.

Maringe, F. and Gibbs, P. (2009) *Marketing Higher Education*. Buckingham: Open University Press.

Maringe, F. and Foskett, N. (eds) (2010) *Globalization and Internationalisation in Higher Education*. London: Continuum.

Maroy, C. and Doray, P. (2000) 'Education-Work Relations: theoretical reference points for a research domain', *Work, Employment and Society*, 14(1): 173–89.

Mason, G. and Bishop, K. (2010) *Adult Training, Skills Updating and Recession in the UK: the implication for competitiveness and social inclusion*, Published by Centre for Learning and Life Chance in Knowledge Economies and Societies. London: Institute for Education.

Mason, G., Williams, G. and Cramner, S. (2009) 'Employability Skills Initiatives in Higher Education: what effects do they have on graduate labour market outcomes?', *Education Economics*, 17(1): 1–30.

McIntosh, S. (2002) *Further Analysis of the Returns to Academic and Vocational Qualifications*, Department for Education and Skills Report 370. London: HMSO.

McNay, I. (2006) *Beyond Mass Higher Education: building on experience*. Buckingham: Open University Press.

McQuaid, D. and Lyndsay, L. (2005) 'The Concept of Employability', *Urban Studies*, 43(2): 197–219.

Meager, A. and Hillage, J. (2010) *Employment and Skills: six key priorities for the next government*, IES Paper, Institute for Employment Studies.

Mendick, H., Moreau, M. P. and Hollinworth, S. (2008) *Mathematical Images and Gender Identities: a report on the gendering of representations of mathematics and mathematicians in popular culture and their influences on learners*. Project Report – UK Resource Centre for Women in Science Engineering and Technology: Bradford.

Moreau, M. P. and Leathwood, C. (2006) 'Graduates' Employment and Discourse of Employability: a critical analysis, *Journal of Education and Work*, 18(4): 305–24.

Morley, L. (2001) 'Producing New Workers: quality, equality and employability in higher education', *Quality in Higher Education*, 7(2): 131–8.

—(2003) *Quality and Power in Higher Education*. Buckingham: Open University Press.

—(2007) 'The X Factor: graduate employability, elitism and equity in graduate recruitment', *Twenty-First Century Society: Journal of the Academy of Social Sciences*, 2(2): 191–207.

Murphy, R. (1988) *Social Closure: the theory of monopolisation and exclusion*. Clarendon Press: Oxford.

Musselin, C. (2005) 'European Academic Labour Markets in Transition', *Higher Education*, 49(1–2): 135–54.

Naidoo, R. and Jamieson, I. (2005) 'Empowering Participants or Corroding Learning: towards a research agenda on the impact of student consumerism in higher education', *Journal of Education Policy*, 20(3): 267–81.

Newman, J. (2005) 'Enter the Transformational Leader: network governance and the micro-politics of modernisation', *Sociology*, 39(4): 717–34.

Newman, J. and Nutley, S. (2003) 'Transforming the Probation Service: "what works", organisational change and professional identity', *Politics and Policy*, 31(4): 547–63.

Olssen, M. (2004) 'Neoliberalism, Globalisation and Democracy: challenges for education', *Globalisation, Societies and Education*, 2(2): 231–75.

Olssen, M. and Peters, M. (2005) 'Neoliberalism, Higher Education and the Knowledge Economy: from free market to knowledge capitalism', *Journal of Education Policy*, 20(3): 313–45.

Olssen, M., Codd, J. and O'Neil, A. M. (2004) *Education Policy: globalisation, citizenship and democracy*. London: Sage.

Organisation for Economic Co-operation and Development (2000) *Schooling for Tomorrow*. Paris: OECD.

—(2003) *Education at a Glance*. Paris: OECD.

—(2009) *Education at a Glance*. Paris: OECD.

Ozga, J. (2000) 'Education: new labour, new teachers', in J. Clarke, J. Newman and E. Mclauglin (eds) *New Managerialism, New Welfare*. London: Sage.

Ozga, J. and Lingard, B. (2007) 'Globalisation, Educational Policy and Politics', in B. Lingard and J. Ozga (eds) *The Routledge Reader in Education Policy and Politics*. London: Routledge.

Parsons, T. (1959) 'The School Class as a Social System: some of its functions in American Society', *Harvard Education Review*, XXIX: 297–318.

Peters, M. (2001) 'National Policy Construction of the "Knowledge Economy": towards a critique', *Journal of Educational Enquiry*, 2(1): 1–22.

Philips, R. and Harper-Jones, G. (2003) 'Whatever Next? Education Policy and New Labour: the first four years, 1997–2001', *British Educational Research Journal*, 29(1): 125–32.

Piore, M. and Sable, C. (1984) *The Second Industrial Divide: possibilities for prosperity*. New York: Basic Books.

Pitcher, J. and Kate, P. (1998) 'Diverse Expectations and Access to Opportunities: is there a graduate labour market?', *Higher Education Quarterly*, 52(2): 179–203.

Pollitt, C. (2007) 'New Labour's Re-Disorganisation: hyper-modernisation and the cost of reform – a cautionary tale', *Public Management Review*, 9(4): 529–43.

Power, S. and Whitty, G. (2006) 'Graduating and Graduations Within the Middle Class: the legacy of an elite higher education', *Cardiff School of Social Sciences Working Paper 118*. Cardiff: Cardiff University, School of Social Sciences.

Power, S., Edwards, T., Whitty, G. and Wigfall, V. (2003) *Education and the Middle Classes*. Buckingham: Open University Press.

Preedy, M., Bennett, N. and Wise, C. (eds) (2011) *Educational Leadership: context, strategy and collaboration*. London: Open University Press.

Pring, R., Hayward, G. Hodgson, A., Johnson, J., Keep, E., Oancea, A., Rees, G., Spours, K. and Wilde, S. (2009) *Educational for All: the future of education for 14–19 year olds*. London: Routledge.

Raffe, D. (2003) 'Pathways Linking Education and Work: a review of concepts, research and policy debates', *Journal of Youth Studies*, 6(1): 3–19.

—(2008) 'The Concept of Transition Institution', *Journal of Education and Work*, 21(4): 277–96.

Rainey, H. (2003) *Understanding and Managing Public Organizations*. San Francisco: Wiley & Sons.

Reay, D. (2001) 'Finding or Losing Yourself: working class relations to education', *Journal of Education Policy*, 16(4): 333–46.

—(2006) 'The Zombie Stalking English Schools: social class and educational inequality', *British Journal of Educational Studies*, 54(3): 288–307.

—(2008) 'Psychosocial Aspects of White Middle Class Identities: desiring and defending against the class and ethic "other" in urban, multi-ethnic schooling', *Sociology*, 42(6): 1072–88.

Reay, D., Ball, S. J. and David, M. (2006) *Degree of Choice: class, gender and race in higher education*. Stoke: Trentham Books.

Reed, M. (2002) 'New Managerialism, Professional Power and Organisational Governance in UK Universities: a review and assessment', in A. Amaral, G. A. Jones and B. Karseth (eds) *Governing Higher Education: national perspective on institutional governance*. New York: Springer.

Rees, G., Gorard, S. Fevre, R. and Furlong, J. (1997) 'History, Place and the Learning Society: towards a sociology of lifetime learning', *Journal of Education Policy*, 12(6): 485–97.

Reich, R. (1991) *The Work of Nations*. London: Simon & Schuster.

—(2002) *The Future of Success: living and working in the new economy*. New York: Vintage.

Renold, E. (2005) *Girls, Boys and Junior Sexualities: exploring children's gender and sexual relations in the primary school*. London: Routledge.

Riddell, S., Baron, S., Stalker, K. and Wilkinson, H. (1997) 'The Concept of the Learning Society for Adults with Learning Difficulties: human and social capital perspectives', *Journal of Education Policy*, 12(6): 473–83.

Rifkin, J. (1996) *The End of Work: the decline of the labour force and the dawn of the new post-market*. New York: Putnam.

Rizvi, F. and Lingard, B. (2010) *Globalizing Education Policy*. London: Routledge.

Robbins Report (1963) *A report for the Committee Appointed by the Prime Minister under the Chairmanship of Lord Robbins, 1962–63 cmns 2154*. London: HMSO.

Roberts, K. (1968) 'The Entry into Employment: an approach towards a general theory', *The Sociological Review*, 16(2): 168–82.

—(1984) *School Leavers and their Prospects: youth in the labour market in the mid 1980s*. Milton Keynes: Open University Press.

—(1995) *Youth and Employment in Modern Britain*. Oxford: Oxford University Press.

—(2001) *Class in Modern Britain*. London: Palgrave.

—(2009) 'Opportunity Structures Then and Now', *Journal of Education and Work*, 22(5): 355–68.

Robertson, R. (1995) 'Glocalization: time-space and hetergeneity-homogeneity', in M. Featherstone, S. Lash and R. Robertson (eds) *Global Modernities*. London: Sage.

Robertson, S. (2005) 'Re-Imaging and Re-Scripting the Future of Education: global knowledge economy discourse and the challenge to education systems', *Comparative Education*, 4(2): 151–70.

—(2009) 'Education, Knowledge and Innovation in the Global Economy: challenges and future direction', *Keynote Address to Launch of Research Centres, VIA University College, Aarthus, Denmark, March, 2009.*

Romer, P. (2007) 'Economic Growth', in D. Henderson (ed.) *The Concise Encyclopaedia of Economics.* New York: Liberty Fund.

Rose, N. (1996) 'Identity, Genealogy, *History*', in S. Hall and P. Du Guy (eds) *Questions of Cultural Identity.* London: Sage.

—(1999) *Powers of Freedom: reframing political thought.* Cambridge: Cambridge University Press.

Savage, M. (2000) *Class Analysis and Social Transformation.* Buckingham: Open University Press.

—(2003) 'A New Class Paradigm?', *British Journal of Sociology of Education,* 24(4): 535–41.

Schomburg, H. and Teichler, U. (2006) *Higher Education and Graduate Employment in Europe: results from the survey of twelve countries.* Dordrecht: Springer.

Schuller, T., Baron, S. and Field, J. (2000) *Social Capital: critical perspectives.* Oxford: Oxford University Press.

Schuller, T., Preston, J., Hammond, C., Brassett-Grundy, A. and Bynner, J. (2004) *The Benefits of Lifelong Learning: the impact on education and health, family life and social capital.* London: Routledge.

Schultz, T. W. (1961) *Investment in Human Capital.* Chicago: University of Chicago Press.

Schumpter, J. (1976) *Capitalism, Socialism and Democracy.* London: Allen & Unwin.

Scott, P. (2005) 'Mass Higher Education – Ten Years on', *Perspectives: policy and practice in higher education,* 9(3): 68–73.

Sennett, R. (1998) *The Corrosion of Character: the personal consequences of work in the new capitalism.* New York: W.W. Norton.

—(2006) *The Culture of New Capitalism.* Yale: Yale University Press.

—(2012) *The Rituals, Pleasures and Politics of Co-operations.* Yale: Yale University Press.

Shain, F. (2003) *The Schooling and Identity of Asian Girls.* Stoke-on-Trent: Trentham Books.

Shain, F. and Gleeson, D. (1999) 'Under New Management: changing conceptions of teacher professionalism and policy in the further education sector', *Journal of Education Policy,* 14(4): 445–62.

Sharpe, S. (1976) *Just Like a Girl: how girls learn to be women.* London: Penguin.

—(1994) *Just Like a Girl: how girls learn to be women: from the seventies to the nineties.* London: Penguin Book.

Sikes, P. (2009) 'In the Shadow of the RAE: working in a new university', in S. Gerwirtz, P. Mahony and I. Cribb (eds) *Changing Teachers Professionalism.* London: Routledge.

Silver, H. and Silver, P. (1997) *Students: changing role, changing lives.* Buckingham: Open University Press.

Skeggs, B. (2004) *Class, Self and Culture.* London: Routledge.

Slaughter, S. and Lesley, L. (1997) *Academic Capitalism: politics, policy and the entrepreneurial university.* Baltimore: John Hopkins University.

Smetherham, C. (2006) 'First Amongst Equals? Evidence of the contemporary relationship between educational credentials and occupational structure', *Journal of Education and Work*, 19(1): 19–35.

Sosteric, M. (1996) 'Subjectivity in the Labour Process: a case study on the restaurant industry', *Work, Employment and Society*, 10: 297–318.

Spender, D. (1982) *Learning to Lose: sexism and education*. London: Women's Press Ltd.

Spours, K. and Young, M. (1988) 'Beyond Vocationalism: a new perspectives on the relationship between education and work', *British Journal of Education and Work*, 2(2): 5–14.

Steedman, H. (2005) *Apprenticeships in Europe: 'fading' or 'flourishing*? CEP Discussion Paper 710, December 2005.

Stevenson, H. (2011) 'Coalition Education Policy: Thatcher's Long Shadow', *Forum*, 53(2): 179–94.

Stokes, H. and Wyn, J. (2007) 'Constructing Identity and Making Careers: young people's perspectives of work and learning', *International Journal of Lifelong Education*, 26(5): 495–511.

Strangleman, T. (2004) *Work Identity at the End of the Line? Privatisation and culture change in the UK rail industry*. Basingstoke: Palgrave.

—(2007) 'The Nostalgia for Permanence at Work: the end of work and its commentators', *The Sociological Review*, 55(1): 81–103.

Stronach, I., Corbin, B., McNamara, O., Stark, S. and Warne, T. (2002) 'Towards an Uncertain Professionalism: teacher and nurse identities in flux', *Journal of Education Policy*, 17(1): 109–38.

Swift, A. and Marshall, G. (1997) 'Meritocractic Equality of Opportunity?', *Policy Studies*, 18(1): 35–48.

Taylor, F. W. (1911) *The Principles of Scientific Management*. New York: Harper and Brothers.

Teichler, U. (2004) 'The Changing Debate on Internationalisation of Higher Education', *Higher Education*, 48(1): 5–26.

Thompson, P. (2004) *Staking on Thin Ice: the knowledge economy myth*. Glasgow: Glasgow University Press.

Thurow, L. C. (1977) Education and Economic Equality, in J. Karabel and A. H. Halsey (eds) *Power and Ideology in Education*. New York: Oxford University Press.

Tight, M. (1998) 'Lifelong Learning: opportunity or compulsion?', *British Journal of Educational Studies*, 46(3): 251–63.

Tomlinson, J. (1999) *Globalisation and Culture*. Chicago: University of Chicago Press.

Tomlinson, S. (2005) *Education in a Post-welfare Society*. Buckingham: Open University Press.

Tomlinson, M. (2007) 'Graduate Employability and Student Attitudes and Orientations to the Labour Market', *Journal of Education and Work*, 20(4): 285–304.

—(2008) 'The Degree is Not Enough: students' perceptions of the role of higher education credentials for graduate work and employability', *British Journal of Sociology of Education*, 29(1): 49–61.

Trow, M. (2006) 'Reflections on the Transition from Elite to Mass to Universal Access: forms and phases of higher education in modern societies since WWII', *International Handbook of Higher Education*, 18(1): 243–80.

Trowler, P. (1998) *Academics Responding to Change: new educational frameworks and academic cultures*. Buckingham: Open University Press.

Unwin, L. (2010) 'Learning and Working form the MSC to New Labour: young people, skills and employment', *National Institute Economic Review*, 212: 49–60.

Unwin, L. and Wellington, J. (2001) *Young People's Perspectives on Education and Employment: realising their potential*. London: Kogan Page.

Vignoles, A. (2008) 'Widening Participation in HE: a quantitative analysis', *Widening Participation in Higher Education: a commentary by the Teaching and Learning Research Programme*. Swindon: Economic and Social Research Council.

Wajcman, J. and Martin, B. (2002) 'Narratives of Identity in Modern Management: the corrosion of gender difference?', *Sociology*, 36(4): 985–1002.

Wallace, M. Wallace, M., Deem, R., O'Reilly, D. and Tomlinson, M. (2011) 'Developing Leadership Capacity in English Secondary Schools and Universities: global positioning and local mediation', *British Journal of Educational Studies*, 59(1): 21–40.

Waller, R. (2006) 'I Don't Feel Like a Student, I Feel Like 'Me'!: the over-simplification of mature student learners' experience(s)', *Research in Post-Compulsory Education*, 11(1): 115–30.

Warhurst, C. (2008) 'The Knowledge Economy, Skills and Government Labour Intervention', *Policy Studies*, 29(1): 71–86.

Warmington, P. (2003) '"You Need a Qualification for Everything These Days": the impact of work welfare and disaffection upon the aspiration of aspirations of access to higher education students', *British Journal of Sociology of Education*, 24(1): 95–108.

Watkins, K. E. and Marsick, V. (1993) 'Sculpting the Learning Organization: consulting using active technology', *New Directions in Adult and Continuing Education*, 58: 81–90.

Watts, A. G. (2006) *Career Development Learning and Employability*, a report to the Higher Education Academy. York: Higher Education Academy.

Weber, M. (1948) *From Max Weber: essays in sociology*, translated, edited and with an introduction by H. H. Gerth and C. W. Mills. London: Routledge and Kegan Paul.

Weil, S. W. (1986) 'Non-traditional Learners Within Higher Education Institutions: discovery and disillusionment', *Studies in Higher Education*, 11(2): 219–35.

Wenger, E. (1998) *Communities of Practice: learning, meaning and identity*. Cambridge: Cambridge University Press.

Whitehead, J. (1996) 'Sex Stereotypes, Gender Identity and Subject Choice at A-level', *Educational Researcher*, 38(2): 147–60.

Whitstone, K. (1998) 'Key Skills and Curriculum Reform', *Studies in Higher Education*, 23(3): 307–19.

Whitty, G. (1989) 'The New Right and the National Curriculum: state control or market forces?', *Journal of Education Policy*, 4(4): 329–41.

— (2000) 'Teacher Professionalism in New Times', *Journal of In-service Education*, 26(2): 281–95.

—(2008) 'Twenty Years of Progress? English Education Policy 1988 to present', *Educational Management Administration and Leadership*, 36(2): 165–84.

Whyte, W. (1956) *The Organization Man*. New York: Simon & Schuster.

Willis, P. E. (1977) *Learning to Labour: how working class kids get working class jobs*. Columbia: Columbia University Press.

— (2003) 'Foot Soldiers of Modernity: the dialectics of cultural consumption and the 21st Century school', *Harvard Education Review*, 73(3): 390–415.

Winch, C. (2002) 'The Economic Aims of Education', *Journal of Philosophy of Education*, 36(1): 101–17.

— (2009) 'Ryle on Knowing and the Possibility of Vocational Education', *Journal of Applied Philosophy*, 26(1): 88–101.

Winch, C. and Clarke, L. (2007) *Vocational Education: international approaches, definitions and systems*. Oxfordshire: Routledge.

Winter, R. (2009) 'Academic Manager or Managed Academic: academic identity schisms in higher education', *Journal of Higher Education Policy and Management*, 31(3): 121–31.

Wolf, A. (2002) *Does Education Matter: myths about education and economic growth*. London: Penguin.

— (2007) 'Round and Round the Houses: The Leitch Review of Skills', *Local Economy*, 22(3): 111–19.

Wolf, A., Jenkins, A. and Vignoles, A. (2006) 'Certifying the Workforce: economic imperative or failed social policy', *Journal of Education Policy*, 21(5): 535–65.

World Bank (2003) *Lifelong Learning in the Global Knowledge Economy: challenges for developing economies*. World Bank: Washington.

Yorke, M. and Knight, P. (2006) 'Curricula for Economic and Social Gain', *Higher Education*, 51(4): 565–88.

Youdell, D. (2003) 'Identity Traps or How Black (1) Pupils Fail: the interaction between biographical, sub-cultural and learner identities', *British Journal of Sociology of Education*, 24(1): 3–20.

Young, M. (2006) 'Curriculum Studies and the Problem of Knowledge: updating the enlightenment', in H. Lauder, P. Brown, J. A. Dillabough and A. H. Halsey (eds) *Education, Globalisation and Social Change*. Oxford: Oxford University.

Young, M. F. (1998) *The Curriculum of the Future: from the 'new' sociology of education to a critical theory of learning*. London: Falmer Press.

— (2009) 'Education, Globalisation and the Voice of Knowledge', *Journal of Education and Work*, 22(3): 193–204.

Zukas, M. and Malcolm, J. (2007) 'Learning From Adult Education', *Academy Exchange*, 6: 20–2.

INDEX

academic drift   81, 102
academics   184–8
   academic capitalism   186
   academic identities   186–8
   hybrid roles   185, 189
   performative pressures   185–7
agency
   action frames   6, 115, 123, 132–4,
      147
   autonomy   23, 25, 144
   interaction with structure   6,
      26, 113
   reflexivity   6
   worker agency   51, 127, 165, 169–70
agenda
   call for change   102
   diplomas   100, 102
apprenticeship   100, 103
   as professional socialization   101–2,
      121–2, 128
attitudes   53, 65, 145
   to education   79, 107, 112–13, 115,
      118, 123, 138, 142, 189
   to work   55–6, 58, 128, 135–6, 198

biography   21, 133, 202
   frame of reference   31
   learning   112, 133, 191
   normal and choice   133–4

capitals *see also* networks
   academic/intellectual, 182, 185–6
   cultural, 8, 67–8, 119, 142, 189, 193
   personal   197
   social   145, 189
careers
   flexibility   9–10, 42, 53, 202
   graduates   193–4
   organization versus
      self-managed   53–5

young people's career
      orientations   137–9, 146–9
choices
   breadth   147
   decision-making   143–5
   educational and school choice   8,
      107, 115, 118–19, 121–2, 131
   pragmatic rationality   142
   structural framing   6, 8, 134, 136,
      144–5, 189
competences   41, 55–6, 86, 89, 126
   behavioural competences   197–8
   limits of   96, 184
   professional competences   126–7
class   6–7, 58, 61, 73–4, 117 *see also*
      middle classes; working
      classes
class-less society   21, 25–6, 117
class politics   24
   division of labour   9, 24, 64,
      66–7, 97–8
   embodied and subjective
      dimension   26–7
communities of practice   126–7
counter-school culture   138
   resistance   117, 123
credentialisim   72–7
   credential inflation   74, 111
   critiques   80–1
   disaffection   75
   over-qualification/under-
      employment   75, 83, 195
   screening   75
   social closure   73
conflict approach   65–6, 68, 73, 76
correspondence theory
   Bowles and Gintis   66–7
corrosion of character   50
   intensification of work   37, 185
curricula   85, 98, 136

challenges for vocational
    education   87, 94,
    97–8, 102
  prescription   155, 159, 166
curriculum
  changes   120, 184
  extra-curriculum   76
  hidden curriculum   7, 67, 120
  teacher relations to   165–6

de-skilling   47–8, 92
digital Taylorism   48

economization   11, 152–4
  critiques of   158–61, 183–4
  discourses   156
  features   154–6
education gospel   153–4
employability   10, 23, 202
  absolute and relative   55–7
  changing career context   53–4
  definitions and dimensions
    55–8, 80
  emergence of concept   53
  policy emphasis on developing
    85–7, 93–4, 99, 155, 158
  subjective aspects   58, 90, 197–8
employers   55, 75
  demands   87–8, 93–5, 99–100,
    102–3
  investment in training   104
  university relations   176, 180,
    195–8
ethnicity   6, 185
ethnic learners' experiences   122–3

feminization of work   42–4
  gender-related skills   92
Feminization   9, 43–5 *see also* gender
  changing opportunities
  critical perspectives   44–5
  female career approaches   43–4
Fordism
  division of labour   40, 63
  educational aspects   63
  Taylorism   39–40

gender   6, 23, 194–5 *see also*
    feminization of work; learner
    Identity

changing opportunities   121
  responses to education   120–2
  socialization   122, 143
  subject choices   121
globalization   3, 17–18, 27–32
  criticisms   29–30
  cultural aspects   29–30
  economic aspects   28–30, 33
  features of   27–8
  globalization of work and
    skills   32–3
  impacts on education   34,
    47–8, 152, 156, 176,
    181, 201
  subjective/experiential aspects
    30–1
graduates   54, 88–9, 103–4, 192–5
  attitudes to work   198
  degrees and graduateness   193
  graduate occupations   194–5
  recruitment and attributes   196–7
  skills   93–4, 184, 196
  Social 'elite'   192

habitus   6, 142
  personal dispositions   26
  vocational habitus   122
human capital   11–12, 43, 87, 151,
    155
  critiques   74–5, 78–80, 113, 203
  marginal product   70
  policy influences   87, 99, 110,
    156, 193
  theory   69–72
higher education   88, 175–99 *see also*
    students
  Browne review   177
  economic goals   93–4, 103
  expansion   135
  globalizing influences   181–3
  institutional performance   89
  part-public institution   177
  Robbins Report   178

identity   4–6, 8 *see also* globalization
    – subjective aspects;
    learner identity; reflexive
    modernization; Work–
    relationship to identity
  life politics and life projects   24–5

ideology 155 *see also* neoliberalism
  economization 161–2
  managerialism 170–1
  universities 183–4
inequality 6, 62, 66–7, 73, 122
  global economic inequality 29
  inegalitarianism 178
  labour market aspects 71
individualization 20–2, 132, 141, 202
  critiques 26–7
  institutionalized
      individualization 22
  labour market as motor of 22
  personal responsibility and
      autonomy 23
individualism 22
  market individualism and
      consumer sovereignty
      155, 160, 162–3
instrumentalism
  approaches to education 11, 71,
      97, 109, 118, 157, 160, 162,
      184, 191, 204
  approaches to work 51, 169,
      171, 186
Internationalization
  policies 34
  student mobility 181

knowledge 8, 78 *see also* work-
      related learning
  knowledge production 47–8, 183,
      186
  late modern society 19, 28–9, 32
  mode 1 and 2 182–3
  operational knowledge 184
  theoretical knowledge 41–2, 98–9
knowledge-based economy 3, 9, 42–3,
      46, 56
  critical perspectives 46–8
  knowledge work/workers 9, 33,
      42, 50, 101, 157
  policy narrative 43, 110, 153, 157
  weightless economy 42

leadership
  characteristics 172–3
  versus management 172
  policy mediation 172–4
learner identities 107, 114–16

biographies and trajectories 115–16,
      129, 133, 143, 146
  class aspects 117–19, 138
  ethnicity 117, 122
  gender aspects 121–2
  learning careers and
      dispositions 115, 144
learning
  formal versus informal 110,
      125–6, 148
learning organizations 124, 157
  learning-supportive organizations,
      128
lifelong learning 12, 42, 92, 157, 202
  critique of 110–11
  learning society rhetoric 108–10

managerialism 51–2, 161, 166, 170–3,
      177, 184–5
  accountability and audit 52,
      164–5, 185
  challenge to professional
      authority 170, 187, 203
  New Public Management 11, 169
  performance management 51, 155,
      159, 161, 166, 169
markets and marketization 34, 155,
      161–4, 202
  choice and competition 162–3
  criticisms 163–4
  market pressures 161, 191
  policy rationale 163
masculinity
  crisis 121
  lads 137–8
mass higher education 94, 176,
      188–9, 192–3, 204
  access and widening
      participation 144, 179
  expansion from elite to mass
      177–80
  policy agenda 178
mature students 109, 144, 189
  adult learners 114, 116
  student experience 116, 119,
      190–1
meritocracy 12, 68, 72
  limits of concept 76–7, 79
  sponsored mobility 79
middle classes 7–8

approaches 76–7, 80, 104, 119–20, 144, 164
   challenges and tensions 32–3, 47, 75–7, 204
   expansion 69, 75, 117, 177–8
modernization 171
   personalization 160
   responsiveness 11, 161, 163, 167, 171
modernity 19, 21, 24–5, 134, 141
   solid and liquid 20

networks 20, 52, 77, 145, 179, 195
network society 18, 19, 28, 31
new growth theory 32–3, 156
neoliberalism 28–9, 72, 162–3, 166, 202–3
   critiques 183, 187
not in education or training (NEETs) 91–2

opportunity 32, 57, 178
   gender 44–5, 121
   hoarding 83
   opportunity traps 4, 7
   social structures of opportunity 18, 33, 63, 73, 103, 119 135–6, 140
   subjective aspects 56
over-qualification 74–5, 83, 103, 195

performativity 168–70, 182, 186
   professional ethic 169–70
personal capital 197
policy approaches
   assessment 34, 102, 143, 159, 166, 169, 203
   globalizing pressures 33–4
   outcomes and outputs 12, 155, 157–9, 166–8, 184
   policy technologies 160–1
   standards reform 158–9, 163–4, 168, 172
   state theory of learning 158–9
polytechnics 178
pool of talent 109, 197
   collective intelligence 64, 152
positional competition 56, 69, 76, 193

post-fordism/post-industrialism 8–10, 20, 27–8, 39–43, 53, 202 see also feminization of work
   communications 41
   educational impacts 62, 70, 157, 180
   theoretical knowledge 41–2
professionals 11, 32, 51–2, 127, 171, 184, 187, 203 see also performativity
   de-professionalization 168
   personnel professionalism 81
   professional identites 164–7
   professional and policy 152, 160, 163, 165–6
public benefits 176

rational choice theories 71–2, 79, 113
recruitment 104, 192, 195–7
   screening 69, 75
   social fit 197–8
reflexive modernization 17–23
   de-traditionalization 19–20, 24
   dis-embedding 19, 22
   modern to late modern society 18–20
   reflexivity 21–2, 24–5
research versus teaching institutions 180

skills 9–10, 65–6, 69–70, 85, 105, 155
   de-skilling 47–8, 168
   disequilibrium 33, 46, 152–3
   high skills economy/work 11, 39–43, 80, 91–2, 110, 124, 182
   key/employability skills 55–6, 87–8, 180
   low skilled work 63, 103, 136–9
   soft skills 92, 198
   vocational learners 97–100
   work-related skills 123–7
skills policy 90, 92–5, 156
   critiques 95–6, 196
   Dearing 93–4
   Leitch 92–3
social change 2, 18, 141
   universities 176

socialization 65 *see also* social
  reproduction
  anticipatory socialization 67,
    120–2, 135–6, 143
  work socialization 124, 127
social justice 12, 62, 92,
    108, 155, 162
  equality of opportunity 6, 86, 178
  life chances 72
social mobility 12, 62, 79–80, 189
social reproduction 2, 7, 66–8, 117,
    137–139, 142
sociology of education
  shift in focus 2, 7, 117–18
status 6, 53, 72–3, 99–100, 119, 146,
    185, 194
  confirmation 178, 193
  relative institutional 180, 183, 186,
    189, 192
students 176
  consumerism of HE 191–2
  diversity 176, 178–9, 189–90
  experience 188–92
  part-time work 191
supply-side 85–8, 95, 151, 156

transitions 21, 110, 131–3, 141–8
  push and pull factors 134
  to higher education 101–2
    116, 144
  traditional youth 135–9
  turning points 115, 133, 145

varieties of capitalism 81–2
  liberal versus occupational
    markets 82
vocational education 13, 64, 96–101

critiques of policy 88, 99, 103–4
German dual system 99–100
vocational versus academic
    pathways 13, 97–8, 100,
    102–4
vocationalism 12, 85–6, 97
  labour market demands 86
  training without jobs 140–1
vocational learners' attitudes 97, 101
  Wolf review 103

welfare state 23, 62, 166
work *see also* professional identities
  changing nature/character 41–2
  future of work debate 13, 37–8,
    45–6
  relationship to identity 8, 48–53
working-class *see also* learner
    identities–class aspects
  working class collectivism 24,
    50–1
work organization *see also*
    communities of practice
  expansive versus restrictive work
    cultures 101, 128
  learning supportive cultures 129
  shop-floor culture 52–3, 137–8
work-related learning 10, 37, 42–3,
    47, 51–2, 55, 74, 80, 89, 97,
    101, 123–8 see also skills

youth 4, 21
  extended youth 145–7
  labour market 96–7, 99, 134,
    136–9
  lifestyle and changing attitudes 146
  ordinary kids 140–1